DISABLED PERSONS

DISABLED PERSONS

Editors

V.V. KRISHNA — B.S.V. DUTT

K.H. RAO

Academy of Communication Culture
Education Science and Service
1-22-10 Srinivasa Nagar,
Guntur 522006
Andhra Pradesh

DISCOVERY PUBLISHING HOUSE
New Delhi

Edition: 2021

ISBN: 978-81-7141-614-1

Disabled Persons

Published by:

DISCOVERY PUBLISHING HOUSE PVT. LTD.
4383/4B, Ansari Road, Darya Ganj
New Delhi-110 002 (India)
Phone: +91-11-23279245, 43596064-65
Fax: +91-11-23253475
E-mail: discoverypublishinghouse@gmail.com
sales@discoverypublishinggroup.com
web: www.discoverypublishinggroup.com

Printed at:
Infinity Imaging Systems
Delhi

Preface

A disability is any restriction or lack of ability to perform an activity in the manner or within the range considered normal for a human being.

One family in four worldwide has a relative with a disability, or in other words more than 500 million persons—10 per cent of the world's total population—suffer from some type of disability. Majority of the disabled persons are segregated and deprived of virtually all their rights, and lead a wretched, marginal life. But, persons with disabilities, as persons like ourselves, have the right to live with us as we do.

This book, in order to disseminate information about disabled persons, contains the United Nations documents, viz., Families and Disability, Human Rights and Disabled Persons, and World Programme of Action concerning Disabled Persons; and UNESCO's legislation pertaining to Special Needs Education. This information will be of great use to people engaged in the programmes—personnel as well as academic—concerned to disabled persons.

We are thankful to United Nations and UNESCO for using their documents in preparing this book.

V.V. Krishna, B.S.V. Dutt
K.H. Rao

Contents

Part-4

LEGISLATION PERTAINING TO SPECIAL NEEDS EDUCATION

PART—1
FAMILIES AND DISABILITY

1
EACH FAMILY IS UNIQUE

"We all come from families. Families are big, small, extended, multigenerational, with one parent, two parents and grandparents. We live under one roof or many. A family can be as temporary as a few weeks, as permanent as forever. We become part of a family by birth, adoption, marriage or from a desire for mutual support. As family members, we nurture, protect and influence each other. A family is a culture unto itself, with different values and unique ways of realising its dream; together, our families become the source of our rich cultural heritage and spiritual diversity. Each family has its strengths and qualities that flow from individual members and from the family as unit. Our families create neighbourhoods, communities, states and nations."

New Mexico Governor's Task Force on Children, Youth and Families, 1991 (23)

One family in four worldwide has a relative with a disability. These families are as different from one another as any other family. But many such families daily experience discrimination and marginalisation in their own immediate neighbourhoods and communities. They are also vulnerable to generalisations about families made by people without personal experience of the actual situation of families. A typical example is the assumption that "a handicapped child means a handicapped family".

The reality is more complex. All families have different strengths and needs. Furthermore, every member of the family also has individual needs, which will differ from person to person, depending on their basic personality, their coping styles and their response to stress in general.

Generalisations about disabled people are as suspect and as dangerous as generalisations about families, and for much the same reason. The experience of disabled people is affected by the social and family environment in which they live as well as by the nature of the disability. Attitudes to disability vary not only from country to country, but also within relatively small areas within a single country. People with visual impairments may be treated very differently from those with speech and hearing impairments. Learning or psychiatric impairments or chronic epilepsy are still relatively the most feared or shunned in both developed and developing countries.

Much depends also on the extent to which disabled people receive the necessary supports, aids and interventions. These range from spectacles and hearing aids, mobility aids, chemotherapy for epilepsy or psychiatric disorders, to schooling and vocational training.

Much of the literature about disability concerns children whose disability was obvious at birth or became apparent at an early age and who are living with their families. In developing countries, a larger proportion of children become disabled after a period of normal development as a direct result of illness or injury (e.g. meningitis, encephalitis or poliomyelitis) or as a consequence of malnutrition. Many more become disabled as a result of road traffic and other accidents, violence, war and its aftermath and as a direct result of abuse. The age of onset and the nature of the impairment will affect different individuals and families to a different extent.

People who become disabled as adults may no longer be living with their own parents but may receive a great deal of support from them or from the extended family. Other adults with an acquired disability may be living a long way away from their families or may no longer be accepted by their families. As a result, many such adults are dependent on the support of the communities where they are living. Local attitudes as well as local services determine whether they continue to be accepted, whether rehabilitation services are available and whether they will be able to resume their work and their place in the community. This applies particularly to soldiers and civilians disabled by wars or armed conflicts, many of whom experience major problems in finding jobs and a valued place in society.

2

DEFINITIONS AND CONCEPTS

Because attitudes to disability are deeply rooted in the social and cultural values of society, definitions of disability are problematic. Scientists and research workers striving for precision and clarity in the use of terminology have developed complex systems of classification, with the aim of facilitating research and scientific communication. The clearest expression of this trend is the classification published by the World Health Organisation (WHO) that is being revised. But the assumptions underlying it has been questioned by disabled people as well as by professionals adhering to a more social model to disability.

The distinction made by WHO (32) in its definitions of impairment, disability and handicap has been widely used and quoted. Briefly, the definitions are as follows:

- An *impairment* is any loss or abnormality of psychological, physiological or anatomical structure or function
- A *disability* is any restriction or lack (resulting from an impairment) of ability to perform an activity in the manner or within the range considered normal for a human being
- A *handicap* is a disadvantage for a given individual, resulting from an impairment or a disability, that limits or prevents the fulfilment of a role that is normal (depending on age, sex and social and cultural factors) for that individual.

These definitions have been increasingly criticised, particularly by organisations of disabled people on the grounds that they focus too much on the individual with the disability and fail to reflect the extent to which the lives of disabled people are disadvantaged by the social structure of the society in which they live. Although the WHO definition of handicap includes the concept of disadvantage, its origins are located in the individual and not in society and its institutions. These definitions also make no direct reference to environmental or family factors.

SOCIAL MODEL OF DISABILITY

The social model of disability insists that social structures and the barriers to which they given rise need to be modified. For example, there are still countries where a child whose intelligence quotient (IQ) falls below a certain point is denied access to education in schools, either ordinary or special. Similarly, many disabled adults are denied the opportunity of obtaining vocational training or of securing paid employment, not because they have been shown to be incapable of work but as a direct result of negative attitudes by decision makers or because the workplace is inaccessible. For disabled people who are denied access to opportunities and facilities, discrimination is a daily experience.

The social model does not seek to minimize or deny the presence of impairments and the restrictions that these may impose on the independence and autonomy of the disabled person. But it does place more emphasis on the importance of society and its institutions being modified to meet the needs of disabled persons. This contrasts with the traditional assumption that it is disabled people who should be trained to adapt or adjust to society. The models can be seen as complementary rather than as mutually exclusive in meeting the needs of individuals within their own social and family settings.

Terms such as disability and handicap are therefore socially and culturally relative. In an example (13) from Mali:

"The most 'disabling condition' for a woman is to be ugly. This condition is defined in very clear terms. These women do not get married and consequently do not fulfil the normal parental role."

In other countries, dwarfs, people missing an eye, toe or finger or having an extra toe or finger or with a facial disfigurement or albinism may have no functional limitations but still be labelled as disabled."

Helander suggests that disability might simply be defined as follows:

"A disabled person is one who in his/her society is regarded or officially recognised as such because of a difference in appearance and/or behaviour, in combination with a functional limitation or activity restriction."

Disabled Peoples' International (DPI), a world federation of organisations of disabled persons, have proposed alternative definitions:

- *Impairment* is the functional limitation within the individual caused by physical, mental or sensory impairment.
- *Disability* is the loss or limitation of opportunities to take part in the normal life of the community on an equal level with others due to physical and social barriers.

The DPI definition therefore dispenses with concept of handicap altogether, regarding it as misleading and discriminatory.

EQUALISATION OF OPPORTUNITIES

The concept of equalisation of opportunities is fundamental not only to definition, but also to the total process of planning and provision and ensuring the full participation of disabled people in society and in determining their own needs and priorities. It is derived from the Universal Declaration of Human Rights.

The most recent United Nations definition of equalisation of opportunities is incorporated in the *Standard Rules on the Equalisation of Opportunities for Persons with Disabilities,* which were adopted by the General Assembly (30) in 1993.

"Equalisation of opportunities means the process through which the various systems of society and the environment, such as services, activities, information and documentation are made available to all, particularly to persons with disabilities."

3

WHAT WE KNOW AND DO NOT KNOW

The quality and quantity of information about disability on a global scale is not impressive and there is some disagreement about the accuracy of such data as are available. The best summary source is the Statistical Office of the United Nations Secretariat in New York, which collects and tabulates information supplied by most Member States of the United Nations. A number of countries have also undertaken detailed surveys and censuses.

It is clear that a major problem in the interpretation of disability statistics arises from the lack of an agreed definition of disability, which would differentiate people with a "marked or significant" disability from people with one that does not seriously impede the day-to-day functioning of the affected individual or that can be easily compensated for (e.g. by spectacles, a hearing aid or a walking stick).

Clearly, such distinctions depend on local customs and attitudes as well as on the availability of aids, appliances and services. For example, people with a mild degree of intellectual disability often participate fully in community activities in most developing counties. In a developed country, however, they are more likely to stand out in schools and may experience difficulty in finding work or taking their place in their local community.

It also goes without saying that in any community much depends on the support provided by the family for their disabled relative in going to school, getting and keeping a job and living with as much independence as possible. In turn, families themselves need support in this task from neighbours and from local services.

ESTIMATES OF PREVALENCE

Most of the published information relates to the number of disabled persons in a country and may also provide information about the nature of their disability. However, little or no statistical information about families as such appears to be available on an international scale.

United Nations sources originally estimated the total number of disabled people in the world to be around 500 million in 1990. These numbers were expected to increase to 600 million by the year 2000, which amounts to approximately one person in ten. The figure of 500 million includes 140 million children, of whom 127 million live in developing countries—including 88 million in Asia, 18 million in Africa and 13 million in Latin America. Another 11 million are in North America and a further 6 millions in Europe.

These figures are now thought to be an overestimate by the United Nations Development Programme (UNDP). Considering only people with "moderate or severe" disability, Helander (13) puts the current total figure at around 276 million, of whom 183 million are in developing countries and 93 million in developed countries. Helander also estimates that an average of 8.5 million severely or moderately disabled people are added to this total every year, or around 23,000 a day. By 2025, the number of disabled people will rise from 183 million to 435 million in developing countries and from 93 million to 138 million in developed countries. Based on these projections, that total number will be 573 million in 2025, or 8.2 per cent of the world's total population.

Each year, 35 million children die and another 35 million become disabled. At least half of all of these occurrences could be prevented by the use of knowledge and skills already in humankind's possession.

Ninety per cent of infant disability is related to environmental causes related to poverty, which include malnutrition, poor sanitation and persistent abuse.

The global prevalence of specific moderate and severe disabilities is estimated as follows:

Type of disability	Percentage
Movement	2.5-3.0
Seeing	0.5-1.0
Hearing/speech	0.5-1.0
Learning	0.2-0.4
Fits	0.3-0.6
Psychiatric	0.1-0.2
Feeling (hands and feet)	0.1-0.2
Combinations of the above	0.2-0.3

Eighty-five per cent of adult disability is caused after the age of 13. Major causes include domestic and industrial accidents, wars and armed conflict and its consequences (particularly undetected plastic land mines), malnutrition and environmental pollution.

The relative increase in the disabled people, particularly in developing countries, can be attributed to a variety of factors. These include not only the rise in the number of births, but also the survival of many children who would previously have died at birth or in the first year of life. This applies particularly to very low birth weight babies and to those with profound and multiple impairments, as well as to children with Down's syndrome or spina bifida who, while not necessarily severely intellectually impaired, are physically vulnerable to respiratory and other infections, unless appropriate medical and nursing treatment is available.

In addition, advances in the quality of health care are associated with increasing life expectancy for both children and adults. Greater longevity in the whole population leads to an increase in the number of older disabled people and in the survival of disabled people who would previously have died at an earlier age. This has clear implications for the need to develop appropriate services to match these demographic trends.

These figures relate to people with marked or significant disabilities. But growing urbanisation and an increase in the complexity of educational and occupational demands will increasingly affect people with relatively mild degrees of impairment. For example, European experience in the early twentieth century and current experience in many developing countries indicates that as more children go to school, those who experience difficulties in learning are more readily noticed. Many are still forced to repeat one or more years, thus singling them out as educational failures and isolating them from their friends. Others are simply excluded from school and left to fend to themselves.

4
EXPERIENCING DISCRIMINATION

For every disabled person in the world, it is estimated that at least four members of the immediate family will be directly affected through having to adapt to and meet the needs of their relative.

All families will be profoundly affected by the nature of the society in which they live and by the value that that society places on the contribution that disabled people can make. These values are reflected in social structures and institutions that may provide pathways or barriers to disabled people taking their place in the community and making a valued contribution to its growth and development. Just as some families are victims of oppression and discrimination, others have been enriched and strengthened by their experiences both within the family and as a consequence of contacts and supports outside the family.

The extent and the manner in which families will be affected will obviously vary in relation to age, gender, degree of dependence and the amount and nature of the support available from the rest of the family, the local community and service agencies as well as depend on social attitudes and structures.

Most societies and cultures discriminate against disabled people and their families to some degree: in the school, the workplace, on the street and in community settings. Many families have encountered stereotyped assumptions about disability. Indeed, as members of their local and national communities, their initial reaction to the experience of disability may well be identical to that of their neighbours.

Although there are few detailed studies on this subject, the many anecdotal accounts from disabled people and their families, as well as the accounts by a range of observers suggest that many people still regard disability as a direct result of magic or of some transgression earlier in life or in a previous life. In many countries, attitudes towards disabled people and their families are still affected by myths and superstitions. These are widespread in the society and are by no means confined to rural areas or to people without education ([16] and [27]).

At one extreme, typified mid-twentieth century Europe, disabled people have been systematically exterminated or permanently incarcerated in institutions. In many developed countries, people with psychiatric or intellectual impairments have been kept in appalling conditions, often without treatment or rehabilitation and with little or no prospect of a return to the community. Some have been (and still are) subjected to compulsory sterilisation or been forced to take part in noxious and illness-inducing drug trials. Many are victims of emotional, physical and sexual abuse.

Just as the Incas banished persons from their cities on festival days, there are still reports of similar practices in some modern States on special occasions such as an international sports event or the visit of a foreign dignitary. There are areas of the world where pregnant women are warned against the risk of encountering a disabled persons because of the risk to their unborn child.

In many countries, disabled people are still isolated from the community and denied access to its resources and facilities. Many have been excluded from work not because their condition precluded work but simply on account of the presence of a disability or because the workplace is not accessible or unsuitable for a disabled person.

Disabled people and their families are also subject to all other forms of discrimination, as are non-disabled members of their communities and countries. Discrimination and disadvantage relating to a family member with a disability may be increased if he or she belongs to a minority ethnic group; if they are female; if they are a member of a low socio-economic group; if they have minority religion; if they are homosexual or lesbian. Some family members with a disability may therefore be subject to multiple severe discriminations and disadvantages.

Poverty is one of the most common forms of disadvantage experienced by disabled people and their families. Disabled people in all countries are economically disadvantaged. Many are living in severe poverty at or beyond the margins of society. This applies also to disabled people in countries with advanced systems of income support, because the allowances available to disabled people are judged to be inadequate to meet basic living costs. An official study in the United Kingdom showed that families of children with disabilities have incomes that are on average 22 per cent lower than those of equivalent families in the population as a whole [26].

The costs of meeting the needs of a disabled person will vary considerably but many studies have demonstrated the need for additional expenditure of clothing (particularly footwear), laundry, transport and additional furniture as well as replacement costs where children may be destructive of household furniture and fittings.

These are examples of direct costs but there are even greater indirect psychological as well as financial costs that arise from the inability of one or more family members to be free to obtain paid employment. It is almost invariably the mother who is prevented from working outside the home, reflecting the stereotype of the community and of the family that it is the mother who must, by definition, be the main carer. In the study of the United Kingdom mentioned above, 32 per cent of parents had no earners within the family unit, compared with 18 per cent of the general population of parents [26].

Yet there are a few societies in which disabled people and their families are regarded as full and equal members of their local community and where the birth of a disabled child may be seen as special gift of God. There are reports of disabled people in Samoa being included in ceremonial dancing and blind people being regarded as being under special divine protection in rural areas of Mexico [9].

A detailed study of proverbs, poems, riddles and folk-songs from Kenya and the United Republic of Tanzania involving references to disability, and interviews with tribal elders and with primary and special school teachers noted that most of the elders attributed disability to God's will or witchcraft and did not believe that education had anything to offer, whereas most of the teachers referred to illness and felt that education would enable children to be accepted and to make a contribution to society [16].

Kisanji concludes that:

"Difficulties notwithstanding, the communities accepted the presence of disabled persons in their midst as part of a continuum of individual differences which must be tolerated, respected and its members assisted to develop within the cultural boundaries."

"The Masai do not stigmatise people who have a disability, however serious the condition may be, by excluding them from the community. Disabled people marry, become parents and perform many other tasks [29]".

Another well-documented example of community acceptance and inclusion is the island of Martha's Vineyard in Massachusetts where a large number of the population have a hereditary form of hearing impairment but where the whole population are easily able to communicate through American Sign Language [10]. In fact, normally hearing families are reported to use sign language when they do not want their children to understand a conversation.

COMBATING DISCRIMINATION

Fortunately, individual families, as well as individuals within families and groups of families working together have themselves, in a variety of ways, worked to modify negative attitudes and striven to secure the acceptance of disabled people into the community. The extent to which they have succeeded varies greatly not only from country to country, but also within countries.

Growth of voluntary organisations

The 1940s and 1950s witnessed the spontaneous development of groupings of parents and family members. At first, these groups provided a foundation for mutual support and learning and a sharing of ideas and experiences. But many developed into effective forces for change, first at the local, then the national and finally at the international level. Their members were not only determined to gain access to basic supports and services for their relatives, but also to create better conditions for families with similar needs in the future. Over the years, they have campaigned vigorously for changes in legislation and provision and often became powerful advocates for changes in social structures [7].

Public attitudes

Voluntary organisations and family members have been at the forefront of the movement to bring about changes in public attitudes to disabled people. They have done so partly by their own example and partly by attempting to influence the way in which disabled people are portrayed in the media: in local and national newspapers and on radio and television.

In general, disabled people are now less often depicted as helpless victims, needing the charity of the public or as fighting bravely to overcome their disability. More and more the emphasis in on their similarity to other people, rather than on differences. Similarly, families are less often depicted as overburdened and handicapped by having to look after a disabled relative. The emphasis is more on the supports that families need in order to help the family as a whole to lead an ordinary life. However, there is still a long way to go in all countries before disabled people and their families are depicted in ways that they themselves can accept. International organisations such as ILSMH have produced some helpful guidelines to this end [28].

Development of self-advocacy organisations

During the 1980s, groups of disabled people themselves began to form their own organisations and to distance themselves from bodies that claimed to represent their interests but that were in fact controlled by a majority of non-disabled people.

Some of these organisations are now highly influential bodies that operate at national and international levels. The best known of these is DPI, which was founded in Singapore in 1981, with some support from the United Nations as a direct consequence of the International Year of Disabled Persons: "Full participation and equality" (1981). It draws its membership from organisation disabled people at the national level and also has strong regional networks.

DPI has been highly influential in the United Nations and played a major part in the development of the World Programme of Action concerning Disabled Persons (1983) and in the launch of the United Nations Decade of Disabled Persons (1983-1992).

The self-advocacy movement tends to be led by articulate or well-educated people with physical, sensory of invisible impairments.

More recently, people with intellectual disabilities have also started to develop self-organisations (e.g. People First) though it is still common for families to advocate on their behalf.

There is a potential source of tension between advocacy and self-advocacy organisations. Organisations of disabled persons wish to speak for themselves and tend to resent and reject statements made on their behalf by organisations for disabled persons. "Nothing about us without us" is the slogan of DPI. However, there is no reason why organisations of disabled people cannot make common cause with other organisations, provided they perceive common goals, and they will be seen to be more effective in securing their aims if they work together rather than separately.

Within families, too, there is a natural tendency for non-disabled members of the family to represent the interests of their disabled relatives, especially if they are children or have significant difficulties in speaking for themselves (e.g. as a result of severe intellectual or language impairments). Many examples of such a tendency can be seen in ordinary social encounters; disabled people have frequently complained that people "talk over the top of their heads", literally if they are in a wheelchair or figuratively in other situations. Many people address the carer or family member in situations where it would be more appropriate to ask the disabled person directly. This is sometimes described as the "Does he take sugar in this tea?" Phenomenon, the title of a weekly radio programme in the United Kingdom.

5

EXPERIENCE OF FAMILIES

Although most disabled people live in families, very little published information or research is available on the situation of such families worldwide. A number of symposia have been held in which reports from different countries have been presented under specific headings (e.g. legislation, family support systems, basic social welfare provisions, respite care etc.) and then analysed for common themes [9]. Despite major cultural and social differences, a number of common themes do emerge from such comparative studies.

Despite the shortage of international and comparative studies, there are many published examples from individual countries in which family members including disabled people have spoken and written eloquently about their needs and aspirations and about the improvements that they would like to see in the ways in which their needs are met and not met.

The stories they tell are not all about isolation, prejudice and discrimination, numerous and moving though these are. They are also about shared learning and growth, about the enrichment of experience of all family members and about the jobs of achievement and success. The experience of disability can be positive and often adds a new dimension to the lives of individuals and families.

FAMILY STORIES COLLECTED BY A TASK FORCE

ILSMH has set up a Task Force to ensure that families who have a relative with a mental handicap are included in activities for the International Year of the Family (IYF) at the local, national and international level. The Task Force consists of one mother and one father from each of the main regions of the world. In order to raise public and professional awareness of the situation of such families, the Task Force has collected a wide range of family stories from the main regions of the world. In addition, members of the Task Force have devised a series of Learning Messages specifically for IYF. These are reproduced in the annex. Although the experience of most members of the Task Force concerned mental handicap, it is felt that both the family stories and the Learning Messages are equally relevant to all disabled persons and their families.

Nearly all Learning Messages demonstrate families' strengths in combating difficulties and discrimination and their ability to learn and develop positively, gaining from their experiences, however difficult and painful they may be. Many, if not all, of their experiences will be similar to those of families with members who have other kinds of disability.

Information given to families

The situation of the families and the condition of their disabled member were found to vary a great deal. Some disabilities had been diagnosed at birth; others were a result of illness, an accident or war. However, learning about the disability presented the first common difficulties. It often took months or even years to obtain an accurate diagnosis, even for families with money, a high level of education and some medical knowledge. Local doctors, even paediatricians were often too ready to offer reassurance that a child who was demonstrably delayed in development would "be all right" or "catch up later". Parents themselves, understandably, wanted to believe this statement and felt unable to challenge it, even when they felt sure that something was wrong. Only the top national hospitals and facilities seemed to have the necessary expertise to assess and diagnose correctly.

The experience of being told that their child is disabled is usually an unforgettable experience for most parents. Parents valued the rare occasions when the specialist told them with sensitivity and enabled them to retain some hope that their child could learn and develop. Too often this was not the case and doctors gave a globally negative picture, telling parents and grandparents only what the child would not be able to do. To these families' credit and the credit of the member with the disability, these gloomy predictions were often disproved.

In Muslim and many Asian cultures, only the father as head of the household was given the information about the disability. Many fathers carry this knowledge alone for weeks, months, even years before they are able to share it with any other member of their family, often another male member and before telling their wife. One Korean father waited for 10 years before informing his wife about the diagnosis he had been given shortly after his son was born.

Advice and support given to families

Very often parents are not given advice about how they can help their child to develop when the disability is diagnosed, nor are they offered adequate support. In developed countries, there is now an understanding that the effects of impairment can be minimised by the provision of learning programmes and appropriate technical aids from the earliest stage. Because of this, support and advice are often offered and educational programmes are available from the age of two years or even earlier. In some developed countries, such as Italy and the United States of America, all children, including the most severely disabled, attend mainstream schools, which is resulting in greater understanding and acceptance from others [24].

In developing countries, access to such support is often rare and problematic. Many families receive no advice or support until their child is of school age, if then. When they seek school or pre-school facilities, they often encounter rejection or teachers who are untrained or unequipped to enable their child to learn. In the local schools, their children are often taunted and even bullied.

In many countries facilities to teach disabled children with learning, sensory and/or behavioural difficulties were set up initially by parents and parent groups themselves. Many mothers of these pioneering families trained as teachers of children with special educational needs and began to help other children and other families as well as their own. Once appropriate educational and, later on, vocational provision was made available, families almost universally reported progress in learning and development. However there is sometimes a mismatch between the diagnoses given and the intelligence test results and the level of progress achieved. Some children assessed at a very low IQ level progress well and achieve considerable independence in self-care skills while other children with a higher tested IQ make little progress ([1] and [20]).

Roles of family members

The day-to-day care that disabled children need varies greatly and depends both on their level of impairment and on the social environment, circumstances and attitudes among which they live. Some young children need much more intensive care because of sleeping, feeding and health difficulties.

Almost universally, responsibility is most likely to fall upon women, usually mothers. Working mothers often give up their jobs to care for their disabled child. In China, after the mother's statutory maternity leave, grandmothers often take over the caring task. Older sisters too have an important role to play and some research suggests that they are the most likely to be adversely affected among brothers and sisters.

While in some cultures the father's main role as a parent is that of breadwinner, there is now greater variety in the way in which fathers parent. In many families the roles are more shared and in cases where both parents shared their fears and feelings and also the care of their disabled child and other children, this also seemed to contribute to a more positive view and outcome. In a minority of families, fathers or grandfathers were the main carers of their disabled child, particularly where this was a son who needed intimate personal care.

A common situation is that of women as single parents, either as unmarried mothers, separated or divorced or widowed parents. Unless they are well supported by their families or communities or are wealthy enough to buy support, they are likely to be among the most financially disadvantaged families.

The reaction of extended family members and of friends and local communities to a disabled child or adult and their family will vary greatly, depending on the values and beliefs, of the society in which they live. Where families are shunned or rejected, this can put an intolerable strain on family members and lead to extreme experiences of isolation and depression. It can also exacerbate marital difficulties and result in separation and marital breakdown.

Where families are supported at least by some members of the extended family and community, this makes a very significant difference to their lives and to the opportunities for the disabled child or adult to interact and have access to ordinary everyday experiences. Supervision and even some practical tasks can be shared, which enables the mother and brothers and sisters also to have some time to participate in the life of the community and to pursue their own interests. Parents and family members greatly appreciate and value such support and count themselves very fortunate to receive it.

Families with a disabled member are often themselves educators in disability issues within their own families and communities. Through their interaction with others and by giving explanations to neighbours and friends, even by involving neighbours and friends in local associations and training events, they are instrumental in raising awareness about disability and in helping the community to increased its knowledge. Contact with disabled children or adults can often enable others to enjoy the relationship when they get to know them and appreciate their personal strengths and qualities.

As their child grows older, families begin to think about the future. Often it is at the stage of adolescence that parents' hopes and expectations for their disabled son or daughter begin to contrast most sharply with those for their children. Sometimes this in itself leads to pressure on mothers to produce more "normal" children and (especially in some cultures) sons to carry on the family name and tradition. In one such case, a mother was persuaded to have eight children, seven of whom were handicapped.

Parents would like their sons and daughters to live as normal a life as possible; to earn their livelihood through employment; to marry and have friends; and to live in their own accommodation with the support they need to lead safe and full lives. In many parts of the world where sufficient local or State services do not exist, families with means band together to set up vocational schemes and, increasingly to set up trust or insurance schemes to provide for their children when they are no longer able to care for them. Often they are again discriminated against in these areas. Few insurance schemes will offer schemes for people with disabilities. The majority of families do not have the means to contemplate any such schemes. Indeed, some have to resort to exploiting their disabled child or family member as beggars, where they are often prey to unscrupulous entrepreneurs.

Many parents look to their non-disabled sons and daughters to provide for their disabled brother or sister. However, both parents' and brothers' and sisters' attitudes to this varies considerably. While some families take this approach for granted, others are very reluctant to place such a major responsibility on their children, who may already have difficulties of their own. Some children who may be the only sibling are also apprehensive and resent the fact that they themselves will receive no support in this task.

Many parents feel the need for facilities when they themselves will no longer be able to provide the necessary care and support to their older family members with a disability. The few institutions that exist are often isolated from family life and do not allow for regular easy contact. Stories of older disabled family members included that of a mentally handicapped man in his sixties who had only recently re-established contact with one brother and whose sister attended his funeral after not having seem him for over 50 years.

Effects on family members

Often there are no major differences to family life. If the disability is not severe, multiple or progressive, it need not interfere with the normal daily routines or with the way families live their lives. Some disabled children, young and older people are well integrated members of their communities, with rewarding relationships and lives that they enjoy and that enrich others. Often they make a valued contribution to the economic and social life of the community. Some disabled people are key members and leaders in their fields, whether it be political, scientific or in the arts. They too are often influential in changing attitudes and social structures for the benefit of disabled people and their families.

Sometimes, however, the interplay of the social environment and severe and/or multiple impairment leads to some restrictions on family life. In addition to the isolation and the increased intensity of caring already mentioned, family members, also report an inability to go out or undertake activities spontaneously, as would other families, unless there are supportive relatives, friends, neighbours living locally or local supportive services that they can access.

The time that parents need to look after their disabled child or relative clearly also affects the time available to devote to their non-disabled children and to each other. Some families do think that their non-disabled children are neglected or held back as a result of this. Sometimes when the needs of all the family members cannot be balanced adequately and the strain is too great, there is family breakdown and either parents separate or disabled children are sent to live outside the family. This can also happen because there are no adequate educational or vocational facilities locally. Again, this affects the closeness of family relationships. But it may have some advantages. As a disabled African leading figure explained, he would not as a non-disabled person have had the advantages of an international education, which enabled him to reach a high post and later return to visit his farming family.

The role of grandparents is often very influential. They can be most supportive and share the care and take a lead in seeking expert opinion and advice, as in a Chinese family that was interviewed. They can often provide support financially and emotionally. They can also be rejecting and oppressive: in blaming the mother; in hiding the truth about a history of disability in the family; in putting pressure on a mother to ignore medical or educational advice or to have more children. Aunts and uncles and other extended family members can also play similar roles.

Brothers and sisters can develop warm, loving relationships with their disabled sisters brothers. They may be the best at understanding them when there are communication difficulties; they may become playfellows. They can be supportive when the disabled child starts school or is taunted or bullied at school. But if this happens then they too can suffer. Some children take on some of the attitudes around them and become ashamed to bring their school friends home to meet their disabled brother or sister and in turn became isolated and withdrawn. Some are disturbed in their activities or their studies by their disabled brother or sister, especially in crowded accommodation.

A key factors seems to be how or whether the disability is explained to them. Some parents are reluctant to do this for a variety of reasons but when explanations are given from an early age children seem better able to cope, perhaps because the parents are sharing their own ability and positive attitude. Being involved in activities and programmes with their disabled brothers and sisters also seems mutually beneficial.

In countries where the standard of living is comparatively high and medical services are more advanced and better equipped, the number of older disabled people are increasing with the increase of life expectancy. This has led to situations where ageing people whose own infirmity may be increasing being in a position of caring for their own disabled parents or other older relatives. The marked increase in the number of older people, who may soon be more numerous than the number of employed people to support them, poses a new and as yet unfamiliar problem both socially and economically for the next millennium.

There are, indeed, important benefits to living with a disabled child or relative. Nearly all parents or family members, no matter how painful or difficult their experiences are or have been, report on important fundamental gains. Many of these relate to knowing and loving the person with disability for his or her unique and individual personality. Many recount with pride the many achievements their child or relative has made in developing independence and in contributing to society. Many report how much such persons are loved and appreciated in their local community. However, there are important gains beyond these.

Some people express this in terms of gaining a different perspective in the way they see life and relate to other people: their experience has given them a new dimension of understanding and humanity. They have shed many of their previously held judgements and are better equipped to understand other disadvantaged people, whether they are disabled, poor or socially weak. Previously, they were critical and perhaps arrogant in their judgements; now they feel better able to understand. Some parents, indeed, offer support and advice to others.

FAMILIES' EXPERIENCE OF PROFESSIONALS

Throughout the life of a disabled person, the family can come into contact with a variety of professionals. Parents and family members are appreciative of those professionals who:

- Treat them and their disabled child or adult relative with consideration and respect

- Communicate with them openly and honestly
- Share their information and skills
- Give clear and full explanations:
  - (a) Of their role and their agencies' responsibilities
  - (b) The legislative framework in which they operate
  - (c) The disabled member's rights and entitlements
- Advocate on their behalf or alongside them for better service provision, more relevant and humane policies and social and economic conditions.
- Explore needs and plan services in conjunction with families.

In many countries there are good examples of true partnership between professionals and family members working and training together and jointly combating discrimination and disadvantage.

However, this is still the experience of only a minority of families. Too many families still complain of inadequate information, both oral and written. When information is given, it is often in a language full of professional jargon, which families have difficulty in understanding. An overly negative view is taken of their disabled child or relative and of themselves. They are often excluded from assessments when these are undertaken and from decision-making and planning when services are delivered. These may be offered on a take-it-or-leave-it basis, with little possibility of choice or negotiation. When consultation does take place, it is often felt to be on an unequal basis and only to a point before "the barriers come down".

Direct communication with the disabled child or adult is not always, or even in the majority of situations, the norm. Even where the law insists that the disabled child or adult's views must be sought, there are limits to how seriously these are considered, especially when there are intellectual impairments or when professionals find it difficult to understand the disabled person.

Low expectations remain a significant form of discrimination and result in reduced life-enhancing opportunities for many disabled children and adults. The arrogance, lack of understanding, insensitivity and judgemental attitudes of some professionals add considerably to the distress of many families.

Many disabled people, parents and other family members, especially those disadvantaged by poverty, low levels of education and low class or status, remain in awe of professionals. Dependence on professionals for those services that exist makes it difficult and risky to challenge their assessments, views and decisions. However, with the gradual growth of United Nations initiatives to promote the rights of disabled people including disabled children and the development of strong parent and self-advocacy groups, families are growing in confidence in their own knowledge, experience and skills and, above all, in the knowledge of the rights of their disabled members to equal social justice. New assertive generations are emerging to claim and work towards these rights, preferably in partnership with professionals but, if this partnership is not forthcoming, without them.

Disabled people and their family members have always had an informal role in raising the awareness of professionals in relation to experience of disability in society and to their needs. Many parents explain to teachers and other professionals how to communicate and respond to their children and also how to explain this to other children and parents. Relatives of older disabled people do the same. In many countries, family members now play an active role in the formal training of professionals.

Recent reviews of research on parental needs has suggested that professionals need to adopt a much wider and more comprehensive perspective in working with families [19]. For example, professionals would be well advised to inform themselves about existing family and social networks, the extent to which individual family members are able to support the child and the parent(s), particularly mothers. Families also differ greatly in their coping style and in their ability to obtain support both from the rest of the family and from their existing social networks. Professionals need to learn to take these factors into account in assessing the social and family context within which the child is living and developing. In the words of this author [19].

"Families differ greatly not only in how they organise themselves and in the resources that they have but in how they perceive the challenges they face. The same event will have different meanings and different effects for different individuals. Ultimately, the implication is that families differ in the types of services which they will find most helpful in supporting their own coping strategies."

6
IMPLICATIONS FOR POLICY AND PRACTICE

The experiences that families have reported throughout the world have profound implications for the ways in which services for families are planned and delivered.

In the following section, examples are given of ways in which professionals have tried to develop services in ways that are more responsive to the needs of families. Attempts have been made to do this by listening to parents and family members and by seeking to work with them on a basis of partnership and quality, where each has complementary expertise.

ACCESS TO INFORMATION

One of the foremost needs of families is for accurate and honest information about the condition of their family member. This may be at the time of birth, if the disability is already apparent; or when it becomes clear that a child's development is delayed or at any time of life when disability is the result of illness or accident, malnutrition, abuse or war.

Because "knowledge is power". Information enables family members to begin to understand their situation and to make choices about what they can do to minimise the effects of the disability on their member's and their own lives. However much of a shock a diagnosis may be, it is often more helpful than uncertainty.

The information that families need is much more than a diagnosis or an account of what impairment is present. Adequate information will include some explanation of biological processes in clear lay language and also some idea of the range of possible prognoses for the person with the disability. An exclusive focus on what the person will not be able to do is experienced as destructive and unhelpful by families. It is even more important to know what they will be able to do and that they are given the range of possibilities, from the most pessimistic to the most optimistic view of the future.

Families also need information about what options for services and supports are available to them. These should include local, regional, national and international organisations; health, education and welfare services; employment and vocational opportunities, as well as informal networks.

The manner in which information is given is almost as important as the information itself. A number of guidelines are offered below, drawn from various sources.

The knowledge gained from assessment, whether it is medical or educational, should be shared with family members as early as possible.

Family members should not, in general, be told alone.

Because such information is likely to be upsetting, telling parents or partners together or enabling a parent to have a relative or friend present is supportive and will enable such support to continue.

The fact that such information is not easy to give or receive should be acknowledged.

There are cultural differences in how emotions are expressed but it is helpful to give opportunities for family members to express their feelings privately and to encourage them to share their feelings with others whom they can trust.

It is important to give opportunities for the first "telling" or information-giving to be repeated or followed up.

If such information comes after birth or a trauma, such as an accident or sudden illness, it is likely to be a shock. In such cases, the information that is given is unlikely to be fully heard or understood. It is therefore important to give some information in writing and to arrange for a second appointment or for a professional such as a doctor or nurse or social worker to visit the family a little later to explain anything that was not understood or to give further information in response to questions that the family want to ask after reflection.

Professionals should demonstrate a positive approach, which reflects respect and valuing of the child or person with the disability. Information should be given honestly but with an emphasis on positives.

Families of disabled persons consistently express the need for a single point of contact to ask for information or advice. Their needs cross traditional departmental boundaries between departments of health, education, housing, social welfare, vocational training and employment.

PRACTICAL ADVICE

Although families value information, they also say that information alone is not enough. They need, from the earliest days, some guidance as to how to support their disabled family member and, wherever possible, how to minimise the disadvantaging effects of the impairment.

Parents of young children appreciate advice on how to stimulate and help their child to learn, explore and socialise. At each age and life stage, there are both common life needs such as the need for loving relationships and a sense of self-worth and security. There are also likely to be particular needs that have to be met: educational needs; sexual and vocational needs; and accommodation and care needs when family members may no longer be in a position to offer the necessary support and care themselves.

Professionals may be able to offer such advice themselves or be in position to direction families to other agencies or organisations who can. Other parents of disabled children of families with a disabled member are often able to support others facing similar issues.

FAMILY SUPPORT

Many families with a disabled child or adult member live their lives and cope in much the same way as other families. However, the availability of support from family, friends, neighbours and communities is a crucial factor in how they do so.

The support that families need and value takes many forms and includes support from informal social networks, local communities and governmental and non-governmental agencies.

Attitudes

The acceptance of and liking or love for the person with the disability is central. Positive attitudes among their family members or from neighbours are of great importance. Families are often instrumental in generating such positive attitudes themselves by giving the people around them an opportunity of getting to know the disabled person.

Practical help

Caring for a disabled child and adult usually takes more time and effort than caring for those without an impairment. In such situations, any help with practical tasks may be supportive, whether it is help with other household duties; help with other children in the family or help in caring for the disabled person, which again may take many forms. It can include looking after the disabled person in the home while other family members are engaged in other activities; undertaking a particular programme with the disabled person to enable him or her to acquire a new skill; or taking the disabled person out of the home for particular activities and experiences to broaden his or her life.

Practical help in the home may also take the form of special aids such as wheelchairs and appliances, and adaptations to the home, such as hoists or wider toilets.

Respite or shared care

The term "respite care" is problematic, since it again reflects the model of disability being an inevitable burden from which relief must be given. Terms such as shared care" or "alternative or second families" are increasingly being used. Similarly, the concept of care may be too limited and under-emphasise the positive aspects of stimulation, new experiences and enjoyment associated with family life.

In a number of countries there are schemes whereby a family with a disabled child or young person is linked with another family who gets to know the child and invites him or her to stay at regular intervals or from time to time. This gives children with a disability an opportunity of mixing with different children and adults in a different environment and of broadening their experiences. It also enables them to gain greater dependence from their own families. At the same time, it gives their own families the opportunity of participating in activities that the disabled member might not be able to undertake or of giving more time than they are usually able to give to other members of the family.

A major national study in the United States showed that although 46 out of the 50 States provided shared care in some form, many families experienced problems in being aware of what was available and in gaining access to the service of their choice [2]. Many of the arrangements were inflexible and failed to meet families' needs. Examples of accessible family support systems from the United Kingdom have recently been reported [25].

In addition to benefits for the family or for the individual, such schemes bring benefits to the community as a whole. Families who offer to share their home with a disabled child or adult demonstrate their commitment to the sharing of such roles and tasks by the community as a whole. They also provide valuable examples to neighbours and fellow citizens.

Financial support

When a family includes a disabled member, the family almost always experiences additional costs. In many countries, financial support is offered only by other members of the family or in some societies by the disabled child or adult begging for alms.

In many developed countries, social welfare provision acknowledges a responsibility for all citizens to support those who are vulnerable and disadvantaged. The State offers some financial support to those who care for disabled children or adults in their family and who may, by so doing, forego their own work or career opportunities. Care within the home is also often seen as a more desirable and certainly also as cheaper form of care then alternative residential care if such support is not available.

When disabled persons reach adulthood, they are also entitled to financial support if they are unable to work of support themselves financially. This includes the cost of any support they need to live in the community, including staff to support them in practical ways by helping them with personal care, shopping, cooking, cleaning etc. and additional costs for travel.

Some families themselves are taking out insurance or setting up trust schemes for their disabled sons and daughters for the future when they are no longer able to offer such children the care they need.

Counselling

In addition to practical support, families or individual family members sometimes need and can benefit from psychological support, particularly when negative reactions to disability persist and/ or become overwhelming. Counselling is a broad term to describe a number of methods of offering such support. The main principles include helping people to express their feelings and thoughts, however negative these may be, in a supportive, non-judgemental environment and to help them to look at all the choices available to them in order to work out what they think is best for themselves and their family. This type of support service is available only to a limited number of people in developed countries and those wealthy enough in developing countries to find and pay for such a service.

Family-to-family support and self-help

Almost all services and policies for disabled people and their families have their origins in families and family members coming together and supporting each other; in initiating programmes to help their disabled children and relatives; and in pressing Governments for social policies to give them the support and services they need.

Families have a unique ability to support others in a similar position to their own. Although all families are different, they can understand better than others the experiences of caring for and living with a disabled family member in their social context and environment. They can empathise with each others' feelings; share ways in which they themselves have coped with any difficulties that arose and how they sought and found solutions. They can be a source of information and advice and offer mutual practical and emotional support. Some of the types of support described in previous sections may be offered by other parents and family members.

Different family members can gain support for their particular situation and role from others: mothers, fathers, grandparents, brothers and sisters. Disabled people gain from the friendship of other disabled children and adults who have had similar experiences of struggle and achievement and of facing prejudice and disadvantage.

Much can be gained from groups and associations of disabled people meeting together and from other family members and families meeting in groups and associations. Not only is there a pooling of knowledge and experience and a breaking down of feelings of isolation, but also such groups can gain strength from each other in initiating new methods of support; in modifying the attitudes of others; in advocating for the rights of people with disability and their families; and in pressing for more appropriate policies to address these rights.

Self-help groups can be appropriate and helpful at any age or stage in the life cycle of the disabled person and his or her family. Children gain from sharing activities; adolescents and young adults from discussing views and experiences as well as having fun together; older people gain from meeting and sharing memories of their past lives, as do all older people.

Groups of parents can meet in each others' homes, in community halls and, as happened in Côte d'Ivoire [11], in the local market-place.

Self-help groups can also invite professionals to give them information, advice or support. They can involve professionals in advocating on their behalf or jointly press for improvements. They can also demonstrate their own abilities to contribute to the training of professionals.

CONFLICT AND ADVOCACY

Conflict may arise from time to time in all families, particularly when children reach the adolescent or young adult stage and may make choices different to those favoured by their parents. Most young people will grow in independence and make their own way. The degree to which they take account of their parents' views and wishes will vary from culture to culture and from individual to individual. This development is even more difficult for those young people who may remain dependent for their physical care on their families throughout their lives.

Common areas for potential conflict include young people's wish to experiment and take risks and try new experiences, even if these are later discarded as mistakes. Young disabled persons may wish to go further afield than their families consider safe; they may wish to try new skills; they may, like other young people, want to form sexual relationships; they may want to marry and to have children of their own.

Their parents and relatives may well be sympathetic to these choices and wishes; they may, indeed, encourage them. However, in other families, young persons may meet with discouragement, disapproval and blocking of their wishes. This negative response may spring from the best of motives: other family members may fear for the disabled young person and wish to protect him or her from harm, upset or emotional pain. However, this may nevertheless constitute a denial of the right of disabled persons to self-determination and to make choices about their own lives.

Similar conflicts may occur when disabled persons are older. They may also want to do things that other family members fell may constitute a risk to themselves.

In such situations, it is important that disabled children, young people and adults have access to an independent person who will act as their advocate and who will argue their cause, try to ensure their rights and enable them to exercise control over their own lives. This may need to be done at the same time as offering some support, advice and/or counselling for the rest of the family.

ABUSE AND PROTECTION

Even more serious and difficult are those situations in which disabled children or adults are abused. While the majority of families care adequately or well for their disabled members, there are family situations in which the disabled member may be scapegoated, neglected or ill-treated.

There is now a growing body of research, at least in developed countries, about the abuse experienced by disabled children and adults. People with disabilities, including older people, have also expressed their feelings and views about their experiences of abuse, which in some cases may have occurred many years ago.

Sexual abuse has been reported in most cultures and all classes of society. As the preconditions for the occurrence of sexual abuse include both the accessibility of a more vulnerable person and the ability to ensure their silence about the abuse, it is clear that these conditions are present in relation to disabled people.

Studies in the United States have estimated that abuse has occurred in up to 25 per cent of adolescents with learning difficulties; 50 per cent of young people in institutions with hearing impairments; and as many as 50 per cent to 75 per cent of children with severe learning difficulties and behaviour problems ([15] and [31]). In the United Kingdom an estimated 5 per cent of adults with learning difficulties have been sexually abused at some time.

There are many reasons for this. Some relate to the negative social attitudes of prejudice and discrimination that lead parents of disabled children to neglect or ill-treat such children or even leave them to die. Family members may adopt the social attitudes and behaviour of others and taunt such children, and criticize or reproach them for their difference and for what they cannot do.

There are many different forms of abuse; abuse is also cumulative and multiple. All sexually abused children and many physically abused children are emotionally abused. About a quarter of the children who are physically abused are also sexually abused. Once a child has been sexually abused he or she is more vulnerable to further abuse.

There is a growing recognition that the abuse of disabled children and adults occurs all too often and more frequently than in other populations. Such abuse occurs not only within families, but also in institutions and with alternative families and carers.

The very dependence of the disabled member may make him or her the target for all the frustrations caused by a variety of stresses in the family such as poverty, overwork, tensions in family relationships, unemployment, poverty and ill health.

Lack of knowledge may also lead to some forms of mistreatment, such as emotional neglect and lack of stimulation, that are likely to affect significantly the disabled person's degree of disability in coping with his or her environment.

Disabled children and adults are perhaps the most vulnerable to abuse of all kinds including severe physical and sexual abuse. Disabled children and adults often require more intimate physical care that enables others to have access to them in private. They may have less access to sexual education and to an understanding of what is normal and acceptable touching and what is sexual behaviour. They are often less free to move about and find independent people to whom they can talk about the abuse and they may also find it harder to communicate and be understood, and, even more crucially, to be believed.

Behavioural signs that indicate the possibility of sexual abuse of other children or adults may be too readily interpreted by professionals as due to the disabling condition. For too long professionals and society at large have failed to consider abuse as a possible origin of changed, perhaps challenging, behaviours in people with disability and have not considered that such behaviour may provide one means–sometimes the only means–by which disabled people can communicate their anger and distress in response to abusive experiences.

Strategies for protection

Many countries have now developed or are developing ways of protecting children and vulnerable adults from abuse both within their families and outside the family by others, including other carers and professional. Such procedures were set up initially for non-disabled children but the frequency of abuse makes it necessary to extend these procedures to disabled children and adults.

There is now greater understanding that professionals, communities and families must be more alert to the possibility of abuse occurring and ways of responding if abuse is suspected. Additional complexities in doing this may be present in investigating and dealing with the abuse of disabled children and adults, particularly in situations where there are difficulties in communication or where the child or adult has an intellectual impairment. Most legal systems discriminate against children and people with learning difficulties or communications impairments, although a few successful prosecutions have been brought in such situations. This remains an area where professionals in all disciplines require more training, knowledge and skills.

Again, training and raising awareness of the possibility of abuse and its damaging long-term consequences are essential, particularly for professionals and carers of disabled children and adults.

Sexual education for disabled children is at least as important as it is for other children. Support for families and for disabled people to increase their opportunities for communication where there are speech, hearing or comprehension difficulties should include signs or symbols that will enable disabled people to tell of abuse if it exists.

Because of the long-term damaging effects of abuse, it is important that all survivors of abuse have the opportunity of working through their feelings and experiences, with the support of a trained

7

SUPPORT IN THE LIFE CYCLE

Arising from what families have reported, some useful general principles can be derived.

GENERAL PRINCIPLES OF SUPPORT

- Support should always be mindful of the rights of the disabled person
- Support should always be offered on the basis of needs identified either by families themselves or in collaboration with families
- Support should be offered in a way that is appropriate to the individual family
- Support should remain flexible. The mode, amount or timing of support should change as the needs of the disabled person and the family change.
- Support should retain a focus on the similarity of needs of the person with the disability and the family to those of others.
- Support should maximize the degree of control exercised by the disabled person and the family
- Support should facilitate the integration of the person with the disability and the family into the life of the local community.

While these principles apply throughout the life span, there are specific aspects to the support offered at key stages in the life cycle.

AT BIRTH

Many parents have written about their experiences and feelings on learning that they had given birth to a child with a disability. It is an experience that is never forgotten, and one that affects their relationships with other professionals for many years. Many parents are still angry and bitter when they remember the pain caused by the manner in which they were first informed that their new baby had a disability. Although there is evidence of considerable improvements over the past 20 years, many parents still complain of insensitivity, lack of information, understanding and support [5].

Some writers automatically assume that giving birth to a child with a disability will always be seen as tragedy and that new parents inevitably pass through periods of mourning and chronic sorrow before they finally adjust to the reality of having a child with a disability. Professionals and well-meaning friends try to help the new parens to accept the disability, somehow implying that parents deny that their child has a disability or that they reject the child.

The reality is that parent's reactions vary greatly. Some will already have been told before birth that their baby will have a particular impairment and will have made a conscious decision to continue with the pregnancy. Some will realise at once that there is an abnormality in the baby before anyone tells them. Others suspect that something is wrong from the behaviour of the staff of the maternity unit or because the hospital procedures are different.

PRESCHOOL YEARS AND EARLY INTERVENTION

Since it is universally accepted that the first five years of a child's life are all important, it is vital that parents of children with disabilities are given every possible support in helping their children's development. The nature and amount of support will vary from family to family, in relation to the needs of the child, the family as a whole and individual members of the family. Each family therefore needs to be aware of what is available and be able to discuss how their needs can best be met.

It is essential that all families should be able to express concerns if they are worried about any aspect of their child's development and that their child should be thoroughly assessed by a multidisciplinary team including doctors, nurses and specialists in child development with a knowledge of assessment of young children. Ideally, such assessments should be carried out in an environment familiar to the child, preferably the child's own home, rather than in the strange environment of a hospital or clinic.

In some countries, specialist child development teams are available to carry out a detailed assessment of the level of development the child has reached in various areas of development (e.g. physical, self-care, social, language development). On this basis, the team suggests activities to assist the child's development that can be carried out at home.

In Kenya, for example, about 30 such teams have been established at the local level to work with families and schools. The teams are themselves supported by the Ministries of Health and Education [27].

At this stage, the team has to have some knowledge of the family situation and to ensure that the suggestions that are made are realistic and manageable. Suggestions for additional family activities, over and above what they would do naturally, should be the outcome of negotiation, rather than prescription. If the parents agree, it may be helpful and informative for a member of the team to visit the family beforehand and to keep in touch with the family to provide support and encouragement and to modify the suggestions if they prove to be unrealistic.

Many of the concerns of families at this point relate to ordinary routines such as feeding and sleeping and the extent to which the baby needs to be treated differently as a consequence of the impairment. At a later stage, they will need support in methods of stimulating the child, the right kinds of activities and play materials, playing with other children etc.

Wherever possible, assessment and early intervention programmes should plan for a multidisciplinary input. It is particularly important to include medical surveillance, in order to identify additional complications. Children with Down's syndrome, for example, frequently have additional impairments involving ocular, auditory, respiratory and cardiac functions. Similarly, children with epilepsy may not obtain access to the right medication. The prevention of secondary impairments is particularly important in children with intellectual impairment. Because these may not be apparent at birth, it is important to provide comprehensive medical monitoring in order to provide timely and effective treatment. It is sometimes difficult to obtain full medical check-ups, as parents' concerns tend to be dismissed as examples of fussiness or over-protectiveness.

Portage home intervention programme

The Portage home intervention programme is perhaps the best-known example of a home-based family support programme for young children with a development delay or disability. This programme was originally developed in rural areas in North America but has since been translated into 30 languages and adapted for use in many developing countries; for example, Guyana, India, Jamaica and Nepal [3].

The Portage programme is based on the parent and home visitor carrying out a joint assessment of the stages that a child has reached in key areas of development; for example, physical, fine and gross motory skills, social, emotional and language development and in a range of spontaneous play activities. This joint assessment is based on the parent's detailed knowledge of the child, supplemented by the home visitor's own observations and experience of other children's development.

The next stage involves discussion and negotiations between the parent and the home visitor concerning priorities for the next steps in the child's learning and, above all, of ways in which the family can help the child to reach these targets in a comparatively short time, within one or two weeks. To this end, the home visitor uses a set of activity cards that suggest ordinary games that can be used by members of the family to help the child achieve short-term targets, mainly using ordinary household routines and activities.

A range of other home–visiting and support programmes have been reported in a number of developing countries. One of the best known of these is the Zimcare project, which has been developed by a voluntary organisation in four rural areas in Zimbabwe [18]. These were run in association with existing locally active organisations (e.g. the Red Cross).

While independent evaluation suggested that this was a successful programme, it is clear that not all families and primary-care givers can commit time and motivation to meeting the demands of such programmes. This raises a general issues about the commitment needed to implement Portage-type programmes by families who are already overwhelmed by the day-to-day demands of work and never-ending domestic tasks. There is also the issue of the nature of the participation demanded by the programme. Even when adapted to suit local conditions, family members (nearly always mothers) have to find time to be alone with the child, to record progress (however simply) and to plan further activities with the home visitor.

It is important for those developing such programmes to take account of the potential resources of the extended family and to adapt them to whatever extent is practicable and desirable. Many grandparents, uncles and aunts and brothers and sisters have become involved in early intervention programmes and have played a major part in helping to give families a sense of common purpose in working together to help children with disabilities to learn and to develop and to be accepted in the neighbourhood and the local community.

Inclusion in mainstream preschool programmes

In addition to specialist initiatives such as Portage, it is important to create opportunities to enable preschool children to be integrated into whatever programmes are available to other preschool children. Many countries have developed a range of preschool facilities: nursery schools, nursery classes in primary classes and day-care centres, as well as many privately run kindergartens and playgroups, often run or controlled by the parents themselves.

Many children with developmental delays and disabilities have been successfully integrated into these programmes. There can be no doubt that they provide a much-needed source of support for parents. Not only do they provide a break from the day-to-day care of the child, but they also provide opportunities for meeting other parents and professional staff on a day-to-day basis, with whom they can exchange ideas and experiences.

Yet preschool provision is not common in developing countries. A summary of provision in Asia indicates that only India, Sri Lanka and Thailand have extensive provision [17], though China seems to be rapidly extending nurseries and including children with developmental delays. There are reports of an experimental integration programme in Anhui Province, with some support from the United Kingdom charity, Save the Children Fund.

Towards partnership with parents

In all projects involving young and preschool children, the utmost care is needed to ensure that professionals and volunteers work with and through full and equal partnership with families at every stage. Parents have frequently complained that professionals have a tendency to take over and to know best, forgetting that it is the family who lives with the child for 24 hours a day and has the experiences of understanding and trying to meet the child's needs. Professionals are there to support not supplant families.

In countries where comprehensive assessment and early intervention programmes are available, it is important to ensure that parents are not overwhelmed and confused by conflicting advice from different professionals whom they encounter in clinics or on home visits. To avoid this, many teams have developed the concept of a key worker. After the initial assessment, this persons provides a single point of contact between the family and the rest of the team. A close relationship develops between the family and the key worker who must be a good listener and mediator, whatever other qualifications they may have. Sometimes this function is carried out by another parent.

Services need to be planned and delivered in order to respond to these individual needs. Services must not be delivered in inflexible packages or be based on a stereotype of family needs and priorities. These have to be discussed and negotiated.

The same dynamic interaction between the needs of families and the nature of available services and supports applies at all stages in the lives of families who have disabled relative.

SCHOOL YEARS

In many developing countries, disabled children do not go to school at all. Surveys conducted by the United Nations Educational, Scientific and Cultural Organisation (UNESCO) indicate that less than 2 per cent of disabled children attend any form of school in many African and Asian countries and that few of those who do so will complete four years of primary education [12]. Yet studies in number of countries have indicated that a certain amount of causal integration does take place. Children have been accepted by the local school, because their parents have taken them and because they and their families were already known to the school ([21] and [22]).

Integration dilemmas

In Western countries, it is widely agreed that all disabled children should attend the same local schools as other children in the neighbourhood. This is probably the view of most parents of younger children and of many parents of older children as well.

But the issues are far from simple from the point of view of families and the children themselves. While the inclusion of children with physical impairments is widely accepted, teachers are less ready to accept children with significant learning or behavioural difficulties and are anxious about teaching children with sensory impairments without additional resources provided by equipment or trained support teachers.

Many industrialised countries have a well-resourced and highly developed special school system, with well-trained staff and staff ratios as low as one adult to three children in some classes. The classrooms are often well equipped and the schools are likely to be visited by speech therapists, physiotherapists, medical and nursing specialists and advisory teachers and psychologists.

Yet however well resourced a special school may be, it still separates its pupils from other children and therefore deprives them of the opportunity of a shared learning environment with other children and of helping them in turn to value and include disabled children. The challenge is one of integrating and combining the educational advantages of special schools with the social benefits of ordinary schools; some call this making ordinary schools special and special schools ordinary.

Many links have been developed between special and ordinary schools. Children from special schools may spend part of each week attending classes in a neighbouring ordinary school. Ordinary schools have in turn set up special classes or developed resource rooms and learning support teams to enable children with disabilities to spend all or most of their time in the ordinary class, with carefully planned support from other teachers.

It is tempting to advise parents in developing countries to avoid the mistakes of developed countries by adopting integrated education from the outset, which is indeed the preferred option for many parents. Others however feel that ordinary schools are simply not ready or properly resourced to meet the needs of children with severe disabilities, particularly those with severe intellectual impairments. Teachers may be hostile or negative, the classes are likely to be too large and the needs of such children may be overlooked. In this situation, some parents prefer to put their energies into lobbying for a special school to be set up, often with funds that they have raised themselves or with limited support from public funds. Many parents have set up their own schools and indeed trained to teach in the schools themselves.

Home-school links

Whether children go to school or not, parents and the wider family are just as much in need of support then as they were during the first few years of the child's life. Some will need support in insisting on the rights of their child to attend school. Others may not be convinced that there will be any benefit in their child attending school. They may feel that little or nothing can be done by schools to help the child and they may fear that the child will be teased, mocked or unhappy both in the classroom and in the playground.

In cases where children do attend school, the development of an active partnership of equals between parents and professionals must be a top priority. Unfortunately, this is far from being a reality in many countries, developing or developed. Indeed, it may well constitute the exception rather than the rule.

In many countries, parents of all children, and not just those with disabilities, are still kept at arm's length by schools. Failure to mobilise the interest of parents and to work for their close involvement in the life of the school and the education of their child is a tragic waste of human resources and family commitment.

Where disabled children are concerned, there is everything to gain from developing close working relationships between teachers and parents and other family members. The rationale for such partnerships is overwhelmingly convincing but, with some notable exceptions, not many examples are to be found throughout the world.

Some years ago, UNESCO commissioned ILSMH to prepare guidelines for collaboration and partnership between parents and professionals working with disabled children and young people [23]. The guidelines reflected the best examples of good practice available from reports by some 70 member societies throughout the world.

The main recommendations concerning school-age children are summarised below. They appear to be relevant to different degrees to children with a wide range of disabilities and to schools and families in many countries.

Guidelines for collaboration between home and school

- There should be opportunities for parents and teachers to discuss their aims and priorities for the child, both in the long term and the short term.
- In order to plan the most appropriate curriculum, teaching objectives and methods, teachers should try to learn about the child's home environment in general and as it relates to the child's learning opportunities in particular.
- Teachers and family members should jointly assess the child's skills, abilities and needs.
- Successful collaboration between parents and teachers depends on the extent to which information is shared.
- Educational goals and methods need to be shared with families.
- Parents and teachers should share and celebrate success.
- Teachers need to find the time to listen to parents' concerns and priorities ("Your choice is our choice", as expressed by teachers in Bangladesh).
- It is useful for parents and teachers to list possible ways in which they can work together; for example, through

teachers visiting parents at home, parents taking part in school activities, recording of children's work through photographs and videos to illustrate progress or share ideas on joint work.

- Parent can be much more fully involved in training professionals.
- Opportunities need to be created to involve both the parents and the student in the formulation and monitoring of plans and policies at the level of the school and in the locality.

NEEDS OF SCHOOL-LEAVERS AND YOUNG ADULTS

The age at which children leave school varies greatly across the world, both for disabled and non-disabled children. In many countries, the majority of children do not complete even four years of primary education and can expect to leave school between 10 and 12 years of age. Many drop out after one or two years and others only attend sporadically. Only a minority proceed to secondary education or beyond.

If this is the norm of many children in developing countries, it is all the more important that a firm foundation of partnership is laid between parents and teachers during the years when children are at school. Many parents will be able to build on these foundations once their child leaves school and transfer what they have learned from this partnership to new challenges and situations that the family will encounter as their son or daughter leaves school and becomes an adult.

Leaving school presents challenges both to the young person and to the family. The routine of daily attendance at school and the structure that this provides are suddenly disrupted. The young person often feels disorientated and confused by the change of routine and lifestyle and may be left with little or nothing to do during the day. It may take time to find a useful role and to adjust to the changes brought about by leaving school.

All this may coincide with the whole range of social, physical and sexual pressures associated with the normal process of adolescence, in this case complicated by disability and by doubts and uncertainties about the future.

The family will also be faced with a number of adjustments. All too often, a member of the family, usually the mother, is forced to give up her work or some of her outside interests, in order to look after a disabled son or daughter. This in itself can be a cause of stress, all the more so because in most countries the prospects of daytime occupation for young disabled people are small. The family situation is therefore potentially tense and explosive.

It is at this time that worries about the long-term future can become prominent; concerns about what arrangements can be made for the young person when the parents are too old or themselves too disabled to look after their son or daughter and what will finally happen after their death. This is a particular concern in cases where the young person is severely intellectually impaired and needs a level of support and care that is not available in the community.

In some countries, housing trusts have been set up to ensure that a home can be provided with appropriate levels of care when this becomes necessary. Parents who can afford to do so may make payments into a trust fund specifically set up for this purpose. Sometimes, all too rarely, plans are made by public authorities to prepare the young person to live in alternative accommodation in the community when the time comes. But schemes such as this are only available to the few and many families cannot see any resolution to this problem and fear that their son or daughter may be sent to an institution for the rest of their lives.

PLANNING FOR THE FUTURE

There are few countries in the world where provision for disabled school-leavers and young people meets the whole range of needs identified at this time in the young person's life or where it is planned in partnership with the family. In most countries, even families who have been reasonably well supported while their child was at school are often neglected and left to fend for themselves. Because few services are available for the young people themselves, the situation at home can be charged and reach crisis point.

Families need to be able to voice these concerns and to know that they will not only be listened to with understanding, but also that plans will be made with their full participation as well as that of the young people concerned, which will result in an exploration of whatever alternatives are available, however limited these may be.

This process needs to begin while the young person is still at school. In some developed countries, there are legal requirements for a transition plan to be developed for all disabled school-leavers. The school is not only responsible for preparing the young person to be as independent as possible, but also for involving parents and the student in discussion and decision-making on future provision, together with other professional staff such as social workers and health professionals who are well placed to advise on these options. Increasingly, schools are helping their students to anticipate some of the problems they will face in finding a job and taking their place in society.

The first need of families is for information about facilities and resources that are or can be made available, however limited these may be. In some countries, this information is summarised in leaflet form, listing the names of key organisations and individuals. These agencies may be scattered and uncoordinated, making it difficult for families to know where and how to begin to secure the support and services that they and their son or daughter need.

Because families are at their most vulnerable at this transition point between school and community services, it is essential to ensure that one person is designated as a single point of contact and that families should have a say in choosing him or her. This person should then try to coordinate the information available from the various agencies and act as a friend or advocate of the family in securing the most appropriate provision for the family as a whole and for the disabled person in particular. Their needs are now, as before, inseparable.

Continuing education

In many developing countries, continuing education facilities are becoming available to disabled young people. These are usually in local community colleges attended by other young people and provide a wide range of vocational and non-vocational courses.

Such colleges provide a fresh start both educationally and socially. Many young people who have attended special schools or classes are more than ready for the more adult and challenging environment that can be presented by a local college.

As most colleges are by definition for all members of the community, the initial assumption is that disabled students will be fully included in the classes of their choice. This means that college staff will need some preparation and support in ensuring that the curriculum and activities of the class and of the college as a whole are fully extended to all disabled students. Some students will need additional support; for example, access to and mobility within the building, taped or Brailled material, sign-language interpretation and learning support. Some of these supports are expensive; others call for a greater degree of awareness, knowledge and skills among all levels of college staff.

The role of parents whose son or daughter is attending college is an ambiguous one. Although they have a great deal of valuable information to share with the college, it is likely that their sons or daughters will be of an age when they ought to be able to speak for themselves and make their own needs known. Staff may therefore be inclined to keep parents at arm's length, in the interests of consistency with other students whose parents may have little or no formal or social contact with the college.

It is important, therefore, that parents should at least be centrally involved at the time of admission to the college. At the stage, other professionals such as teachers, health professionals or social workers may also be involved with the young person and the family in developing a transition plan in collaboration with college staff. Parents should then have an opportunity of sharing their views and information on a basis of equality with other partners in the transition process.

Because choosing the right courses is one of the most difficult decisions facing any student entering college, it is essential that all concerned are made aware of what is available and that the choice really meets the needs of the student who should have the final say. There is a risk of underestimating the student's abilities and of assuming that certain courses may be too difficult for one reason or another or that vocational courses may not lead to employment at the end of the course. Family members, college staff and former teachers may all have different views. In this situation, the voice of the student is sometimes drowned in a chorus of well-intentioned advice.

Preparation for employment

Despite world recession and high levels of unemployment, disabled people insist on their rights to paid employment. This is in line with International Labour Organisation Convention 159 of 1983 concerning Vocational Rehabilitation and Employment (Disabled Persons) [14] and also with the Standard Rules on the Equalisation of Opportunities for Persons with Disabilities [30]. A small number of countries have introduced legislation making it illegal to discriminate against disabled people in respect of employment, as well as housing, education, leisure, transport etc. (e.g. the Americans with Disabilities Act, 1990). Others have introduced disability quotas and levies (e.g. Germany).

In reality, the number of disabled people in full employment is very low in most countries. Nevertheless, a growing number of disabled people have found and kept jobs, despite the underestimation of the likelihood of their doing so by families or professionals.

In developing countries, many disabled people are working with their family, especially in rural areas. In other cases, they are working in family businesses or selling goods from a family stall in the market-place. This not only benefits the individual and the family, but also provides a good example to the general public that disabled people can make a positive contribution to society.

In other cases, parents and voluntary organisations have themselves set up sheltered workshops and vocational training centres to ensure that disabled people have access to some form of training and vocational preparation (e.g. Kenya). Some of these workshops specialise in making certain products and then marketing them directly to the general public. This aim may at times conflict with that of preparing people to work in the open market or at least of securing supported employment.

Many industrialised countries have long established day centres or sheltered workshops but their success in placing people in open employment is limited. A number of countries, however, have reported successful schemes where a disabled person is given whatever support is needed to enable them to do a particular job in a given environment. The support may be in the form of grants for the employer to adapt the workplace or for individuals to acquire physical or electronic supports to enable them to operate machinery or to carry out tasks that would otherwise be difficult or impossible for them.

In some countries, human support is given to enable a disabled person to learn and become proficient in the tasks required in the work setting. This support is sometimes provided by a staff member from the day centre or sheltered workshop or by a volunteer from the workplace who provides essential social support in helping particularly those with intellectual impairments to make friends and join informal social networks (e.g. Pathway scheme in the United Kingdom, started by the voluntary agency, the Royal Society for Mentally Handicapped Children and Adults (MENCAP) but later developed from public funds).

Living in the community

In developed countries, the principle of living an ordinary life implies that disabled people should be supported in leaving their families and living as independently as possible. Some progress has been made to this end. An increasing number of adults, including some with severe physical and intellectual impairments, are living in their own homes and apartments, with as much support as they need as individuals. This comes from publicly funded social-care assistants who help them with those tasks and activities that they cannot carry out for themselves.

In most developing countries, however, it is traditional for young people to remain with their families until they marry. In these situations, the concept of moving out of the family in late adolescence would not be considered appropriate, as the family expects to provide a home for some years and also to include new daughters-in-law as the sons marry, at least for a period. Furthermore, the extended family has a key role in supporting all members of the family, including those with a disability. This may include a job and a home being provided by a member of the extended family. Although a greater number of small nuclear families are now found in developing countries, the traditional supporting role of the extended family remains strong in most countries.

MARRIAGE AND PARENTHOOD

Disabled people often have restricted opportunities to meet people of their own age and background. Similarly, families of young disabled people may over-protect their son or daughter and discourage friendships and more intimate relationships, for fear of exploitation or disappointment.

In the past, there has been little open recognition of the sexual needs of disabled people and of the fact that these are no different from those of the rest of the population. Disabled people, particularly those with intellectual impairments, have been regarded as asexual both their families and by professionals, despite clear evidence to the contrary. Consequently, sexuality, sex education and support in personal relationships generally have rarely been provided for young people or discussed by their families.

More recently, the social and sexual needs of disabled people of all ages have received increasing recognition, stimulated in part by growing evidence of their vulnerability to exploitation and sexual abuse as well as by the more positive motivation of supporting them in forming relationships, in marrying and in becoming parents.

Recognising, respecting and supporting disabled people in forming relationships, marrying and becoming parents again calls for understanding and collaboration between disabled people themselves, their families and the various professionals with whom they may be in contact. Although many disabled people will need relatively little help, others, particularly those with intellectual or communication impairments, may well encounter greater obstacles and need sensitive support.

Many disabled people marry and become successful parents, and some marriage partners and some parents may become disabled when they already have a family. Again there will be a great variety of experience, just as among the non-disabled population and depending on the social environment.

Although many disabled people have married and become parens, they face many obstacles. In part these spring directly from cultural and social attitudes to disability. For example, there may be fears about the extent to which the disability may be inherited and may be passed to children, or there may be concerns about the ability of the disabled person to support a family.

Disabled people who have pioneered by pressing for their right to share these common human experiences have helped to shape society's thinking on these issues and some disabled parents and some children of disabled parents have begun to document their experiences.

CHALLENGE OF AGEING

The increasing life expectancy both of disabled people and their parents is bringing new challenges. It is not uncommon for ageing disabled people themselves to become carers of their elderly and infirm parents. This may provide a valued and indeed indispensable role for them, but it also creates barriers to their own independence and autonomy in the community. Their situation parallels that of countless women who have sacrificed opportunities for a career, marriage and motherhood in order to devote themselves to the care of their or their spouses' elderly and dependent parents.

Some disabled people enter willingly into such a role but others will feel that new restrictions are being imposed on them against their will. It is important, therefore, that these issues are considered by the whole family in advance of emergencies and that the disabled member of the family should express a clear view and take appropriate action. Families should expect to receive support from professionals and service agencies in the community.

The process of ageing can be particularly difficult for disabled people. It is all too often assumed that any physical or psychological difficulties that they experience are an integral part of their disability. When this happens, they may find it hard to obtain investigation and treatment for conditions that are not directly related to their disability at all.

A further dilemma arises in individuals with Down's syndrome who show signs of rapid ageing consistent with Alzheimer's disease at a comparatively early age. Although many have lived successfully and with varying degrees of support in the community, the ageing process can affect them so severely that some form of residential care becomes necessary. Should they then be integrated into ordinary old people's homes and geriatric hospitals where they will be much young than other residents and where they might have to live in poor conditions for many more years? A preferred solutio is to provide them with an increasing amount of support to enable them to remain either in their own homes or in supported accommodation. Funds for this option are hand to come by.

Preparing for death and bereavement

Children and adults with disabilities are as, or perhaps even more, likely to experience the death of their relatives, carers and friends as anyone else. They themselves may have a progressive, terminal condition. It may be particularly painful for carers to explain and prepare disabled people for death and bereavement, as well as to support them through their grief and mourning. This is understandable when attachments may be all the more crucial because of the additional dependency needs. However, it is all the more important to involve the disabled person in what is happening, to explain and to provide opportunities for them to express their feelings, fears and anxieties as well as the confusion, anger and powerlessness that are well-known features of bereavement. Giving information and explanation, and involvement in planning for their own future, are all ways in which those supporting disabled people can enable them to retain as much control over their own lives as possible.

8

CONCLUSIONS

Disabled people themselves and their families have already made and are continuing to make a significant and powerful impact on the way the societies in which they live think about and respond to disabled people. An increasing number of disabled people are making an outstanding and inspirational contribution to the life of their communities as teachers, politicians and artists. The various United Nations conventions and charters and guidance to Governments in relation to disability issues are a useful spur to further action. But profound changes are needed before disabled people are granted equal rights and can fully take their place in society and, most importantly, before society itself can fully benefit from the creativity, strengths and abilities of disabled people and their families. IYF can provide a starting-point for a major reappraisal of the extent to which families can be better supported in helping their relatives to take their place in the community and to make a significant contribution to society.

In preceding sections, the focus has been on individual families and services to support people with disabilities and their families in particular. But what disabled people and their families most want is to have the same access and rights to life-enhancing opportunities as their non-disabled friends and neighbours. In order for this to be possible, the needs of disabled people must be considered alongside those of all other groups.

For this to happen, the built environment will need to change to enable disabled people to become as mobile and as able to use buildings, transport and other facilities as everyone else.

Education, employment, housing, health, social welfare, income security and all other services must also become as accessible to disabled people and to members of their families as to all other members of society.

About all, social attitudes in all cultures must become informed by true knowledge about disabled people and their families, their strengths, their needs, their difficulties and their gifts.

These changes can come about in a variety of ways through:

- National and local policies and social education
- A more informed portrayal of disabled people and their families by the media
- A greater degree of interaction between disabled people and their families
- The perseverance of disabled people, their families and supportive professionals in continuing to campaign for all these necessary changes.

More positive social attitudes, policies and structures will bring about a greater contribution from disabled people and their families. This in turn will provide a foundation for the achievement of the goal of a Society for All in the twenty-first century.

REFERENCES

1. Baine, D. Handicapped children in developing countries. Edmonton, Canada, University of Edmonton Press, 1988.

2. Bradley, V., J. Knoll *and* J. Agosta, *eds*. Emerging issues in family support Wahington, D.C., American Association on Mental Retardation, 1992.

3. Brouilletee, J., M. Thorburn *and* K. Yamaguchi. Early Intervention. *In* P. Mittler, R. Brouillette and D. Hornis, *eds*. World yearbook of education: special needs education. London, Kogan Page, 1993.

4. Byrne, E., C. Cunningham *and* P. Sloper, Families of children with Down's syndrome: One feature in common. London, Routledge, 1988.

5. Carr, J. The effect on the family of a severely mentally handicapped child. *In* A. Charke, A.D.B. Clarke and J. Berg. *eds*. Mental deficiency: The changing outlook, 4th ed. London, Methuen, 1985.

6. Dunn, W. Personal communication. 1993.

7. Dybwad, R. Voluntary organisations in the field of mental handicap. Boston, Brookline Publications, 1989.

8. Fryers, T. Epidemiological thinking in mental retardation: Issues in taxonomy and population frequency. *In* N. Bray, *ed. International review of research in mental retardation* (New York and London, Academic Press, 1993).

9. Gartner, A., D. Lipsky *and* A. Turnbull, *eds.* Supporting families with a child with a disability: An international outlook. Baltimore, Maryland., Paul H. Brookes, 1991.

10. Groce, N. Everybody here spoke sign language: Hereditary deafness on Martha's Vineyard. Cambridge, Massachusetts, Harvard University Press, 1985

11. Haddad, H. Personal communication. 1993.

12. Hegarty, S. Education of children with disabilities. *In* P. Mittler. R. Brouillette and D. Harris, *eds.* World yearbook of education: special needs education. London, Kogan Page, 1993.

13. Helander, E. Beyond prejudice and dignity: An introduction to community based rehabilitation. Geneva, United Nations Development Programme, 1993.

14. International Labour Organisation. *International labour conventions and recommendations, 1919–*. Geneva, International Labour Office.

15. Kelly, L. The connection between disability and child abuse: a review of the research evidence. Child *abuse review,* 1:157-167, 1992.

16. Kisanji, J. Interface between culture and disability in the Tanzanian context. *International journal of development, disability and education:* 41, 1994 (in press).

17. Kohili, T. Special education in Asia. *In* P. Mittler, R. Brouillette *and* D. Harris, *eds.* World yearbook of education: special needs education. London, Kogan Page, 1993.

18. Mariga, L. and R. McConkey. Home based learning programmes for mentally handicapped people in rural areas of Zimbabwe. *International review of rehabilitation research,* 10:175-183, 1987.

19. McConachie, H. Implications of a model of stress and coping for services to families of young disabled children. *Children: care, health and development,* 20, 1994.

20. Milies, C. Educating mentally handicapped children. 2. ed. Peshawar, Pakistan, Mission Hospital, 1991.

21. Milies, C. *and* M. Milies. Children with learning difficulties. *In* P. Mittler, R. Brouillette and D. Harris, *eds.* World yearbook of education: special needs education. London, Kogan Page, 1993.

22. Milies, M. Action study on integration of handicapped children in Pakistan. Peshawar, North-West Frontier Province, Mission Hospital, 1985.

23. Mittler, P., H. Mittler *and* H. McConachie, Working together: Guidelines for collaboration between professionals and families of children and young people with disabilities. UNESCO Guides to Special Education No. 2. Paris, United Nations Educational, Scientific and Cultural Organisation, 1986.

24. P. Mittler, R. Brouillette *and* D. Harris, *eds.* World yearbook of education: special needs education. London, Kogan Page, 1993.

25. Mittler, P. *and* H. Mittler, *eds. Innovations in family support.* Chorley, Lancashire, Lisieux Hall Publications, 1994.

26. Office of Population Censuses and Surveys, Survey of disability in Great Britian; Part 5: Financial circumstances of families. London, Her Majesty's Stationary Office, 1988.

27. Serpell, R., L. Marige *and* K. Harvey. Mental retardation in African countries: Conceptualisation, services and research. *In* N. Bray, *ed. International review of research in mental retardation* (New York and London, Academic Press, 1993).

28. Shearer, A. *Think positive: Presenting a positive image of people with mental handicap.* Brussels, International League of Societies for Persons with Mental Handicap, 1984.

29. Talle, A. Notes on the concept of disability among the pastoral Masai in Kenya. *In* F. J. Brown and B. Ingstad, *eds.* Disability in a cross-cultural perspective: Working Paper No. 4 Oslo, Department of Social Anthropology, 1990. pp. 61-78.

30. United Nations, *Official Records of the General Assembly, Forty -eighth Session, Supplement No. 49* (A/48/49), resolution 48/49, annex.

31. Westcott, H. The abuse of disabled children and adults. London, National Society for the Prevention of Cruelty to Children, 1993.

32. World Health Organisation. International classification of impairments, disabilities and handicaps; A manual of classification relating to the consequences of disease, Geneva, 1980.

Annex

LEARNING MESSAGES

The Learning Messages that the IYF Task Force of ILSMH wants to communicate to its member societies, and to Governments, international agencies and to all individuals and organisations concerned with IYF are as follows:

(a) All people are valued members of their communities;

(b) People with a disability and their families are equal participating members of their communities and have the same rights:

(i) To participate in decisions that affect their lives;

(ii) To diversity of choice of housing, education, work, recreation and leisure;

a. To equity and justice;

b. To be empowered to take their full place in the community;

c. To dignity and privacy in all aspects of their lives;

(c) Everyone is likely to experience disability at some time in their lives, either personally or through members of their family or community;

(d) Society can add to or lesson disability;

(e) People with disabilities have abilities;

(f) People with a disability have the right to be consulted, to make informed choices and to exercise control in planning their lives;

(g) People with a disability and their families and carers have an important contribution to make to policy development, planning and delivery of services and to training about disability issues;

(h) It is normal to be different;

(i) People with a disability have useful knowledge about their own needs, strengths and abilities;

(j) Families with a member who has a disability have knowledge about their own strengths, needs and abilities;

(k) Families need information;

(l) Support for families with a member who has a disability makes economic sense;

(m) Definitions of the family must reflect the wide range of family arrangements and forms found in society;

(n) Usually it is in the best interests of the family member with a disability to remain within the family environment, at least during childhood. Families require practical support in order to fulfil this role. Exploitation of families by the State needs to be avoided;

(o) The interests, safety and welfare of the person with a disability must always be safeguarded;

(p) In two-parent families, the task of caring for family member with a disability should as far as possible be shared by both parents. Fathers and mothers both have a vital role in creating a beneficial family environment. Both can make a valuable contribution to the functioning of supportive organisations and where possible should be actively involved in such organisations.

PART—2
HUMAN RIGHTS AND DISABLED PERSONS

INTRODUCTION

1. By way of introduction it might be useful to go back into the past and to mention the names of Franklin D. Roosevelt, Goya, Frida Kahlo, Beethoven, Helen Keller and so many other famous men and women who in addition to their achievements have bequeathed us the living testimony of the fact that even those who had to cope with pain, adversity or particular physical or mental disabilities were also able to move humanity through their art, science and genius. To support this statement and to show that it is still valid today, it would suffice to mention the name of Stephen W. Hawking, the well known author of the best-seller A *Brief History of Time**, who is regarded as one of the world's major theoretical physicists and who, despite having suffered from a progressive and incurable motor neuron disease for more than 25 years, is currently active as a professor at the University of Cambridge, in the same chair held by Isaac Newton two centuries ago.

2. However, there is no doubt that the mere mention of historical or outstanding figures is not enough to understand fully the immense problems facing millions and million of persons who, either permanently or for a prolonged period, suffer from some type of disability. In fat, the above references, in addition to being of some illustrative value, are designed to explain our intention of departing from the classic approach to disability—which traditionally confines it strictly to the person affected and does not regard it as something which concerns us all—and of treating it as a problem that involves the community as a whole.

3. More than 500 million persons[1]—10 per cent of the world's total population—suffer from some type of disability. In the majority of countries, at least 1 out of 10 persons has a physical, mental or sensory impairment, and at least 25 per cent of the entire population

are adversely affected by the presence of disabilities. These figures show with considerable eloquence the enormous size of the problem and, in addition to its universal scope, highlight the well-known impact of this phenomenon on any society as a whole. However, this quantification alone is not a sufficient basis for evaluating the actual gravity of the problem, since these persons frequently live in deplorable conditions, owing to the presence of physical and social barriers which prevent their integration and full participation in the community. As a result millions of children and adults throughout the world are segregated and deprived of virtually all their rights, and lead a wretched, marginal life.

4. Therefore, we do not consider it too bold to begin this study by immediately stressing the social question involved and the inherent problem of human rights.

5. As a preliminary warning, it should be pointed out that to deal correctly with this topic it is essential to rid ourselves of any feelings of pity or commiseration. We are not dealing with a strictly humanitarian problem, still less with a situation requiring our charity. Far from that, the treatment given to disabled persons defines the innermost characteristics of a society and highlights the cultural values that sustain it.

6. It might appear elementary to point out that persons with disabilities are human beings—as human as, and usually even more human than, the rest. The daily effort to overcome impediments and the discriminatory treatment they regularly receive usually provides them with special personality features, the most obvious and common of which are integrity, perseverance, and a deep spirit of comprehension and patience in the face of a lack of understanding and intolerance. However, this last feature should not lead us to overlook the fact that as subjects of law that enjoy all the legal attributes inherent in human beings and hold specific rights in addition.

7. In a work, persons with disabilities, as persons like ourselves, have the right to live with us and as we do. From the legal point of view, there are three dimensions to this statement: (a) the recognition that persons with disabilities have specific rights; (b) respect for these and all their rights; and (c) the obligation to do what is necessary to enable persons with disabilities to enjoy the effective exercise of all their human rights on an equal footing with others.

A. ORIGINS OF STUDY

8. On 12 March 1984, the Commission on Human Rights adopted resolution 1984/31 recommending to the Economic and Social Council that it request the Sub-Commission to appoint a Special Rapporteur to undertake a thorough study, in consultation with the Centre for Social Development and Humanitarian Affairs, of the causal connection between serious violations of human rights fundamental freedoms and disability as well as of the progress made to alleviate problems, and to submit its views and recommendations, through the Commission on Human Rights and the Commission on Social Development, to the Economic and Social Council. The Council endorsed the Commission's request by its resolution 1984/26 of 24 May 1984.

9. On 29 August 1984, in response to a request by the Economic and Social Council and the Commission of Human Rights, the Sub-Commission adopted resolution 1984/20 in which it decided to appoint Mr. Leandro Despouy as Special Rapporteur to conduct a comprehensive study on the relationship between human rights and disability.

B. BACKGROUND

10. Recently, beginning in the late 1970s, the international community, pressed by the enormous suffering caused by widespread hunger, ecological disasters, wars, etc., became increasingly aware of the problems afflicting persons with disabilities. The beginning of the new multilateral concern with disability can be seen as the adoption by the General Assembly of the Declaration on the Rights of Disabled Persons, on 9 December, 1975, following the Declaration on the Rights of Mentally Retarded Persons, adopted on 20 December 1971.[2]

11. As will be recalled, on 16 December 1976 the General Assembly proclaimed 1981 as the International Year of Disabled Persons,[3] later known under the theme "full participation and equality", and there was established a United Nations Trust Fund to finance those activities whose purpose was, in particular, to draw the attention of the international community to the situation and the needs of persons with disabilities. The main result of the actions undertaken before and during the celebration of that year was the elaboration of the "World Programme of Action concerning Disabled Persons",[4]

which the General Assembly adopted by consensus through its resolution 37/52 of 3 December 1982. The Programme sets the guidelines for a world strategy to promote the adoption of effective measures for prevention of disability, rehabilitation and the achievement of "equality" and "full participation" of disabled persons in social life and development.

12. It is important to mention that the World Programme of Action explicitly recognises the right of every human being to equal opportunity, which in fact means a broadening of the concept of human rights. This explains why, the year following the adoption of the plan, the General Assembly, through its resolution 37/53, entitled "Implementation of the World Programme of Action concerning Disabled Persons", stipulated that United Nations human rights bodies should take into account the unfavourable conditions in which most disabled persons are living and urged those bodies to adopt measures to correct the situation.

13. However, the point of departure of the work of the relevant United Nations human rights bodies is essentially Sub-Commission resolution 1982/1, in which the Sub-Commission recommended that Governments give consideration to difficulties encountered by disabled persons in the enjoyment of universally-proclaimed human rights as well as to the need to strengthen procedures for them to bring allegations of violations of their human rights to a competent body vested with the authority to act on such complaints or to draw them to the attention of the Government.

14. One year before the appointment of the Special Rapporteur, the Sub-Commission, at its thirty-sixth session, explicitly highlighted, in resolution 1983/15, the relationship between human rights and disability, in particular between human rights violations and disability.

C. MANDATE OF THE SPECIAL RAPPORTEUR

15. As mentioned earlier, the original mandate of the Special Rapporteur derived from Commission on Human Rights resolution 1984/31, Economic and Social Council resolution 1984/26 and Sub-Commission resolution 1984/20. These resolutions call for a thorough study to be undertaken of the causal connection between serious violations of human rights and fundamental freedoms and disability, focusing on recommendations and/or progress achieved in remedying

that situation. The mandate also includes a request to make an in-depth analysis of all forms of discrimination against disabled persons, as well as the existing or possible relationship between the system of apartheid and disability.

16. Guided by the principles of equality of opportunity, full participation and an independent living for disabled persons, the Sub-Commission requested the Special Rapporteur to examine closely the treatment afforded to disabled persons by public and private institutions, and any cases of institutional abuse, and to examine the situation of economic, social and cultural rights in relation to disability. Lastly, the Sub-Commission's resolution requested the inclusion in the study of a preliminary outline on the subject of scientific experimentation as it relates to disability.

17. The Special Rapporteur's mandate was subsequently extended and refined thanks to guidance and input from members of the Sub-Commission, observer Government, non-governmental organisations, etc., during the discussions which took place at the thirty-eighth and fortieth sessions of the Sub-Commission in 1985 and 1988 respectively, which provided an opportunity for examination of the Special Rapporteur's preliminary report (E/CN.4/Sub.2/1985/32) and his progress report (E/CN.4/Sub.2/1988/11). Particularly noteworthy, in this connection, were observations on the need for indepth study of the various types of conflict, wars and other forms of violence as causal factors of disability, the relationship between the latter and peace; the repudiation of penalties or punishments, such as amputation, deliberately designed to cause disability; and the desirability of providing an adequate legal definition and more precise statistical data on the number of disabled persons.

18. The discussions which were held brought out clearly the desirability of including in the study the particularly complex and serious problems which arise in regard to disability in particular groups, such as women, [5] indigenous populations, [6] immigrant workers and refugees, [7] and also the acute problems experienced by disabled persons in the developing countries. This report also reflects the concern expressed by various participants in regard to the relationship between extreme poverty, underdevelopment [8] and social inequalities and the emergence and intensification of disabilities and also the enjoyment of human rights by disabled persons.

19. Finally, it is to be noted that the Economic and Social Council, during its session held in New York from 29 June to 31 July 1992, approved the request made by the Commission on Human Rights, in its resolution 1992/48 of 3 March 1992. To the Secretary-General asking him to take all measures needed to ensure that the Special Rapporteur's final report on human rights and disabled persons be published by the United Nations in all the official languages and be transmitted to the Commission for Social Development for its consideration.

D. SOURCES AND INFORMATION RECEIVED

20. In compliance with the mandate conferred on him by the preceding resolutions, the Special Rapporteur has, since 1984, circulated requests, based initially on a provisional list of questions and subsequently on a questionnaire, for information and suggestions from Governments, various United Nations bodies, in particular the Centre for Special Development and Humanitarian Affairs in Vineena, the specialised agencies, regional organisations and non-governmental organisations concerned, in particular organisations for disabled persons. The large number of responses received supplement the information received by the United Nations prior to the appointment of the Special Rapporteur, as published in documents E/CN.4/Sub.2/1983/36 and Add. 1-4 and E/CN.4/Sub.2/1984/9 and Add. 1. The Special Rapporteur has also followed closely intergovernmental activities, national policies and activities on non-governmental organisations aimed at ensuring the prevention of disability and greater integration and participation by disabled persons. Close contact has been maintained in particular—directly or through the Centre for Human Rights—with activities undertaken under the aegis of the Centre for Social Development and Humanitarian Affairs in implementation of the World Programme of Action concerning Disabled Persons.

21. The main sources used in compiling this report have basically been the relevant international instruments, in particular those of universal scope, and the replies sent by Governments and intergovernmental and non-governmental organisations to the questionnaire and to the numerous additional requests made of them. Account has also been taken of documents prepared by experts on disability and meetings of experts held mainly under the auspices

of the United Nations. For purely methodological reasons it has been found preferable to group together in an annex all the replies received and the extensive reference material.

22. Lastly, the Special Rapporteur would like to express his appreciation to the members of the Sub-Commission for the information provided, and in particular for their suggestions and valuable advice on both technical and substantive matters. He would also like to emphasise the contribution made by delegations from observer Governments, various United Nations bodies, in particular the Centre for Social Development and Humanitarian Affairs, specialised agencies such as ILO and WHO, and in particular the assistance received from non-governmental organisations headed by disabled persons, without whose decisive support this report could never have been written and to whom it is only right that it should be dedicated.

E. PLAN OF WORK

In the light of the foregoing, the present study has been broken down into five chapters and has been prepared in accordance with the plan of work contained in the progress report of 1988 which, it will be recalled, was discussed by the Sub-Commission at its fortieth session. Chapter I deals in particular with legal issues regarding disabled persons and the formulation of an adequate definition of disability. Chapter II discusses factors causing disability, with particular reference to violations of human rights and humanitarian law as such factors. Chapter III describes the prejudices, discrimination and other violations of human rights to which disabled persons are subjected. Chapter IV sets out the national and international policies and measures designed to eradicate discriminatory practices and guarantee the disabled the full enjoyment of human rights. Chapter V is concerned with public information and education. Lastly, attention is drawn to the conclusions and recommendations of the Special Rapporteur based on the study.

9

BASIC LEGAL CONCEPTS

A. ADDRESSING THE QUESTION

24. This chapter will comprise a preliminary discussion of a number of basic issues, which relate to the main subject of this paper. Thus, for example, an attempt is made to answer the following questions: Do disabled persons enjoy the same rights as others? Do they have specific rights? If they do have such rights, where are those rights established? Are they to be found mostly in declaratory provisions which afford no legal protection? In the case of certain legally "identifiable" groups, such as disabled persons, its mere recognition of equality before the law enough or should some other requirements be added to allow the disabled to exercise their full range of recognised human rights effectively and on an equal basis? Finally, is the right to equal opportunity really that, or just an aspiration?

25. Bearing in mind that this is a study of universal scope, we must concentrate mainly on examining the various relevant international instruments. Of these, we will review both those which set forth broad guidelines (for example, declarations) and those which contain binding and generally applicable standards for all individuals (such as the International Covenants). Naturally we will also include a discussion of those instruments which lay down specific standards regarding disability or which refer to particular categories of disabled persons (such as the Convention on the Rights of the Child).

26. Lastly, it is important to stress that some of the provisions of those instruments are preventive while others are compensatory, although in every instance the common denominator is the protective

function. In addition, some standards are designed to attack the factors which cause disability, whereas others seek to protect persons who already suffer from some form of disability. In still other cases, both objectives are combined. Only by reading the entire body of these provisions—and using the rules which are characteristic of human rights as the criterion for interpreting them—will we be able to grasp fully the core concepts of the subject and its true legal dimension.

B. INTERNATIONAL HUMAN RIGHTS STANDARDS*

27. In accordance with purposes and principles of the Charter of the United Nations and the International Bill of Human Rights, not only are persons suffering from any form of disability entitled to exercise all the civil, political, economic, social and cultural rights embodied in these and other instruments, but they are recognised as being entitled to exercise them on an equal basis with other persons.

28. These two statements are founded both on general provisions, such as Articles 55 and 56 of the Charter of the United Nations—which refer to the fact that all Member States have undertaken to promote "higher standards of living, full employment, and conditions of economic and social progress and development"—and on specific provisions, such as article 25 of the Universal Declaration of Human Rights, which recognises that everyone has "the right to a standard of living adequate for the health and well-being of himself and of his family" as well as "the right to security in the event of unemployment, sickness, *disability,* widowhood, old age or other lack of livelihood in circumstances beyond his control" (emphasis added).

29. Regarding the principle of equal rights, the imperative form of each article of the Universal Declaration is highly instructive. Article 1 stipulates that "All human beings are born free and equal in dignity and right...". Article 2 state that "Everyone is entitled to all the rights and freedoms set forth in this Declaration, without distinction of any kind, such as race, colour, sex, language, religion, political or other opinion...". Articles 3 and 6 in turn use the expression "Everyone has the right to...". Article 7 states that "All are equal before the law and are entitled without any discrimination to equal protection of the law. All are entitled to equal protection against any discrimination...and against any incitement to such discrimination."

30. Although only one of the provisions of the Universal Declaration that has been quoted refers specifically to disability, this instrument has been and is of vital importance in promoting and protecting the human rights of the disabled, because these persons have the same dignity and the same rights as all other human beings. Furthermore, the Declaration has served as the basis and the point of reference for many other subsequent instruments and resolutions adopted on the subject.

31. The International Covenant on Economic, Social and Cultural Rights and the International Covenant on Civil and Political Rights came into force in 1976. Together they form the most comprehensive international code of binding legal provisions in the area of human rights. The two Covenants develop and supplement the provisions of the Universal Declaration, and the three instruments together make up what has come to be known as the International Bill of Human Rights. Disability is perhaps the area in which the importance of recognising the indivisibility and interdependence of human rights and fundamental freedoms, as both Covenant do, is most evident and sharp. This means recognising the urgent need to give equal attention and consideration to the application, promotion and protection of civil and political rights, on the one hand, and economic, social and cultural rights on the other.

(a) International Covenant on Economic, Social and Cultural Rights

32. Beginning with its preamble, this Covenant refers to the need to create conditions "whereby everyone may enjoy" the full range of human rights. Article 1 establishes the right of self-determination and article 2 guarantees that the rights enunciated in the Covenant will be exercised by all without discrimination of any kind. Article 6 recognises "the right to work, which includes the right of everyone to the opportunity to gain his living by work which he freely chooses and accepts". Thus, for example, if a disabled person who is able to earn his living by working is in a position of inequality *vis-a-via* others, this would represent a violation of that right.

33. Article 7 refers to the rights of everyone to the enjoyment of just and favourable conditions of work which ensure adequate remuneration. The principle of "equal remuneration for work of equal

value without distinction of any kind" is established. The unacceptable distinctions obviously extend to those applied to disabled persons, although such distinctions are commonly applied to the disabled, who are customarily paid less because of their condition, despite the fact that their disability does not prevent them from doing the same work as a non-disabled person.

34. Article 10 (2) states that "Special protection should be accorded to mothers during a reasonable period before and after childbirth". This matter is closely connected with the subject of disability because many cases of disability occur on account of pregnancy or childbirth difficulties.

35. Article 11 recognises that everyone has the right to an adequate standard of living for himself and his family, including adequate food, clothing and housing. This study present information which shows that, in the majority of cases, this right is very far from being respected where the disabled are concerned.

36. Article 12 recognises the right of everyone to the enjoyment of the highest attainable standard of physical and mental health. This right is obviously violated when the necessary measures are not taken to prevent undernourishment or malnutrition, when proper medical care is not provided, when the disabled are not given rehabilitation services, when general living conditions are not conducive to mental health, when immunisation campaigns to prevent certain diseases that cause perfectly avoidable disabilities are not carried out, when people live in squalid and overcrowded accommodation, etc.

37. Article 13 recognises the right of everyone to education. In the case of disabled persons, this means both that they must have effective access to education in the communal schools and that special education should be provided for them where necessary.

38. Finally, article 15 recognises that right of everyone to take part in cultural life. This right is violated, for example, when access is not possible to facilities in which cultural activities take place (cinemas, theatres, libraries, sports stadiums, museums, etc.), when not alternatives are provided to enable the disabled to participate, or when they are excluded on account of prejudices in respect of their ability to participate.

(b) International Covenant on Civil and Political Rights

39. This instrument ensures to all individuals without distinction of any kind, such as race, colour or sex, all the rights established therein, and its article 2 establishes that everyone shall have an effective remedy to put an end to any violation of those rights. This provision, as we shall see later, is of fundamental importance for the disabled, because Governments do not always recognise the legal protection of their rights and almost never provide any special measures to assist the disabled in taking action against any violations of those rights.

40. The Covenant, which uses language similar to that of the Universal Declaration of Human Rights (art. 5) and to the actual title of the United Nations Convention against Torture and Other Cruel, Inhuman or Degrading Treatment or Punishment, establishes in its article 7 that "No one shall be subjected to torture or to cruel, inhuman or degrading treatment or punishment". It further provides that "no one shall be subjected without his free consent to medical or scientific experimentation". It is common knowledge that both phenomena today are a major cause of various kinds of disability.

41. Article 9 refers to the whole area of criminal judicial proceedings, the right to defence and the right to be informed of the reasons for one's arrest. This article is of considerable importance as far as protection is concerned, especially for those persons who suffer any kind of mental disability, to prevent them from being subjected to arbitrary and unnecessary arrest or any other kind of institutional abuse.

42. In article 17, it is stated that "No one shall be subjected to arbitrary or unlawful interference with his privacy, family, home or correspondence, nor to unlawful attacks on his honour and reputation". This article is directly linked to the situation of persons who are committed to institutions and whose most elementary rights are habitually infringed, as for example their right to privacy. Article 23 recognises the right of men and women of marriageable age to marry and to found a family. Especially in the case of the mentally ill, this article is often violated all over the world, for apart from the fact that in a great many instances the persons have no real disability, their families or the authorities of the institution to which they are committed infringe the right, which everyone has, to marry and found a family. This right is also violated in cases of enforced sterilisation.

43. Article 25 establishes the right of everyone to take part in the conduct of public affairs, directly or through freely chosen representatives; to vote and be elected at periodic elections by universal suffrage; and to have access, on general terms of equality, to public service in his country. This right is violated, for example, when a mentally disabled person is not allowed to exercise his right to vote, even though he is in a position to do so; or when the blind are denied the vote on the pretext that secrecy will not be maintained; or when the polling station is not accessible to persons with restricted movement: or when a candidate for position in the public service is discriminated against and denied this opportunity on account of the prejudice that because he has a particular disability he is not qualified to hold that post.

44. Lastly, and as indicated at the beginning of this chapter, only by reading both instruments consecutively can one appreciate the interdependence between civil and political rights and economic, social and cultural rights, and above all, the importance of that interdependence in all matters relating to persons with a disability. It can happen, and has in fact happened, that some Governments ensure optimum living standards for disabled persons but limit their exercise of certain political rights, such as the vote.

C. OTHER CONVENTIONS OF UNIVERSAL SCOPE

45. In addition to those basic instruments, the International Convention on the Suppression and Punishment of the Crime of Apartheid provides in article II, that the term "the crime of apartheid" shall apply to "the infliction upon the members of a racial group or groups of serious bodily or mental harm, by the infringement of their freedom or dignity, or by subjecting them to torture or to cruel, inhuman or degrading treatment or punishment."

46. The Convention against Torture and Other Cruel, Inhuman or Degrading Treatment or Punishment, which was adopted in 1984, contains universally applicable standards which are of great importance for preventing disability. Under article 2, each State party undertakes to adopt effective legislative, administrative, judicial or other measures to prevent acts of torture in any territory under its jurisdiction. Under no circumstances may an order from a superior officers, or exceptional circumstances such as a state of war or a threat of war, internal

political instability or any other public emergency, be invoked as a justification for torture. Article 14 of the Convention goes beyond the purely preventive aspect and contains binding provisions for compensation whereby Governments ensure that the victim of an act of torture obtains redress and has a right to fair and adequate compensation, including the means for as full rehabilitation as possible.

47. The United Nations human rights bodies have paid particular attention to the need to prevent injury to children and to afford disabled children adequate protection. This attention was largely responsible for the inclusion of special provisions in the Convention on the Rights of the Child. Thus, for example, article 19 of the Convention provides for the protection of the child from all forms of physical or mental violence, injury or abuse, including sexual abuse.

48. Its article 23 provides that:

1. States Parties recognise that a mentally or physically disabled child should enjoy a full and decent life, in conditions which ensure dignity, promote self-reliance and facilitate the child's active participation in the community.
2. States Parties recognise the right of the disabled child to special care and shall encourage and ensure the extension, subject to available resources, to the eligible child and those responsible for his or her care, of assistance for which application is made and which is appropriate to the child's condition and to the circumstances of the parents or others caring for the child.
3. Recognising the special needs of a disabled child, assistance extended in accordance with paragraph 2 of the present article shall be provided free of charge, whenever possible, taking into account the financial resources of the parents or others caring for the child, and shall be designed to ensure that the disabled child has effective access to and receives education, training, health care services, rehabilitation services, preparation for employment and recreation opportunities in a manner conducive to the child's achieving the fullest possible social integration and individual development, including his or her cultural and spiritual development.

4. States Parties shall promote, in the spirit of international cooperation, the exchange of appropriate information in the field of preventive health care and of medical, psychological and functional treatment of disabled children, including dissemination of and access to information concerning methods of rehabilitation, education and vocational services, with the aim of enabling States Parties to improve their capabilities and skills and to widen their experience in these areas. In this regard, particular account shall be taken of the needs of developing countries.

49. Some provisions of the International Convention on the Protection of the Rights of All Migrant Workers and Members of Their Families may be regarded as relevant to the protection of this group of persons from disability. In particular, article 16(2) provides that migrant workers and members of their families shall be entitled to effective protection by the State against violence, physical injury, threats and intimidation, whether by public officials or by private individuals, groups or institutions. Under article 28 of the Convention, migrant workers and members of their families shall have the right to receive any medical care that is urgently required for the preservation of their life or the avoidance of irreparable harm to their health on the basis of equality of treatment with nationals of the State concerned.

50. Since its establishment over 70 years ago, the International Labour Organisation (ILO) has never ceased to advocate that disabled persons, whatever the cause or nature of their disability, should be afforded every opportunity for vocational rehabilitation, including vocational guidance, training or readaptation as well as opportunities for employment, whether open or under sheltered conditions.

51. ILO Recommendation No. 99 of 1955 concerning Vocational Rehabilitation of the Disabled was a landmark in the promotion of the right of the disabled to participate fully in opportunities for training and employment. Moreover, the fact that many countries the world over have based their vocational rehabilitation laws and practices on this recommendation proves what a wide impact this ILO instrument has had. The same recommendation gave impetus to the ILO's technical cooperation activities in this field.

52. On 20 June 1983, the plenary International Labour Conference adopted a Convention (No. 159) and a Recommendation (No. 168)

concerning vocational rehabilitation of the disabled. Both instruments made an appeal for renewed efforts to ensure that disabled persons are ensured equal access to training and employment. They also emphasised the important role of employers' and workers' organisations and of the community itself in attaining this goal. The direct intervention of these organisations should be of considerable influence in ending the discriminatory practices which unfortunately still hamper the access of disabled workers to the labour market. The Convention and the Recommendation also stress the need to pay greater attention to the training and employment of disabled persons in rural areas, outline new criteria for creating jobs and, perhaps most importantly, point out the need to consult disabled persons themselves in planning and formulating policies and programmes that will affect their integration or reintegration into active working life.

53. As was mentioned before, these ILO standards opened up for the organisation, its member States and all those involved in the vocational rehabilitation of disabled persons, a wide area where practical steps could be taken within the framework of the United Nations Decade of Disabled Persons. At the same time, the implementation of these provisions will be of great assistance in helping disabled persons to enjoy their human rights, especially those related to their social and economic welfare.

D. REGIONAL INSTRUMENTS

54. Three regional intergovernmental organisations—the Council of Europe, the Organisation of African Unity and the Organisation of American States—have adopted international instruments concerning human rights, including the human rights of the disabled.

55. On 4 November 1950, under the auspices of the Council of Europe, the Convention for the Protection of Human Rights and Fundamental Freedoms was adopted in Rome. This Convention incorporates many of the rights set forth in the Universal Declaration of Human Rights and includes the prohibition of torture and cruel, inhuman or degrading treatment or punishment, stipulated in its article 3.

56. Particular reference was made to the rights of disabled persons in the European Social Charter, adopted in Turin on 18 October 1961, article 15 of which is entitled: "The right of physically or mentally disabled persons to vocational training, rehabilitation and social resettlement."

57. On 24 July 1986 the Council of the European Communities adopted a Recommendation on the employment of disabled people in the European Community.[9] The Recommendation is based on the principle that disabled people have the right to equal opportunity in training and employment. The Council of the European Communities, the Commission and the Committee of Ministers have adopted various resolutions on an appropriate policy for the rehabilitation of disabled persons, in which member States are called on to step up preventive measures to eliminate impairments, disabilities and handicaps, implement a comprehensive and coordinated policy of rehabilitation, and encourage the full participation of disabled persons in their rehabilitation and in the life of the community.

58. The African Charter on Human and Peoples' Rights adopted in 1981 in Nairobi, stipulates in article 18.4: "The aged and the disabled shall also have the right to special measures of protection in keeping with their physical or moral needs."

59. The American Convention on Human Rights does not explicitly address the subject of disability, referring to it implicitly as do the European Convention, the International Covenant on Civil and Political Rights, etc. However, two articles of the American Declaration of the Rights and Duties of Man, adopted in Bogotá in 1948, are clearly relevant. Article XI states that: "Every person has the right to the preservation of his health through sanitary and social measures relating to food, clothing housing and medical care, to the extent permitted by public and community resources". In addition, article XVI proclaims the right of every person to enjoy the protection of the State from the consequences of "unemployment, old age, and any *disabilities* arising from causes beyond his control that make it physically and mentally impossible for him to earn a living" (emphasis added).

60. On 14 November 1988 the Additional Protocol to the American Convention on Human Rights in the Area of Economic, Social and Cultural Rights was adopted. In arricle 18 the Protocol states that disabled persons have the right to special protection. It declares that they have the right to appropriate work programmes, special training for their families, social groups and the consideration of the requirements of disabled persons in urban development plans.

E. STANDARDS OF INTERNATIONAL HUMANITARIAN LAW

61. As examples of standards of international humanitarian law, whose violation often results in or aggravates disability or has particular consequences for disabled persons, it would be appropriate to mention the Third and Fourth Geneva Conventions of 1949, relative tot he Treatment of Prisoners of War and the Protection of Civilian Persons in Time of War, respectively.[10] Furthermore, article 3, which is common to the four Geneva Conventions and governs armed conflict not of an international character, prohibits at any time and in any place whatsoever violence to life and person, *mutilation,* cruel treatment, etc.

62. Part II of Protocol I, additional tot he Geneva Conventions of 1949, in articles 8 to 34, contains provisions intended to ameliorate the condition of the wounded, sick and shipwrecked in time of international armed conflict. Article 35 prohibits the employment of methods and material of warfare of a nature to cause superfluous injury, unnecessary suffering, or widespread, long-term and severe damage to the natural environment. In accordance with article 44, any combatant who falls into the power of an adverse Party shall be a prisoner of war; article 45 provides measures for the protection of prisoners of war.

63. Part IV (article 48-79) provides for the protection of civilian populations who fall into the power of an adverse Party. Articles 48-71 are additional to the provisions of the Fourth Geneva Convention concerning the protection of the civilian population and civilian objects against the dangers of military operations, and set out a series of norms to achieve this. The main one of these (art. 48) is to ensure that the Parties to a conflict shall at all times distinguish between the civilian population and combatants and shall direct their operations only against military objectives. Methods of warfare such as the starvation of civilians and attacks on the natural environment are specifically prohibited. Articles 72-79 deal with the treatment of persons in the power of a party to the conflict. Articles 76-78 are measures designed to protect women and children, in particular against rape, forced prostitution and any other form of indecent assault. Article 79 states that journalists engaged in dangerous professional missions in areas of armed conflict shall be considered as civilians and shall be protected under the Conventions and the Protocol.

64. Protocol II relates to armed conflicts not of an international character, including conflicts between the armed forces of a government and dissident armed forces or other organised armed groups which exercise control over a part of its territory. Article 4 provides that all persons who do not take a direct part or who have ceased to take part in hostilities, whether or not their liberty has been restricted, shall be treated humanely, without any adverse distinction. It includes a list of acts which shall remain prohibited at any time and in any place whatsoever, in particular murder, torture, *mutilation* and corporal punishment. Article 5 lays down minimum provisions with regard to persons deprived of their liberty for reasons related to armed conflict and norms for the protection of persons prosecuted and punished for criminal offences related to the armed conflict.

F. NON-CONVENTIONAL PROVISIONS

65. Over more than 20 years, the General Assembly, Economic and Social Council and other bodies concerned with human rights have adopted various declarations and resolutions aimed directly or indirectly at promoting and protecting the human rights of disabled persons.

66. The Declaration on Social Progress and Development, adopted by the General Assembly by resolution 2542 (XXIV) of 11 December 1969, states in article 10 that social progress and development shall aim at the continuous raising of the material and spiritual standards of living of all members of society, with respect for and in compliance with human rights and fundamental freedoms, through the attainment of the Declaration's main goals. These goals include the assurance of a steady improvement in levels of living, the achievement of the highest standards of health and the provision of health protection for the entire population, if possible free of charge. In article 11, section (c) of the Declaration, the goal of the protection of the rights and the assuring of the welfare of the disabled and protection for the physically or mentally disadvantaged is included.

67. In resolution 2856 (XXVI) of 20 December 1971, the General Assembly proclaimed the Declaration on the Rights of Mentally Retarded Persons and called for national and international action to ensure that it would be used as a common basis and frame of

reference for the rights contained in it. According to the Declaration, the mentally retarded person should enjoy the same rights as other human beings, including the right to proper medical care, economic security, the right to training and rehabilitation, and the right to live with his own family or with foster parents. Furthermore, the Assembly declared that there should be proper legal safeguards to protect the mentally retarded person against every form of abuse if it should become necessary to restrict or deny his or her rights.

68. The relevant bodies of the United Nations are currently considering the Principles for the Protection of Persons with Mental Illness and for the Improvement of Mental Health Care, which are intended to serve, *inter alia*, as a guide to Governments, specialised agencies, national, regional and international organisations, competent non-governmental organisations and individuals and to stimulate a constant endeavour to overcome economic and other practical difficulties in the way of their adoption and application, since they represent minimum United Nations standards for the protection of fundamental freedoms and human and legal rights of persons with mental illness,

69. In resolution 3318 (XXIX) of 14 December 1974 the General Assembly adopted and proclaimed the Declaration on the Protection of Women and Children in Emergency and Armed Conflict, and called for the strict observance of the Declaration by all Member States. In article 1 the Declaration states that attacks and bombings on the civilian population, inflicting incalculable suffering, especially on women and children, who are the most vulnerable members of the population, shall be prohibited and condemned. Article 2 condemns the use of chemical and bacteriological weapons in the course of military operations as this constitutes one of the most flagrant violations of the Geneva Protocol of 1925,[11] the Geneva Conventions of 1949 and the principles of international humanitarian law.

70. The Declaration also states that "All efforts shall be made by States involved in armed conflicts... to spare women and children from the ravages of war", and that "All the necessary steps shall be taken to ensure the prohibition of measures such as persecution, torture, punitive measures, degrading treatment and violence, particularly against that part of the civilian population that consists of women and children".

71. In 1975 the General Assembly adopted the Declaration on the Rights of Disabled Persons, which proclaimed that disabled persons have the same civil and political rights as other human beings. The Declaration states that disabled persons should receive equal treatment and services which will enable them to develop their capabilities and skills to the maximum and will hasten the process of their social integration or reintegration.

72. As they are particularly relevant, article 5-11 are reproduced in full:

Article 5

Disabled persons are entitled to the measures designed to enable them to become as self-reliant as possible.

Article 6

Disabled persons have the right to medical, psychological and functional treatment, including prosthetic and orthetic appliances, to medical and social rehabilitation, education, vocational training and rehabilitation, aid, counselling, placement services and other services which will enable them to develop their capability and skills to the maximum and will hasten the process of their social integration or reintegration.

Article 7

Disabled persons have the right to economic and social security and to a decent level of living. They have the right, according to their capabilities, to secure and retain employment or to engage in a useful, productive and remunerative occupation and to join trade unions.

Article 8

Disabled persons are entitled to have their special needs taken into consideration at all stages of economic and social planning.

Article 9

Disabled persons have the right to live with their families or with foster parents and to participate in all social, creative or recreational activities. No disabled person shall be subjected, as far as his or her residence is concerned, to differential treatment other than that required by his or her condition or by the improvement which he or she many derive therefrom. If the stay of a disabled person in a speacialised establishment is indispensable, the environment and living conditions therein shall be as close as possible to those of the normal life of a person of his or her age.

Article 10

Disabled persons shall be protected against all exploitation, all regulations and all treatment of a discriminatory, abusive or degrading nature.

Article 11

Disabled persons shall be able to avail themselves of qualified legal aid when such aid proves indispensable for the protection of their persons and property. If judicial proceedings are instituted against them, the legal procedure applied shall take their physical and mental condition fully into account.

73. In resolution 31/82 of 13 December 1976, the General Assembly recommended that "all Member States should take account of the rights and principles laid down in the Declaration on the Rights of Disabled Persons in establishing their policies, plans and programmes" and that "all international organisations and agencies concerned should include in their programmes provisions ensuring the effective implementation of those rights and principles."

74. In decision 1979/24, adopted on 9 May 1979, the Economic and Social Council took note of the Declaration on the Rights of Deaf-Blind Persons, which had been formulated and adopted by the Helen Keller World Conference on Services to Deaf-Blind Youths and Adults on 16 September 1997, and decided to bring it to the attention of the General Assembly as part of the documentation submitted under the question of the International Year of Disabled Persons.

75. Article 1 of the Declaration reiterated the fundamental principle that:

Every deaf-blind person is entitled to enjoy the universal rights that are guaranteed to all people by the Universal Declaration of Human Rights and the rights provided for all disabled persons by the Declaration on the Rights of Disabled Persons.

76. In addition to the provisions already mentioned, there are many other international instruments protecting human rights which, inasmuch as they are designed to prevent certain abuses which might cause disability, deserve recognition for their preventive value. For example, in 1955 the First United Nations Congress for the Prevention of Crime and the Treatment of Offenders adopted the Standard Minimum Rules for the Treatment of Prisoners, article 31 of which states that corporal punishment, punishment by placing in a dark cell, and all cruel, inhuman or degrading punishments shall be completely prohibited as punishments for disciplinary offences.

77. In resolution 34/169 of 17 December 1979, the General Assembly adopted the Code of Conduct for Law Enforcement Officials and transmitted it to Governments with the recommendation that favourable consideration should be given to its use within the framework of national legislation or practice as a body of principles for observance by law enforcement officials. Article 5 of the Code reads as follows:

No law enforcement official may inflict, instigate or tolerate any act of torture or other cruel, inhuman or degrading treatment or punishment, nor may any law enforcement official invoke superior orders or exceptional circumstances such as a state of war or a threat of war, a threat to national security internal political instability or any other public emergency as a justification of torture or other cruel, human or degrading treatment or punishment.

78. In resolution 37/194 of 18 December 1982, the General Assembly adopted the Principles of Medical Ethics relevant to the role of health personnel, particularly physicians, in the protection of prisoners and detainees against torture and other cruel, inhuman or degrading treatment or punishment. The first of the Principles of Medical Ethics states that:

Health personnel, particularly physicians, charged with the medical care of prisoners and detainees have a duty to provide them with protection of their physical and mental health and treatment of disease of the same quality and standard as is afforded to those who are not imprisoned or detained.

79. Principle 2 states that:

It is a gross contravention of medical ethics, as well as an offence under applicable international instruments, for health personnel, particularly physicians, to engage, actively or passively, in acts which constitute participation in, complicity in, incitement to or attempts to commit torture or other cruel, inhuman or degrading treatment or punishment.

80. Further to what was stated in the introduction, it should be noted that on 16 December 1976 the General Assembly, in resolution 31/123, proclaimed the year 1981 International Year of Disabled Persons. The theme and objective of the Year were "full participation and equality", defined as the right of disabled persons to participate fully in the social life and development of their societies, to enjoy living conditions equal to those of their fellow citizens, and to have an equal share in improved conditions resulting from socio-economic development. Other objectives included increasing public awareness, understanding and acceptance of disabled persons and encouraging them to form organisations through which they could effectively express their views and call for action to improve their situation.

81. On 3 December 1982, the General Assembly, in resolution 37/53, proclaimed the period 1983-1992 United Nations Decade of Disabled Persons and encouraged Member States to utilise this period as one of the means to implement the World Programme of Action concerning Disabled Persons. This programme, which is currently being implemented and to which we will make numerous references throughout this document, recognises "equalisation of opportunities" as an objective as well as a means of achieving full participation in all areas of social, cultural and economic life. The explicit recognition of the right of every human being to the "equalisation of opportunities" gives a clear legal consistency to the juridical treatment of issues concerning disabled persons, and adds a human rights dimension which, previously there was an unwillingness to acknowledge.

82. The most important development in recent times has been Economic and Social Council resolution 1990/26 of 24 May 1990, authorising the Commission for Social Development to establish an ad hoc working group of government experts to elaborate standard rules on the equalisation of opportunities for disabled children, youth and adults[12]. This instrument, which is in the process of formulation, is of fundamental interest to us. It will in fact be the first international instrument, not only to be universal in scope and to refer specifically to disabled persons, but to contain an extremely broad and

comprehensive statement of the right of disabled persons to equal opportunities. Furthermore, the standard nature of the rules to be formulated emphasises their highly legal and imperative character.

G. SUMMARY AND ASSESSMENT

83. The three main conclusions to emerge from the extensive catalogue of international instruments which we have analysed are:

(a) The principle of equality of rights—inherent in the concept of human rights and expressly embodies in all the instruments—confers on disabled persons the same rights as on other persons in general;

(b) Disabled persons also have specific rights, See, for example, the next paragraph and chapter IV;

(c) These rights do not appear in any formal listing but are scattered throughout a number of legal instruments, or have been recognised by the courts. In fact, what might be termed the specific rights of disabled persons are only the material and legal expression of the minimum contribution which the community or the State should make towards ensuring that such persons can enjoy on an equal basis all the human rights enjoyed by individuals in general. Strictly speaking, this is not even what is known in legal terminology as "positive discrimination" (affirmative action) but simply equalisation.

84. Lastly, the specific rights of disabled persons—the right of a deaf-mute to have an interpreter during trial proceedings, etc.—in addition to being rights *per se,* are also the means of realising other fundamental human rights on an equal basis, such as, in this case, the right of defence. The lack of an interpreter in criminal proceedings where the accused is a deaf-mute not only infringes a procedural norm, but purely and simply negates the right of defence.

85. Lastly, the question of the protection of the human rights of disabled persons has a dual dimensions. On the one hand, there is the problem of specific legal guarantees—interpreter, specialised legal assistance, etc. so as to guarantee a fair and equitable judgement—and on the other hand there is the acute problem of the lack of specific effective resources to put an end to the violations of which, as disabled persons, they are victims. These two issues will be dealt with in chapter IV.

H. TERMINOLOGY, DEFINITION AND STATISTICS

1. Terminology

86. In his preliminary report (E/CN.4/Sub.2/1985/32), the Special Rapporteur described the unduly narrow interpretation and, in some cases, the pejorative connotation of the terms used in everyday language and in legal texts to refer to disability and disabled persons.[13] Spanish, for example, has numerous terms to describe disabled persons: *minusválidos, inválidos, impedidos, lisiados, incapacitados, paraliticos, mutilados, restrasados,* etc., and while each expression has its own connotation, the terms may on occasion be used indiscriminately and in many cases involve what amounts to a devaluation of the person. For example, the Spanish term *invalido,* means "without value". However, this latter expression has become current internationally with a sense other than its literal meaning. The International Labour Organisation (ILO) in its various conventions generally uses in Spanish the expression *inválidos o personas inválidas,* while the various United Nations bodies tend to use the term *impedidos,* The present trend is to discourage any reference which describes a person in terms of his functional limitations, for example, *los ciegos* ("the blind") and to prefer expressions such as *una persona con una deficiencia visual* ("a person with impaired vision"). French shows similar trends and the expression *non voyant* is more and more tending to replace the word *aveugle.*

87. The keen controversy over terminology which exists in Spanish does not seem to be as fierce in other languages. On the basis of his own analysis which appears in paragraphs 8 and 9 of his preliminary report and in view of the comments and suggestions made at earlier sessions of the Sub-Commission, the Special Rapporteur decided to use as equivalent terms the expressions "disabled" (in English), *handicapé* (in French), (in Russian) and *personas con discapacidad* (in Spanish). Although the Sub-Commission's resolution 1984/20, like the World Programme of Action, refers to *impedidos,* the Special Rapporteur has preferred the above expression in Spanish since the term *discapacidad* is a clearer and more scientifically accurate way of describing an ability different from the norm, which when preceded by the words persona *con* removes all pejorative connotations. Lastly, where, thankful, some terminological standardisation has begun to appear is in the expression *enfermos*

mentales, since the Working Group of the Commission on Human Rights on the Question of the Draft Body of principles and guarantees for the Protection of Mentally-Ill Persons adopted the use of this term by consensus.[14]

88. This is the moment to point out that the terminology issue is closely related to the problem of the definition and neither can fail to take account of the international instruments in force or the domestic legislation of different States. It is therefore necessary to take account of existing definitions and to respect the terminology used by each body, organisation or Government. This explains why the Special Rapporteur, having expressed his preference for the expression *personas con discapacidad,* uses many other terms in the course of the study, particularly when quoting, international Instruments, provisions of domestic law, or documents or replies from Governments or organisations.

2. Criteria for a definition

89. The World Health Organisation (WHO), in the context of its health epxerience, makes the following distinction between impairment, disability and handicap which was included in the World Programme of Action:

Impairment: Any loss or abnormality of psychological, physiological, or anatomical structure or function.

Disability: Any restriction or lack (resulting from an impairment) of ability to perform an activity in the manner or within the range considered normal for a human being.

Handicap: A disadvantage for a given individual, resulting from an impairment or disability, that limits or prevents the fulfilment of a role that is normal, depending on age, sex, social and cultural factors, for that individual.

90. According to the definition contained in the Declaration on the Rights of Disabled Persons, the term "disabled person" means "any person unable to ensure by himself or herself, wholly or partly, the necessities of a normal individual and/or social life, as a result of a deficiency, either congenital or not, in his or her physical or mental capabilities". The International Labour Organisation (ILO), in its Vocational Rehabilitation and Employment (Disabled Persons) Convention No.

159, Recommendation No. 99 concerning Vocational Rehabilitation of the Disabled and Recommendation No. 168 on Vocational Rehabilitation and Employment (Disabled Persons) states that "'disabled person' means an individual whose prospects of securing, retaining and advancing in suitable employment are substantially reduced as a result of a duly recognised physical or mental impairment". In its explanatory notes on the implementation of the above instruments, ILO reproduced the definitions of the World Health Organisation for clarification purposes. However, it was pointed out that the use of the words "impairment", "disability" and "handicap" might give rise to some difficulty of interpretation when applied to the provisions of those ILO instruments.

91. According to the World Programme of Action, handicap is a function of the relationship between disabled persons and their environment. It occurs when they encounter cultural, physical or social barriers which prevent their access to the various systems of society that are available to other citizens. Thus, handicap is the loss or limitation of opportunities to take part in the life of the community on an equal level with others, representing socialisation of an impairment or disability.

92. A WHO Expert Committee on Disability Prevention and Rehabilitation,[15] meeting in 1981, agreed with reference to the definitions of the International Classification of Impairments, Disabilities and Handicaps (ICIDH) that impairments and disabilities may be visible or invisible, temporary or permanent and progressive ore regressive. Members gave the following examples to illustrate their interpretation of the terms. A patient with hypertension (*disease*) is affected by cerebral haemorrhage (*impairment*) which leads to right-sides hemiplegia causing walking, writing and speech difficulties (*disabilities*). If the patient does not recover sufficiently to resume work or to be able to live an independent life, his disadvantage is considered a handicap.[16]

93. The Committee pointed out that classifications, characterising long-term consequences of disease and trauma, such as WHO's ICIDH, had been tried only recently. The disease process was described at points in its progression beyond its active state in the following way:

(i) From its cause or origin (etiology);

(ii) To its active state (pathology);

(iii) To the long-term consequences of health status or organic function (impairment);

(iv) In terms of long-term functional change in body appearance or movement (disability);

(v) From the perspective of limitations confronted in socio-economic or life-supporting roles attributable to the interaction between the person with impairments or disabilities and environmental constraints (handicaps).[17]

94. Reasonable agreement among the health and medical community on specific parts of the ICIDH concepts and classifications was expressed. For example, it was generally agreed[18] that: *impairment* includes description of the loss or abnormality of psychological, physiological, or anatomical structure or function at the level of the organ or anatomical structure or function; *disability* includes description of human function and activity at the level of the person; and *handicap* includes description of restrictive circumstances or disadvantages at the level of social and economic roles. However, disagreements do arise when linking these concepts to specific operational definitions and also problems occur when applying the ICIDH in social policy and programme formulation and implementation.

95. The Special Rapporteur wishes to point out that there is a close relationship and considerable overlap between elements in the impairment, disability and handicap definitions. This is exemplified in the failure to specify the degree of severity of disability which is often a predictor of handicap and in the problems of grading and problems of boundaries with handicap and impairment which are particularly important in the filed of mental disability. In any case, the WHO definition has been extremely useful, at least for statistical purposes, in giving some degree of homogeneity to domestic legislation and even in standardising criteria internationally. The Statistical Office of the United Nations uses this definition as well as country classifications in disability cross-tabulations for censuses and surveys.

96. It is essential to bear in mind that the definitions of the WHO Classification were made in the context of health experience and are therefore basically clinical and do not incorporate the social and

cultural aspects which are necessarily present in disability and impairment. For example, persons may be treated as if they were disabled and subjected to many kinds of restrictions (occupational, social, educational etc.) although from a clinical point of view they are not actually disabled. Frequently, persons who have been disfigured by burns, although not incapacitated, are treated as disabled persons simply because of the external effects. Something similar is usually the case with persons who have abnormal heads or facial features, but whose mental and physical faculties are unimpaired.

97. Since WHO adopted and published the ICIDH in 1976, the organisation has been encouraged to continue to revise the Classification, and particularly to incorporate social and environmental factors in the definition of handicap and give special attention to the problem of impairments and disabilities regarding mental health and mental handicap. General Assembly resolution 37/53 may in particular be recalled in this context along with WHO's proposals in this regard which were put forward at the fifth inter-agency meeting at Vienna from 18 to 20 February 1987.[19] The revision has not materialised, however,[20] and it is to be hoped that it will do so before 1993, the final year of the United Nations Decade of Disabled Persons.

98. The importance of refining the definition is obvious when it is observed that two thirds of the Governments which sent replies to the Special Rapporteur use the international WHO definition contained in the World Programme of Action. Compared to the developed countries, an even greater proportion of developing and least developed countries reported that they used those definitions. Furthermore, 18 countries reported that, while their Governments had adopted no legal definitions of those terms, they nonetheless used the international definitions. Sixteen of these also happened to be among the developing or least developed countries. Other States which submitted information to the Centre did not have general legal definitions to disability or disabled persons but there were legal definitions in respect of different legal regime (Social Insurance Act, Special Education Act, Labour Act) and applied to different disabled groups (victims of labour accidents and injuries, disabled children, mentally ill persons).[21]

99. At the same time, the domestic legislation of many States provides a concept of "disabled person" based on the qualifications

referred to above, but in relation to the individual's functional capacities in the social, labour and other types of environment. The definition of "disabled person" varies considerably from one country to another, and even within the same State it can differ from one legislative sector to another. The concept of total or partial incapacity for work due to illness or accident appears as a universal criterion in systems of disability insurance and workers' compensation for industrial accidents,[22] and it also seems to constitute the basis of all the legislation on the disabled in a number of countries.[23] Some of the replies reveal a tendency to adopt broader concepts, which take into account the possibility of participating on an equal basis and in an independent manner in all spheres of social life,[24] including—as is sometimes expressly stated—leisure and recreational activities. It remains to be determined how far these new concepts have permeated into the law, administrative practice and judicial decisions.

100. In defining a disabled person, domestic laws use different criteria, characteristics or classifications. For example, some include total and partial impairment of senses, and physical and intellectual capacities.[25] Others refer to a handicap or deviation of a social nature,[26] injury or illness,[27] or incapacity to accomplish physiological functions[28] or to obtain and keep employment.[29] Some definitions refer to age as a factor of disability.[30] These definitions usually also reflect the consequences for the individual—cultural, social, economic and environmental—that stem from the disability. Of these the following may be mentioned: inability to function normally in certain areas of social life,[31] and restricted possibilities of education, rehabilitation and employment.[32]

101. Since the revision of the WHO International Classification has not yet taken place and since a set of standard rules on the equalistation of opportunities for disabled persons is in preparation, the Special Rapporteur considers that it will be sufficient to restrict himself to outlining some basic criteria which the future definition should contain so that it will encompass, in addition to the medical and clinical aspects of disability, the social and cultural factors attendant on disability. It may be recalled here that the members of the Sub-Commission at its fortieth session agreed with the proposal to formulate a definition, the essential criterion of which would be the existence of specific long-term problems affecting the person or

behaviour of the disabled person and constituting major long-term obstacles to the enjoyment of human rights, to equality of opportunity and treatment, to social participation and to independent living.

102. During the discussion many of the experts stressed the advantages of this formula[33] as being neither too broad nor too restrictive. The balance which was required in the definition involved both clinical and socio-cultural aspects. Too broad or too vague a formula from the clinical point of view ran the risk of undermining its primary objective, which was to protect the human rights of persons who really needed protection, in other words, those who suffered from some type of disability and were therefore in a situation of genuine disadvantage. It was this that justified, or rather required, special attention (regulation). On the other hand, a narrow definition from the socio-cultural point of view meant that a large number of persons who obviously needed protection might be cut off from it. In other words, where this aspect was concerned, the definition needed to be capable of a broad interpretation in order to be compatible with concepts applicable to human rights and to serve as a universal reference.

103. From the medical point of view, the Special Rapporteur considers that the expressions "functional change" or "disorder", "permanent or prolonged", "physical or mental" reflect simply, clearly and generically the clinical elements contained in the WHO International Classification. The notion of "considerable disadvantages" (having regard to age and social environment), "for the purposes of his family, social, educational and occupational integration and/or the enjoyment of human rights", introduces the socio-cultural factors which are missing from the International Classification, but which have been incorporated into the domestic legislation of many countries.

104. While the Special Rapporteur makes no claim to formulate a universally valid definition—the drafting of which should be the responsibility of the Ad Hoc open-ended working group of government experts to elaborate standard rules on the equalisation of opportunities for disabled persons—he considers that the conjunction of these clinical and socio-cultural elements, on which there is a clear consensus, enables a disabled person to be defined as follows: "Any person suffering from a permanent or prolonged functional disorder, whether physical or mental, which having regard to his age and social

environment entails considerable disadvantages for the purpose of his family, social, educational or occupational integration, and for the effective enjoyment of his human rights; shall be considered disabled." This formula, it should be reiterated, not only takes clinical aspects into account, but also the specific issues which affect disabled persons and create certain obstacles to the enjoyment of their human rights, to equality of opportunities and treatment, to their participation in society and to their independence.

3. Statistical estimates

105. Differences in definitions, both within countries (and sometimes from one agency or service to another) and among countries, as well as the technical shortcomings of censuses (in some countries, population censuses do not even identify disabled persons) and particular social attitudes of uneasiness or shame towards disabled persons, make it very difficult to establish reliable statistics on the number of persons composing this population, the origin of its problems and, still less, the way disabilities will develop over time. The Government reports thus vary greatly in this regard and the only common feature they have is that they all accept WHO estimates as valid.

106. If these are correct and we accept as valid the figure of 500 million disabled persons in the world, 140 million of them are children. In addition, some 300 million live in developing countries and therefore have to cope with their disability in what are usually adverse economic and social conditions. It is estimated that only I per cent of these 300 million persons have access to assistance, rehabilitation and appropriate services, with the result that there may well be 297 million disabled persons in these countries who have no possibility of living a dignified life, with full participation in society and equality of opportunity. According to an ILO estimate, one third of the total number of disabled persons are women, i.e. about 160 million. In referring to the causes of disability in the nest chapter, we shall give a much fuller statistical picture.

107. Many replies, particularly those from developing countries, consider that the number of disabled persons as a percentage of the total population—estimated at between 6 and 10 per cent at present—will increase in the years to come despite the progress some

of them have made in respect of health and rehabilitation. One reason is that life expectancy is longer in much of the world and the number of disabled persons increases with age. In the developing countries, moreover, account must be taken of the high rate of population growth. It is estimated that, during the next 40 years, the world population will increase from 5 billion to slightly more than 8 billion, but the group of persons aged 65 and over is expected to double in the developed countries and to quadruple in the developing countries and, in all countries, this is the group with the largest proportion of disabled persons. It should also be pointed out that economic and technological advances are leading to new causes of disability, such as traffic accidents, industrial accidents, heart and circulatory disease, drug abuse and environmental pollution. This means that there are countries which are beginning, as a result of the progress made, to eliminate some causes of disability (malnutrition, poliomyelitis, measles, etc.), but new causes are emerging and they require different policies of prevention.

108. It should also be recalled that the World Programme of Action concerning Disabled Persons recommends that Governments should collect data on disabled persons through national population censuses, household surveys, etc., and disseminate the information obtained. In accordance with this recommendation, the Statistical Office completed a microcomputer database in 1988 called "United Nations Disability Statistics Database" (DISTAT). The first statistical compendium on disabled persons was published in 1990[34] it contains detailed information on 55 countries and covers 12 demographic and socio-economic topics, namely, age, sex, residence, educational level, economic activity, marital status, family environment, causes of disability and special auxiliary means used. The main objective of the publication is to draw attention to the work being done at the national level in favour of disabled persons, but, above all, to make headway in the preparation of international statistics.[35] Perhaps the key aspect of the compendium is the valuable information it provides on various methods of obtaining new statistics to facilitate the comparison of data and the broader use of the conclusions by persons responsible for planning, policy-making and research.

10

FACTORS CAUSING DISABILITY

A. MULTIPLE CAUSES

109. In the replies received from governmental and non-governmental sources, the causes of disability mentioned most often are the following: heredity, birth defects, lack of care during pregnancy and childbirth because of lack of coverage or ignorance, insalubrious housing, natural disasters, illiteracy and the resulting lack of information on available health services, poor sanitation and hygiene, congenital diseases, malnutrition, traffic accidents, work-related accidents and illnesses, sports accidents, the so-called diseases of "civilization" (cardiovascular disease, mental and nervous disorders, the use of certain chemicals, change of diet and lifestyle, etc.), marriage between close relatives, accidents in the home, respiratory diseases, metabolic diseases (diabetes, kidney failure, etc.), drugs, alcohol, smoking , high blood pressure, old age, Chagas' disease, poliomyelitis, measles, etc. Non-governmental sources also place particular emphasis on factors related to the environment, air and water pollution, scientific experiments conducted, without the informed consent of the victims, terrorist violence, wars, intentional physical mutilations carried out by the authorities and other attacks on the physical and mental integrity of persons, as well as violations of human rights and humanitarian law in general.

110. Although the following table prepared by WHO is based on very different criteria from those used in this study, it gives an idea of the number of cases of disability to which the various causes give rise.[36]

	In million
Non-contagious somatic illnesses	100
Injuries/wounds	78
Malnutrition	100
Functional psychiatric disorders	40
Chronic alcoholism and drug abuse	100
Congenital diseases	100
Contagious diseases	56

111. For purely pedagogical reasons, the Special Rapporteur decided in his preliminary report to divide the causes of disability into general and specific ones in order to distinguish, to the extent possible, between causes which do not necessarily entail violations of human rights, such as natural disasters, irreversible diseases and old age, and "specific" causes, such as torture, ill treatment, amputation, environmental pollution, etc., where disability is the direct or indirect consequence of a violation of human rights. The purpose of this distinction is simply to place emphasis on the latter causes and to focus on the two aspects of this problem, namely, human rights violations as causes of disability (chap. 10) and violations of which disabled persons are the victims (chap. 11).

General causes which do not necessarily entail violations of human rights

112. By way of illustration, we will briefly describe some of the general causes of disability to which the Special Rapporteur's attention has been drawn in particular because they are so frequent or so serious. For example, cardiovascular diseases are referred to in some of the reports received as the cause of a great many cases of disability. The way of life in large cities and the tension it produces, as well as the new needs constantly being created and the keen competition in consumer societies, are the cause of these diseases, which are usually regarded as diseases of civilisation, development and urban living, and this is why they are much more frequent in industrialised countries.

113. Neuromuscular diseases are also the cause of many disabilities. There is, unfortunately, no way of preventing or combating

many of them. The most common symptom of these diseases is a loss of strength, which may be apparent at birth or start gradually at any age. One of the best known is Duchenne's dystrophy, which, for still unknown reasons, leads to the progressive destruction of the skeletal muscles. It affects men, but is transmitted by women.

114. Traffic accidents are referred to in nearly all the reports as a cause of disability, although they are obviously more frequent in the more developed countries. According to WHO, 500,000 persons are seriously injured in traffic accidents each year and many of these 500,000 seriously injured persons are probably permanently or temporarily disabled. Industrial accidents are also mentioned in a number of reports as a cause of disability, although to a lesser extent than traffic accidents. According to the International Labour Organisation, 50 million accidents occurs annually in industry and many cause disability. Industrial accidents have stayed at the same level in the developed countries, but are on the increase in countries which are in the process of industrialising. This is a result of the difference in the strict application of work safety standards in developed and developing countries. It is also a result of the fact that, when a country is constantly taking on more workers in the industrial sector, they go through a learning period when they are more accident-prone.

115. Natural disasters are also a very important cause of disability, although their quantitative effect is not known, since persons who are disabled as a result of an earthquake, flood or other disaster are not identified according to the source of their disability. During the International Year of Disabled Persons, the Office of the United Nations Disaster Relief Coordinator (UNDRO) conducted research in four developing countries where disasters occurred during the period 1976-1980 for the purpose of studying the conditions of persons who had been disabled in some way as a result of a disaster and it reached the conclusion that the scientific and medical community pays little or no attention to victims who have been disabled. The four countries are Algeria and Guatermala, where earthquakes occurred, and Santo Domingo and Haiti, which were hit by hurricanes, and, according to the report (included in the UNDRO publication on disasters and disability), the long-term effects of disasters on health are not well-documented and this is why the reconstruction plans of disaster-stricken countries include many aspects relating to renovation, but

often overlook the physical and mental rehabilitation of persons. The consequences of disasters are usually expressed in monetary terms and human suffering is expressed quantitatively as the number of persons killed or left homeless and injured, but the latter is an amorphous category that is difficult to define and includes many persons who are affected by some kind of disability, whether temporary or permanent. During earthquakes, there is usually one person killed for every three injured; the earthquake at Skopje, Yugoslavia, in 1963, left 1,070 dead and 3,500 injured, 1,200 of whom were permanently disabled.

116. The reports also refer to diseases such as poliomyelitis, which has been eradicated in much of the world, but still strikes more than 400,000 persons in Africa, Asia and Latin America each year. Of the diseases which mainly affect children, reference is also made to measles, which not only kills 2 million children each year, but is also one of the main causes of blindness, deafness and mental defects. Over 800 newborn children die as a result of tetanus each year and an even greater number survive with major handicaps, German measles is also a major cause of blindness and deafness. One of the causes of mental defects is the lack of iodine, which, in the first year of life, leads to deafness and dumbness and mental impairments, especially in mountain regions. Vitamin A deficiency is another of the main causes of blindness in developing countries and it weakens children's defences, thus promoting all kinds of infections, which, in many cases, cause death.

117. Chagas' disease is referred to by only one country (Argentina) as a cause of disability, but it has spread throughout Latin America and affects millions of persons. Chagas-Mazza disease affects 4 million persons in Brazil; 3 million in Argentina; and 700,000 in Colombia. In Ecuador, it is estimated that between 10 and 12 per cent of the population is infected, while, in Chile, 300,000 persons and, in Venezuela, 1.2 million persons are affected. All in all, the experts calculate that the *Trypanosoma cruzi* parasite may be carried in the blood of about 30 per cent of the population of Latin America. Although only between 20 and 30 per cent of the persons infected show unmistakable signs of the disease, they are a serious potential danger, since it has been demonstrated that one of the most common ways the parasite spreads is through blood transfusions, although it may also be spread by the insect vector popularly known in

Argentina as *vinchuca*. The disease prevents persons from leading a normal life and, especially, from working and is also a cause of death.

118. Some replies refers to Down's syndrome (mongolism) and dwarfism (achondroplasia) as non-preventable and incurable diseases which affect children. Others regard old age as a cause of disability because of the gradual loss of various abilities as the human organism deteriorates.

B. VIOLATIONS OF HUMAN RIGHTS AND OF HUMANITARIAN LAW AS FACTORS CAUSING DISABILITY

119. The role of violations of human rights and of humanitarian law as causes of disability is the main focus of this chapter, which has been divided into sub-topics in order to deal with the problem in all its complexity, i.e. starting with the most obvious manifestations, such as torture and other attacks on the physical or psychological integrity of persons, going on to less specific causes, such as malnutrition, the lack of sanitation and of proper medical care and underdevelopment in general, and then considering the deplorable situation of many disabled persons who also belong to other particularly vulnerable categories or groups, such as immigrants, refugees, etc.

120. The existence of a causal link between the two phenomena (violations and disability) was first highlighted by some special rapporteurs appointed by the Sub-Commission and the Commission on Human Rights, who drew attention to this twofold problem on a number of occasions in referring to the topics entrusted to them (torture, arbitrary detentions, for example) or the situation of the countries within their terms of reference (Chile, Iran, Afghanistan, El Salvador, etc.) However, it was at the urging of the non-governmental organisations concerned that the admissibility of this question was recognised and the problem of disability could be considered by bodies responsible for the protection of human rights from the standpoint of and in connection with violations.

121. In addition to the lengthy bibliography that now exists and is composed of reports and studies to which we have referred on the relationship between violations of human rights and disability, it should be noted that the mandate of the bodies affording protection

has been expanding and now even includes specific undertakings, as, for example, in resolution 1988/13 entitled "The situation of human rights in El Salvador", by which the Sub-Commission requested the Special Rapporteur on Human Rights and Disability "to undertake all measures that are within his reach tending towards achieving the prompt and regular evacuation of the war wounded and disabled and inform the Sub-Commission...as to the result of his humanitarian effort". The Government of El Salvador cooperated with the Special Rapporteur and informed him of the measures it had adopted in that regard, drawing particular attention to those of a legislative and practical nature.

122. There are quite a few examples of widespread violations of the rules of humanitarian law which may cause temporary or permanent disability and have particular effects on disabled persons. In the preceding chapter (paras. 61-64), we referred to the Third and Fourth Geneva Conventions of 1949 and Protocols I and II additional thereto, placing particular emphasis on the prohibition of violations of humanitarian law which might cause disability or have a particular impact on disabled persons.

123. According to Hans Hoegh, Special Representative of the Secretary-General for the Promotion of the United Nations Decade of Disabled Persons, under normal circumstances, disabled persons represent approximately 7 per cent of the population of the developing countries.[37] In conflict situations, however, this figure increases to approximately 10 per cent. In Cambodia, for example, tens of thousands of persons have been left disabled as a result of the serious war injuries received since 1970. Although there are no national statistics available on the number of war cripples, local statistics show that persons who have had limbs amputated represent a significant proportion of the disabled population (over 80 per cent). The affected population in the refugee camps is estimated at 6,000 persons.

124. It is obvious that the nature and extent of the harm suffered by the victims of a situation of violence or an armed conflict depends to a large extent on the combat methods used and the use of certain particularly harmful firearms, bombs, explosives, etc. Land mines are one of the most frequent sources of disability, both in international armed conflicts such as the Iran-Iraq war and in internal armed conflicts, for example in El Salvador, and also in conflicts of

a mixed nature, as in Afghanistan before the withdrawal of Soviet troops. Unfortunately this conflict is continuing in the form of a civil war, and the number of victims is increasing. In Afghanistan, but especially in Pakistan, there are special sections in hospitals that are filled with persons injured by exploding mines.[38]

125. The devastating effects of the use of chemical weapons on life, the environment and the survivors' health is a topic of growing concern for the international community and the United Nations in particular. Thus, at its fortieth session, the Sub-Commission adopted resolution 1988/27 of 1 September 1988, entitled "Respect for the right to life: elimination of chemical, weapons". The resolution stated that the Sub-Commission was deeply shocked and saddened by the destruction of human life, life-long disabilities and great suffering caused by chemical weapons and indicated the necessity for the international community to take urgent and effective measures to prevent the future use of chemical weapons in violation of international law in order to protect human life.

126. In a specially-prepared report on violations of international humanitarian law, Disabled Peoples' International (DPI) indiated that, although all wars have their wounded, very frequently a large number of permanent disabilities are the result of illegal military operations, ill-treatment of prisoners of war, refusal to attend to the wounded or interference with the humanitarian action of civilians. The report goes on to indicate the gravity and frequency of certain attacks on refugees or places of refuge housing defenceless persons often deprived of any food aid or medical supplies. It also mentions the repeated armed attacks on hospitals and health staff assigned to wounded, ill or disabled persons. These are reprehensible acts from every point of view, says the organisation, and no strategic considerations can justify them. What is more, persons who have suffered serious injury or have any type of disability are not only defenceless but are obviously at a disadvantage in terms of escaping the attack.

C. SUFFERING INFLICTED ON NON-COMBATANTS IN SITUATIONS OF ARMED CONFLICT OR CIVIL STRIFE

127. Unlike the past, when wars generally took place on the battlefield and most victims were soldiers or combatants, today, as

a result of the proliferation of internal conflicts (in which the civilian population is much more exposed) and because of the development of certain weapons with enormous destructive power, the number of civilians affected by the violence is considerably greater than the number of combatants themselves.[39] According to available information, women and children account for over three quarters of the victims of armed conflicts in over 50 countries.[40] In the last decade over 1 million children in poor countries have died as a direct consequence of war. For each dead child, three more are estimated to have been injured or physically disabled and many more psychologically damaged.[41]

128. Although the most relevant aspects relating to women and children will be dealt with specifically in section D of this chapter, the above-mentioned information clearly illustrates the huge influence of armed conflicts and situations of violence in creating disabilities and also highlights their negative impact on the population in general and on disabled persons in particular. In this connection, we also believe it is important to stress the extremely complex and delicate situation in which persons with any type of mental disability frequently find themselves during these conflicts. Under such circumstances persons with disabilities are often deprived of all care and even of their most vital needs. Obviously this state of affairs usually leads to isolation, depression, distress, and therefore an increase in mental disturbances. At other times persons opt for concealment and, terrorized, flee society in the hope of finding refuge in places where they are not always safe and where it is difficult for them to find any help.

129. Also in connection with the suffering inflicted on non-combatants, the Special Rapporteur has received extensive information on events in Afghanistan, Angola, Cambodia, East Timor, El Salvador, Ethiopia, Mozambique, Sri Lanka, Etc. However, most of the communications he has received on this question refer to the situations in the Israeli-occupied Arab territories. By way of illustration, some 1,000 Palestinians have died and tens of thousands have been injured since the intifada began. According to a letter addressed to the Special Rapporteur by the representative of Palestine to the United Nations, between December 1987 and February 1991 over 8,000 Palestinians were permanently disabled as a result of Israeli policy in the occupied territories.[42]

D. INSUFFICIENT CARE AND CRUELTY TOWARDS CHILDREN AND WOMEN

130. The non-governmental organisations stress the fact that the rising wave of terrorism, the increase in military repression in certain regions, the frequent use of weapons with high destructive power and shortages imposed by war have truly devastating consequences for the most vulnerable and defenceless groups of society such as women and children. A recent survey of Afghan refugees and persons displaced within their own country highlighted the fact that the main victims of air bombing were women, children, adolescents and elderly people.

1. Children

131. The Special Rapporteur on States of Emergency indicates in his latest report that in South Africa, which has systematically resorted to the adoption of emergency measures, between June 1986 and August 1987 approximately 30,000 persons were detained for periods of more than 30 days, of whom 40 per cent were children under 18 years of age. The reports of the Ad Hoc Working Group of Experts on Southern Africa mention many cases of torture and inhuman treatment of civilians and young children. The thousands and thousands of child soldiers in Iran, Afghanistan and many other countries in the world complete this partial listing of acts of cruelty towards children.

132. It would not be right to ignore the tragic situation of displaced or refugee children, of whom there are approximately 15 million today and who, in addition to the risks from the conflicts themselves, must suffer the heart-rending trauma of being uprooted. In many cases they are also forced to change residence frequently. The displaced are frequently subjected to military controls when travelling from one temporary camp to another, and they are not allowed to resume their normal lives. Unlike refugees, who because they have crossed frontiers can have the immediate support and protection of the United Nations High Commissioner for Refugees, displaced persons usually have greater difficulty in obtaining international protection since they remain in their own countries. This raises a series of problems when one or both parties to the conflict limit or prevent access to aid and rehabilitation.[43]

133. Among the injuries that are usual causes of permanent disabilities in children during armed conflicts are injuries to the brain and spinal cord, bone deformities in the arms and legs and loss of sight, hearing or mental capacity. That is to say, diseases producing disabilities that have not yet been eradicated, such as menngitis, tuberculosis, poliomyelitis, etc., have now been joined by diseases that are the result of war and of lack of care, such as: compound fractures, bone and tendon infections and deformities due to delay in medical care or lack of proper treatment. In the case of children, it is particularly serious when the bones in the deformed limbs begin to grow.

134. From the psychosocial point of view, the traumas caused in children by conflicts usually have a very harmful effect on them psychologically. Many children, deprived of the security that is the basis for a child's natural development and subjected to constant tension for a lengthy period of time, become chronically sad and anxious and display behavioural disturbances of varying degrees of intensity.[44]

135. Unfortunately, during armed conflicts some developing countries assign all existing rehabilitation services to adults, especially combatants and the military. In such circumstances, children and women are generally given no assistance at all, while in other cases assistance is minimal. In the armed conflicts in Angola and Mozambique, for example, less than 10 to 20 per cent of the children received inexpensive prosthetic devices. In Nicaragua and El Salvador, only 20 per cent of children in need were provided with the necessary services. From 1 to 10 per cent of the Afghan refugees receiving care in Afghanistan were children.[45]

136. The Special Rapporteur wishes to pay a tribute to the UNICEF strategy for the prevention of disability since it includes a higher degree of early detection of disability and intervention at the community level to respond adequately in cases of children with traumatic injuries. It also includes greater supply of prosthetic devices, the production of wheelchairs and inexpensive prosthetic and orthopaedic devices and the training of highly-skilled therapists able to deal with emergency situations.

137. In addition to situations of violence and their effects on children, emphasis should also be placed on other factors that might

have a negative influence on children, such as child labour. Working at a young age can have terrible consequences for the child's mental and physical development. Children are not physically equipped to withstand long hours of exhausting and monotonous work. Their bodies are much less resistant to the effects of fatigue and effort than are those of adults. Many of them are already suffering from malnutrition, which further saps their stamina and makes them more vulnerable to disease. Carrying heavy weights and working in uncomfortable circumstances in small factories can produce deformities, especially of the bones. Children working in the manufacturing sector are more exposed to accidents and occupational hazards than adults. They have less experience in handling tools, tire much more easily than adults and have shorter attention span: a split second's carelessness can mean a permanent disability.[46]

138. In most of the world, prenatal diseases and diseases in infancy as a result of malnutrition are cited as major causes of disability in children. Infants who are given food of low nutritional value and drink non-potable water suffer from severe diarrhoea which, if the child survives, leads to chronic anaemia due to lack of iron, which in turn contributes to a poor state of general health and is a factor in learning disorders. Lack of proper nutrition is mentioned in the majority of the replies received as one of the factors most affecting children's mental or physical growth. As mentioned earlier, lack of vitamin A causes blindness in hundreds of thousands of children every year and lack of iodine causes loss of hearing, goitre, a marked decline in mental faculties and cretinism. In this connection, the provisions of article 24 of the Convention on the Rights of Child, which in paragraph 2 (c) recognises the child's right to "the provision of adequate nutritious foods and clean drinking-water, taking into consideration the dangers and risks of environmental pollution;" are very encouraging.

139. The human rights protection bodies, and the Sub-Commission in particular, have taken a deep interest in the prevention of certain traditional practices, such as female circumcision, which because if causes injuries in children is considered to be a serious abuse of children. This have contributed considerably to the adoption of various provisions in the Convention on the Rights of the Child. One of them, contained in article 19, stipulates that children shall be protected from all form of physical or mental violence, injury or

abuse...including sexual abuse. Similarly, under article 24, paragraph 3, States parties shall take all effective and appropriate measures "with a view to abolishing traditional practices prejudicial to the health of children". Finally, the physical and psychological ill-treatment of children, both within and outside the family, is a topic that has been poorly understood in the past but that is an extremely serious cause of disability in both developed and developing countries. The harm that can be caused in children by their parents or other persons beating, insulting, humiliating and maltreating them can be so great that in many cases it causes mental illness, social maladjustment, difficulties in school or at work, sexual impairment, etc. Another problem, of a complexity requiring a separate study, is the traffic in children's organs that is taking place in developing countries especially.

2. Women

140. Much of what has been said concerning the situation of children during armed conflicts also applies to women as a sector of the civilian population that is particularly affected by violence. Thus we would now like to focus our attention on the negative consequences for women of the persistence of certain cultural barriers that make them the victims of a twofold discrimination: as women and as disabled persons. Much has been written on discrimination against women, but very little has so far been done to deal adequately with the problem of disabled women. The few attempts made have been based on a mistaken approach, since they treat the acute problem of disability as part of the general topic of discrimination against women. However, sex and disability are two separate factors which, when combined tin the same person, usually reinforce each other and compound prejudices.

141. It has been proved that women in many countries are disadvantaged with respect to men from the social, cultural and economic points of view, which makes it very difficult for them to have access to health services, education, vocational training, employment, etc. This statement, which is valid for women in general, also applies to disabled women. For the latter, however, the lack of access to health services will certainly aggravate their disability or make it difficult for them to be rehabilitated quickly by making their participation in community life even more problematic.

142. All the arguments adduced in favour of women's full participation in the various spheres of cultural, political, economic life, etc., are doubly applicable to disabled women, not only regarding equal rights, but also with respect to the negative consequences for society in general of neglecting any human resource, for the community's failure to use it turns it into a burden for that community. It is sufficient to realise that over 250 million disabled persons throughout the world are women to understand the importance of the issue and its close links to all development questions. Women make up three quarters of disabled persons in the developing countries, with the highest proportion in Asia. From 65 per cent to 70 per cent, i.e. the great majority, live in rural areas.[47]

143. The Nairobi Forward-looking Strategies for the Advancement of Women mention women with physical and mental disability under the "areas of special concern". Paragraph 296, after identifying the factors that contribute to the rising numbers of disabled persons, states that the recognition of their human dignity and human rights and the full participation by disabled persons in society are still limited. These are additional problems for disabled women who have domestic and other responsibilities. Among the recommendations to Governments are the adoption of the Declaration on the Rights of Disabled Persons and the World Programme of Action, which provide an overall framework for action, especially regarding problems specific to women that have not been fully appreciated by society because they are still not well known or understood.

144. Paragraph 296 concludes by recommending that: "Community-based occupational and social rehabilitation measures, support services to help them with their domestic responsibilities, as well as opportunities for the participation of such women in all aspects of life should be provided. The rights of intellectually disabled women to obtain health information and advice and to consent to or refuse medical treatment should be respected; similarly, the rights of intellectually disabled minors should be respected."

145. Finally the Special Rapporteur would like to express his disappointment at the virtually total lack of bibliographic material on the specific problem of women with disabilities. It is all the more surprising to find such a lack in women's literature, which is obviously very familiar with discrimination.

E. SPECIFIC PROBLEMS OF SOME OTHER VULNERABLE GROUPS

1. Refugees

146. The situation of refugees has at least two readily recognisable points of contact with the subject of disability. Firstly, these are persons who have had to leave their country in order to escape from wars, armed conflicts, political persecution and so on: in other words, who in one way or another have experienced violence at close range and who have accordingly run all the risks and encountered all the dangers it involves as a causative factor in disability. Secondly, even when the refugees are already settled in the receiving country, they have in any case, as rule, to cope with various difficulties which *per se* make them a particularly vulnerable population.

147. The additional obstacles faced by a refugee who is also a disabled person have to be assessed against this background. What is more, in many countries the fact that an applicant for refugee status is disabled is customarily taken as grounds for rejecting his application; everyone will remember with sadness the tragic situation of thousands upon thousands of disabled refugees who have spent years in transit status in Thailand and other countries of South-East Asia awaiting a visa that never arrives, or that arrives only for those refugees who satisfy the conditions of physical and mental wholeness bureaucratically required by immigration laws.

148. Until the establishment of the Trust Fund for Handicapped Refugees (TFHR), set up with funds originating from the Nobel Peace Prize granted to the United Nations High Commissioner for Refugees in 1981 and donated for that purpose, little or nothing was known about the tragic situation of disabled persons in refugee and displaced persons' camps. This noble gesture by UNHCR threw some light on what was happening, although none of the mass media showed any great interest in the matter. It is nevertheless true that the resources allotted to the Trust Fund are used to alleviate the unhappy situation of these refugees. For examples, disabled persons in need of special treatment that cannot be provided in the country where they have taken refugee have been moved. A total of 322 persons were moved in the first four years and number have been increasing since then.

149. There are no detailed figures for the number of refugees suffering from this or that disability, and the piecemeal information at the Special Rapporteur's disposal is not up to date. A few figures can, however, be quoted to illustrate the scale of the problem. According to a UNHCR report, 22 projects concerning disabled persons were in the process of implementation at a total outlay of $983,396 at the end of 1986. These projects were being carried out in Africa, Asia, Europe and Latin America and their combined beneficiaries totalled 10,755. These 22 projects covered 19 countries and were serving twice as many people in 1986 as the year before. Even then Pakistan was the country with the largest number of disabled refugees (3,088 with mental impairment, 4,050 with physical disabilities).

150. The same report states that some 300 handicapped persons, 65 per cent with physical and organic disabilities and the remaining 35 per cent suffering from psychiatric disorders, mental retardation or psychosomatic consequences of torture, arrived in third world countries in 1986. It is also reported that between 1985 and 1986 the figure increased. Some developed countries have concluded agreements to receive disabled refugees. The Netherlands, for example, informed the Special Rapporteur that it had launched such a policy in 1978 and increased its scope with effect from 1981.

151. Among the causes of disability, apart from the common causes, the report states that refugees are most affected by poverty, poor health and hygiene and inadequate health education. It is stated further that they suffer more than the rest of the population from hereditary physical and mental disabilities, congenital diseases, malnutrition and accidents. UNHCR encourages rehabilitation projects, emphasising refugee participation. It makes it a practice to subsidise rehabilitation communities, although it provides direct subsidies only in exceptional cases. It purpose is always to facilitate contact for the disabled refugees with the local associations concerned. Under the heading of special education it also subsidises programmes and employs teams of instructors, therapists, counsellors, etc. As to employment, it always endeavours to place the refugees concerned in work, either by setting up small businesses or through productive participation, especially in the informal sector of the economy.

152. The United Nations Relief and Works Agency for Palestine Refugees in the Near East (UNRWA) reported that it provides education, health care and auxiliary services for disabled persons registered in five areas: Jordan, Lebanon, Syrian Arab Republic and Israeli-occupied territories. Prevention and the rehabilitation of disabled persons are included in UNRWA regular programmes, in collaboration with local and international non-governmental organisations. These measures comprise maternal and child health care, preventive programmes that include immunisation, nutrition and supplementary feeding, and health education. Medical services of care, prevention and cure were rendered to a total of 1,845,175 refugees in 1986 and 3.5 million children received health education in 635 schools run by the organisation.

2. Indigenous inhabitants

153. At various sessions of the Sub-Commission, non-governmental organisations concerned with protection of the human rights of indigenous populations have reported that the risk of disability among those population is extremely high because their working conditions are often exhausting and highly dangerous, their level of living is usually lower than that of the rest of the population and the preventive medical services available to them are often of very poor quality. Furthermore, disabled persons belonging to such groups do not usually have access to suitable rehabilitation services or adequate government help. In short, the characteristics making up a vulnerable group which in the case of disabled persons in subject to twofold discrimination were highlighted by almost everyone who spoke on this topic.

154. Settlement, the expansion of extractive industries such as mining and logging, large-scale development projects, such as hydroelectric dams, and so on, are affecting an increasing number of indigenous populations that until very recently depended essentially on hunting and fishing for their livelihood. These activities result in loss of land, the enclosure of hunting grounds and the destruction of wild fauna and flora, making the indigenous communities increasingly dependent on prepared foods containing large quantities of unwholesome sugars and fats. These, and excessive glucides, greatly increase the incidence of cardiovascular diseases and cancer[48] and

may also be a factor in diabetes.[49] To sum up, the systematic changes in diet brought about by industrial projects imposed on the population, or by emigration, not merely destroy the indigenous economy but can also enslave the mind.

155. Although they may seem much less obvious than any physical disability, learning disorders are a particular source of danger because they may affect an entire population and even impair its capacity to resist exploitation. Consequently, ILO Convention No. 169 concerning Indigenous and Tribal Peoples in Independent Countries marks a genuine step forward; it recognises the right of such peoples to take control of their own development, to administer their territories and to require the State to take steps to protect their environment. Special rules are laid down to these ends in articles 4 and 7 and in part II of the Convention. Be that as it may, the Convention has attracted very few ratifications, and indigenous peoples and non-governmental organisations are urging the need for a greater United Nations commitment in this connection. The Conference on Environment and Development which is to be held in Brazil in June 1992 will provide an exceptional opportunity to spell out rights and responsibilities with regard to the environment of indigenous populations.

3. Migrant workers

156. The special situation of migrant workers and their families as groups falling victim to discrimination is a topic which has long been a focus of attention in the United Nations, to the point where, as already stated, the International Convention on the Protection of the Rights of All Migrant Workers and Members of Their Families was adopted on 18 December 1990. Over and above the rules laid down in that instrument, the *travaux preparatories* are very illuminating, for they draw attention to the precarious situation that frequently overtakes persons in this category and the increased discrimination which disabilities often bring with them.

157. At the national level, paradoxically, certain immigration laws have been the means of revealing the discriminatory criteria applied against persons with a disability, since in many cases they were—and, as we shall see later on, still are—denied admission to the country.

F. UNDERDEVELOPMENT AND ITS VARIOUS MANIFESTATIONS CONSIDERED AS A VIOLATION OF HUMAN RIGHTS

158. Both the Sub-Commission's discussions and most of the replies received emphasise the important role of underdevelopment in the occurrence and intensification of disabilities.[50] Owing to a vicious circle, mass shortcomings in the area of education, nutrition and health care bring about an increase in the disabled population that cannot contribute to development, thus increasing the public burden on third-world countries. The problem is therefore generally presented as a denial of the right to development as recognised by the United Nations: a right whose fulfilment is considered one of the most effective means of overcoming disabilities and strengthening protection of the human rights of disabled persons.

159. Many of the replies agree in singling out the following among the causative factors of underdevelopment-related disability: indigence, poor food and housing, lack of public hygiene, degradation of the environment, inadequate education and health information, the well-known effect of illiteracy, etc.

160. Unlike the factors making for disability which we have identified at the beginning of this chapter and elsewhere in it—torture, amputation, etc.—the causes we are examining now certainly justify reference to a cause-and-effect relationship between the phenomenon (hunger, malnutrition, etc.) and the resultant disability, but in this case the direct relationship between victim and victimizer apparent in the case of torture, for example, is missing. In essentials, the difference lies firstly in the distinctive nature of the causes of disability (violation of civil rights in the one case and of economic, social or cultural rights in the other) and secondly in the practical difficulties of fixing the blame. It is easier to punish the perpetrators of an inhuman, cruel or degrading act than to identify those responsible for hunger or poverty. There is no doubt, however, that death from starvation constitutes a denial of the right to life and an act of cruelty as blameworthy as torture.

161. Hunger is a scourge that is still ravaging a large proportion of mankind; where it does not lead to the early death of the hungry, it results in a chronic state of malnutrition that slowly reduces people's mental and physical capacity. It has consequently come to be said that hunger is the sickness of slaves, for it affects those who, by their very status, are subjected to the hardest, heaviest and most dangerous

kinds of work, with the result that they consume more energy and need to be better fed. According to the table prepared by WHO and referred to above (see para, 110), more than 100 million persons—that is to say, more than 20 per cent of all disabled persons—are suffering from disabilities of various kinds resulting from dietary deficiencies. The replies, in their turn, make it clear that the commonest causes of disability in most parts of the world are prenatal diseases or diseases of early infancy due to malnutrition.

162. The lack of an adequate health system has repeatedly been ranked among the main causes of disability. Not only does it impede the decisive task of prevention, but many avoidable disabilities grow worse or become permanent for lack of attention. Furthermore the lack or inadequacy of medical attention during pregnancy or confinement is, according to UNICEF, one of the most powerful factors in disabilities among children. The non-governmental organisations emphasise that the problems resulting from inadequate health care can be solved only through the establishment of a network of health services where basic care is accessible to all, regardless of economic circumstances or geographical location. Similarly several Governments and non-governmental organisations include insalubrious housing among the causes of many disabilities since it serves as a breeding-ground for a great many diseases, makes for accidents, leaves its inhabitants exposed to the worst fates in the event of natural disasters, and so on. Lastly, many replies refer to article 8 of the Declaration on the Right to Development, which provides that States should undertake all necessary measures for the realisation of the right to development and shall ensure, *inter alia,* equality of opportunity for all in their access to basic resources, education, health services, food, housing, employment and the fair distribution of income.

163. The extraordinarily rapid progress of science and technology proceeding in disregard of nature's laws and nature's capacity for self-cleaning and self-reproduction, has resulted in an alarming deterioration and degradation of our natural environment. Yet only in the last few years has it come to be realised more and more that desertification,[51] uncontrolled deforestation, soil exhaustion, depletion of the ozone layer, pollution and toxic wastes produce a wide range of adverse effects on human health and are the causes of disabilities of various kinds. Disasters such as the fire at the Chernobyl nuclear power station in the Soviet Union and the accident

at the Bhopal chemical plant in India are no more than examples of the tragic effect which contamination and environmental pollution have on health and the generation of disabilities.

164. It should also be remembered that at several sessions of the Sub-Commission growing concern has been expressed about the use of pesticides and feeding-stuffs that contain hormones, antibiotics or other additives and that are still being exported to developing countries even after they have been prohibited in their country of origin as a result of their harmful effects. Furthermore the preliminary report submitted by the Special Rapporteur on "Human rights and the environment" (E/CN.4/Sub.2/1991/8) gives a series of similar examples which clearly illustrate this point.

165. Another of the main causes of disability consists of injuries or diseases caused by working with dangerous substances or under unsuitable conditions. Problems are created in this connection by the transfer of unsuitable, defective or obsolete technology or equipment from developed to developing countries, by excessively long hours of work with inadequate rest breaks, etc. Some participants in the Sub-Commission's sessions have expressed their deep concern at the degree of non-compliance with safety standards in industrial and agricultural work. It has been said that, in countries where those standards had recently been lowered, there had been a striking increase in work-related disabilities.[52] The effects of dangerous substances often go beyond the actual worker and are felt by his entire family. For example, reports from Bhopal refer to a high incidence of disabled babies, miscarriages and stillbirths due to exposure of the parents to chemicals which, as we know, killed more than 2,000 people and left many thousands permanently disabled.

166. Lastly the Special Rapporteur draws some encouragement from the measures taken by United Nations bodies to prohibit the movement of toxic and dangerous products and wastes to, and their dumping in, other countries and the export of dangerous chemicals or pharmaceuticals. Many disabilities are due to defective baby foods and to the distribution in developing countries of drugs which have been superseded or prohibited in the developed countries owing to their dangerous side-effects. Such acts, whatever they many be called, are genuine violations of human rights and should be treated as such by the international community.

167. A factor which is intimately bound up with disability, and which in some degree combines many of those already examined is indigence: extreme poverty, or "the supreme evil" as it used to be called by Father Joseph Wresinski, the founder of the International Movement ATD Fourth World, which has been doing commendable work on behalf of the poorest for several decades. Indigence, besides being in itself the most palpable expression of social exclusion and denial of the enjoyment of all human rights, is a direct cause of disability as well as a factor that worsens both disability and discrimination against disabled persons.

168. In a letter addressed to the Special Rapporteur by the non-governmental organisation ATD Fourth World it is stated that:

Disability in all its forms, being present in all social settings, is nevertheless part of the daily life of families and groups in a situation of extreme poverty, whether in the poorest regions of the world or in poverty-stricken areas industrialised countries. Indeed, disability is so intimately bound up with poverty that it is difficult to isolate as a problem. Is it a cause of poverty? Is it a result? The greater the poverty, the greater the risks of disability become. Through their living conditions, working conditions state of health, ignorance and so on. The poorest are especially exposed to the onset of various disabilities, not merely at birth and in infancy but at every stage in life. As a result, infirmities and handicaps accumulate in the course of a single person's or a single groups's life. This is illustrated by various statistics, for example those indicating the increased risk of disability incurred by certain categories of workers in the most dangerous and unhealthiest sectors. Similarly the leprosy map of Africa covers much the same territory as the hunger map. While the correlation between extreme poverty and disability is very widely acknowledged in the case of the developing countries, it is less clearly perceived with reference to the poorest milieux in the industrialized countries.

169. The organisation goes on to state that:

Indigence worsens the consequences of disability and leads to situations of multiple discrimination. The consequences of disability are more serious, longer-lasting and harder to bear for the poorest and their families, while entire groups are weakened by the fact that a large number of their members are afflicted in this way. This is especially true in that the means of overcoming the difficulties of living with certain physical or mental deficiencies—the prevention, re-education and vocational training services—are largely lacking in the most underprivileged ranks of society. Thus one and the same disability or infirmity may have very different consequences according to the victim's socio-economic status and level of training. For example, a lawyer who has partly lost the use of one leg will be able to keep his practice, whereas an unskilled agricultural labourer may well be left with no source of livelihood. Furthermore, the low level or even complete absence of education in the poorest circles virtually rules out access to the resources of vocational retraining, all the more so since those resources are rarely designed with the situation of the poorest in mind. In the industrialised countries there is a tendency for children, young people and adults in a situation of extreme poverty to be hedged about with administrative rules on disability that allow no scope for promotion, training or integration in society.

G. APARTHEID

170. There are two main reasons why it is relevant to include apartheid in this study: firstly, the prevailing system in South Africa is the cause of many disabilities among the majority black population of the country; and, secondly, disabled persons who belong to that majority are in turn victims of a twofold discrimination. The living conditions of the vast majority of the coloured population, especially in Soweto and the Bantustans, are characterised by a lack of drinking water and of adequate sewerage. Moreover, malnutrition and generally poor sanitation mean that the number of disabled persons is very high in this community. Furthermore, the constant oppression and permanent violence practised by the white minority against the coloured population significantly increase the number of disabled persons.

171. In connection with this twofold discrimination, Disabled Peoples' International (DPI) reported to the Commission on Human Rights an incident which received much publicity at the time and which provides a particularly graphic example of such an aberration. It concerned a group of foreigners who were visiting South Africa and were involved in a car accident. All the members of the group received immediate medical care except for one, who was black and was denied medical care by the emergency services, as a result of which he will be quadriplegic for the rest of his life. The DPI stated that this

incident illustrates the relationship between apartheid and disability and expressed its distress at the fact that this is happening daily to the majority population in the country and only came to light in this case because the victim was a foreigner.

172. According to a WHO report, the tension that apartheid creates in the black population is affecting mental health. It gives as an example the massive forced expulsions which have been ordered to achieve the bantustanisation of some unpopulated areas of the country in order to perpetuate white economic and political supremacy through the creation of a mobile group of migrant labourers with wretched living conditions. Furthermore, the situation of coloured people with mental disabilities is extremely serious and goes so far as to include their employment as free labour by private enterprise with the agreement of the Government. Although the Special Rapporteur lacks recent information, until a few years ago there was not a single black psychiatrist in the whole of South Africa, and vital decisions concerning thousands of African mental patients were taken by doctors working part-time who, in addition to having been trained in another culture with racist characteristics, did not even speak the language of their patients. The availability of beds for psychiatric care per 1,000 inhabitants of the white population is 3.3 times greater than for the black population.

173. While considerable progress has recently been made in South Africa in the field of human rights, and particularly in the legal abolition of apartheid, the Special Rapporteur believes that the situation is still far from satisfactory and for this reason has preferred to fulfil his mandate by highlighting aspects linking disability with apartheid, as he was asked to do by the Sub-Commission.

H. PROBLEMS RELATED TO SOME DELIBERATELY INFLICTED FORMS OF PUNISHMENT AND OTHER TREATMENT

174. On various occasions in the Sub-Commission, representatives of non-governmental organisations for disabled persons and other participants have joined in identifying the following practices as serious violations of international law and human rights:[53] amputation as punishment; the institutionalisation of disabled persons; institutional abuse, including the use of drugs; forced sterilisation, castration and female circumcision; and the blinding of detainees as an alternative

to detention. Many speakers have emphasised that no religious tenet or other cultural factor could justify or excuse such acts, which they regard as being contrary to binding human rights standards prohibiting torture and other cruel, inhuman or degrading treatment or punishment.

175. Mutilations, particularly the amputation of the extremities of captured combatants in time of armed conflict, have been condemned as an aberrant practice, common in some regions, which is contrary to the Geneva Conventions and human rights standards. Several non-governmental organisations have pointed out that forced sterilisation is more often used on disabled women than men in order to prevent them from having children. Often, disabled women are sterilised for eugenic reasons or simply because they are often victims of rape. Indeed, sterilisation is sometimes a prerequisite for entry into an institution.[54]

176. For many years the Sub-Commission has been closely studying traditional practices, for example sexual mutilation, which affect human rights, as well as ways of eradicating those which harm families and the community, and of encouraging practices that are beneficial.[55] In that regard, particular attention should be paid to relevant aspects of the report submitted on the subject by the Special Rapporteur, Mrs. Halima Warzazi (E/CN.4/Sub.2/1991/6).

177. Finally, among the institutional abuses of which disabled persons are often victims, as well as maltreatment, the administration of drugs and other aspects which will be looked at in chapter 11, the use of psychiatry for political ends and the improper detention in psychiatric hospitals of political opponents or disabled persons when it is not needed or not advisable, have been condemned.

178. In conclusion, the Special Rapporteur would like to reaffirm his belief, already expressed in his preliminary report,[56] that certain punishments, such as amputation, which are deliberately intended to disable the individual, are contrary to international humanitarian law. A correct interpretation of article 4 of the International Covenant on Civil and Political Rights—and, in the same context, articles 15 and 27 of the European Convention on Human Rights and the American Convention on Human Rights, respectively—allows us to conclude that cruel, inhuman or degrading treatment or punishment is prohibited at all times and in all circumstances and that no emergency situation can authorise them. Any penalty, whether based on principles that

are legal or religious or both, which entails cruel or inhuman punishment or treatment is a violation of human rights in the light of the international norms in force.

I. SCIENTIFIC EXPERIMENTS

179. Without question some of the most serious human rights violations that cause disability are scientific experiments conducted without the victims' informed consent. Such acts are prohibited particularly by the Geneva Conventions and article 7 of the International Covenant on Civil and Political Rights. Earlier they formed the subject of important decisions by the allied military tribunals set up to punish Second World War criminals on the basis of the Charter and the Judgement of the Nuremberg Tribunal.[57] At the moment the transplantation of children's organs is one of the most sensitive of a great many complex problems. According to a WHO report there has always been a shortage of organs available for transplants and for this reason many countries have established procedures intended to increase supply. Nevertheless there is sufficient evidence to indicate an increase in the commercial traffic in human organs, particularly from living donors who are unrelated to the recipients. There are grounds for fearing that as a result there could exist a traffic in human beings of which children, as always, are the main victims.[58]

180. - It is felt that these problems call for further in-depth study of an ethical and normative nature, particularly in view of recent genetic and biological developments. The Special Rapporteur considers that such an analysis, which is extremely necessary, should take the form of a separate study because of the highly complex technical problems involved. Cooperation with WHO and various bioethical and life sciences associations would be desirable for such an undertaking.

11
PREJUDICES AND DISCRIMINATION AGAINST DISABLED PERSONS: AREAS, FORM AND SCOPE

A. INTRODUCTION

181. This chapter, perhaps more than any other, should highlight the relationship between the goals of "full participation" by disabled persons and the strategies for guaranteeing the "equality" of opportunity and treatment, as well as the link between both these aims and one of the most cherished goals of organisations of disabled persons, namely, to ensure the maximum degree of autonomy and independence for the disabled. This means developing and capacities of the individual to the full, rather than adopting the traditional approach of emphasising disabilities or handicaps to classify individuals, since these tend to be the direct or aggravated result of the attitude of the community itself towards persons who suffer from some real or apparent[59] physical or mental disorder or functional problem.

182. - Clearly, the disabilities of a person who has not received proper rehabilitation treatment will grow worse and, in some cases, become acute. If he is discriminated against in the work place because of his disability or he is simply afforded no employment opportunity, his dependence and his isolation will be greater. If the educational system does not provide for his specific situation, a disabled person finds himself excluded from it, and without proper instruction his disabilities worsen. If the cultural and sporting activities of society are designed solely for a standard category of person which does not include him, he will be barred from culture and sport. If means of transport, pavements and buildings are inaccessible to such a person,

he will be unable to move about freely. In short, it is such barriers and discrimination which to a large extent create or aggravate disabilities and actually set people apart from society, in many cases making them a burden to the community. This demonstrates conclusively the importance of efforts to achieve the maximum degree of autonomy and independence for disabled persons, not only for their benefit, but also for the benefit of society as a whole.

183. Mr. Bengt Lindquist, Swedish Minister for Family Affairs and Matters concerning the Disabled and the Elderly, told a group of specialists[63] that:

The ideas and concepts of equality and full participation for persons with disabilities have been developed very far on paper, but not in reality. In all our countries, in all types of living conditions, the consequences of disability interfere in the lives of disabled persons to degree which is not at all acceptable. Many of the existing obstacles and limitations occur in areas of fundamental importance to our situation as citizens of our societies. If a person in a wheelchair wants to attend a public meeting, be it social, cultural or political, and if he cannot get into the meeting room because the building is not accessible, his rights as a citizen have been violated. A blind person interested in a public debate who has no access to the daily paper in which the discussion takes place is in a similar situation. When a person is excluded from employment because of the fact that he is disabled, he is being discriminated against as a human being. If a general education system is developed in a developing country and disabled children are excluded, their rights are being violated.

B. AREAS AND SCOPE OF DISCRIMINATION

184. Among the information provided by non-governmental organisations was a document prepared by the World Veterans Federation listing the areas or spheres in which disabled persons find themselves at a distinct disadvantage. They are:

(a) *Education*. In all countries, educational institutions are not always accessible to disabled persons and in many cases such persons are not admitted to the same schools as other people. The same applies to vocational training and to academic studies;

(b) *Employment.* In addition to the fact that many work places are not physically accessible to severely disabled persons, employers often fail to understand that a physical disability does not necessarily involve mental impairment and even fellow workers themselves may be opposed to the employment of disabled persons;

(c) *Transport.* Attention is drawn to the highly discriminatory effect of the failure to provide accessible means of transport and the obstacle which that presents to an independent life for disabled persons;

(d) *Housing.* It is noted with astonishment that even now, in highly developed countries, buildings which are not accessible to disabled persons are still being constructed. The use of wheelchairs, for instance, in extremely difficult, or even impossible, in many apartment buildings;

(e) *Buildings in general.* The above observations also apply to other premises such as public office buildings, restaurants, cinemas, theatres, libraries, hotels, sports facilities etc. Apart from the obstacles presented by building design, prejudices often exist which render the access of disabled persons to premises such as restaurants or bars difficult or impossible. It is common to hear the management of such establishments say that there are no tables free when a group of disabled persons attempts to enter.

C. CULTURAL BARRIERS

185. Although in most of the replies it is recognised, at least implicitly, that prejudices and discrimination against disabled persons exist, few Governments have made a study of the causes and forms of such practices. However, with regard to causes, some replies were objective enough to single out traditional attitudes which expose some categories of disabled persons to feelings of shame, superstitious fear and rejection.[61] It is worth noting that both governmental and non-governmental sources point to cultural barriers as one of the main obstacles to the integration and full participation of disabled persons in all aspects of social life.

1. Access to education

186. Further to the information provided by the World Veterans Federation, the Special Rapporteur considers it worthwhile emphasising the impact of such cultural barriers on all aspects of the economic, working, educational and everyday life of disabled persons. With regard to education, for example, paragraph 120 of the World Programme of Action stipulates that education should, as far as possible, to provided within the ordinary school system, without any discrimination against handicapped children or adults. However, this condition is not always met, because of the prejudices of the authorities and teachers, of the parents of other children, or even of the parents of disabled children. Consequently, in many instances where the child's disability does not constitute an obstacle in itself, discrimination prevents him from entering the ordinary school system. In some cases, it is the law itself which stipulates that disabled children must attend special schools, which is tantamount to official segregation. In other cases, the obstacle to school attendance is the lack of means of transport, both in cities and in rural areas, although the phenomenon is much more common in the latter. Shortcomings in building design have a similar effect, making access to school buildings and movement inside them difficult, and also barring access to toilets etc., a very common phenomenon.

2. Unemployment

187. From the reports received, it emerges that unemployment is one of the main problems of disabled persons. According to ILO, the level of unemployment among disabled persons is two or three times as high as for other persons, and in many developing countries where unemployment is very widespread, the employment prospects of disabled persons are minimal or nonexistent. For example, the unemployment figures for Europe are as follows: in the United Kingdom, the estimated level of unemployment amongst disabled persons in 1978 was 14 per cent, compared with 5.5 per cent for the rest of the population; in France in the same year, the unemployment rate amongst disabled persons was three times as high as for the rest of the population; the Netherlands and Denmark had unemployment rates of 7 per cent in 1978, and only 11.5 per cent and 17.5 per cent respectively of their registered workers with disabilities were able to find work; in the Federal Republic of Germany,

the average period of unemployment for workers with disabilities is 16 months, compared with 10 months for the rest of the population.[62] Although these figures are 10 years old, they provide a clear indication of the comparative levels of unemployment among disabled persons and for the rest of the population.

188. Still with regard to the major problem of unemployment. Finland, which is a developed country and highly advanced with regard to the treatment of disabled persons, recognises in its official report that, while a special employment service does exist and employers receive subsidies for employing disabled persons, their conditions continue to deteriorate in relation to the general rise in unemployment. The official report of Canada states that, despite the fact that the law prohibits discrimination against disabled persons, many cases of unequal treatment on the labour market have been discovered and the unemployed rate is estimated at more than 50 per cent. The Australian authorities state that there is some labour discrimination against disabled persons in regard to equal opportunities to acquire skills and training, equal employment opportunities, equality in working conditions and career advancement. They also state that many disabled persons live below the poverty line.

189. In the developing countries, the extremely high percentage of unemployed disabled persons means that they are forced to resort to begging in order to survive or that the favoured few who obtain jobs are forced to accept very low levels of pay. Moreover, in some countries, employers compel disabled persons to refrain from joining unions if they want a job. The World Federation of the Deaf notes that, in addition to the lack of technical assistance and necessary interpretation services, prejudices in general are one of the main factors making it difficult or impossible for persons with hearing disabilities to become fully integrated into the labour market.

3. Private life

190. The example provided by governmental and non-governmental sources on the negative effect of prejudices on the daily lives of disabled persons are many and varied. With regard to marriage, the Government of China provides an authentic illustration of the special situation that can arise when a disabled young man and an able-bodied girl have a love affair. White there is nothing

abnormal or reproachable in such a situation, it is commonly disapproved of by both sets of parents, friends and relatives. In such circumstances, it is easy to imagine the marriage ending in separation or divorce. In this as in many other similar cases, it is not only the disorder or functional disability that generally prevents integration or lasting marriage, but the behaviour of society towards disabled persons (other examples can be found in paras. 197 and 198).

4. Legal barriers

191. As stated earlier, because of the special situation of disabled persons, a number of "positive actions" must be taken to ensure that they are genuinely able to enjoy their most fundamental rights on a basis of equality. Nevertheless, many non-governmental organisations have informed the Special Rapporteur of failures to meet this requirement. In some countries, for example, deaf and dumb persons are deprived of the right to a defence because the judicial and investigating authorities do not have permanent interpreters, which are essential in such cases.

192. At the other extreme, there are also fairly numerous complaints from non-governmental sources concerning what might be termed "negative actors" resulting in the legal exclusion of disabled persons from many acts of daily life. In many countries, even today, deaf and dumb persons who are unable to express themselves in writing are considered legally incapacitated, although other effective means of communication, such as sign language, already exist or have been developed. Another similar example is the barring of blind persons from acting as guardians, when they are actually perfectly able to act as parents, and thus also as guardians. Finally the Pan-American Congress of the Blind reports that, in some Latin American countries, sightless persons are no permitted to vote or stand for election, on the grounds that it is difficult for them to vote responsibly or preserve secrecy.

D. PARTICULARLY VULNERABLE SITUATION OF THE MENTALLY ILL

193. However, it is in the sphere of mental disability that these legal barriers are most in evidence. There is general agreement that persons with mental disabilities are among the groups most discriminated against and the special report prepared by Mrs.. Erica-

Irene Daes entitled "Principles, guidelines and guarantees for the protection of persons detained on grounds of mental ill-health or suffering from mental disorder" fully confirms this view.[63]

194. According to information received from the International League of Societies for Persons with Mental Handicap, a meeting of lawyers representing various associations held at Marburg, Germany, in June 1989, reached the following conclusions.

(a) In everyday life, mentally handicapped persons are not treated equally with their neighbours, colleagues, etc. In addition to being frequently refused entry to bars, restaurants, swimming pools, discotheques, etc., they are often not allowed into hotels and regularly face enormous difficulties in finding accommodation, even in apartments, particularly when they are in groups;

(b) In the legal sphere, for example many instances of discrimination can be found in immigration laws. Many national laws prevent mentally handicapped persons from entering the country, not only as permanent residents, but even as tourists, for a limited period of time. Attention is drawn to the fact that it is in the most developed Western countries (Canada, France, Switzerland, United States) that this type of restrictive legislation is most frequently applied on the grounds, in many cases, that the presence of mentally handicapped persons from abroad will impose "excessive demands on health or social services";[64]

(c) It is also regrettable that, in some countries, mentally handicapped children are denied the opportunity to develop and learn, although there is abundant evidence to show that even seriously mentally handicapped persons can acquire practical skills and attain a high level of proficiency in manual work;

(d) The worst form of discrimination against the mentally handicapped is the campaign to legalise the termination of life of severely handicapped new-born children;

(e) Finally, attention is drawn to deplorable treatment to which mentally handicapped persons are frequently subjected in psychiatric hospitals, a question which is dealt with specifically below.

E. INSTITUTIONALISATION

195. In this connection, it should be recalled that the Sub-Commission's Special Rapporteur, Mrs. Erica-Irene Daes, in her report relating specifically to persons detained on grounds of mental ill-health or suffering from mental disorder, showed that some persons had been subjected to privation in psychiatric institutions, as well as to many other forms of psychiatric maltreatment and misuses of psychiatry, including even torture by drugs, in contravention of medical ethics and of the relevant international instruments.[65]

196. As this is a question which has been duly considered in the above-mentioned report and in the various discussions in the Working Group on the Principles for the Protection of Persons with Mental Illness and for the Improvement of Mental Health Care, we shall refer only briefly here to the acute problem of the abuses and problems which regularly arise from the internment of the mentally ill in psychiatric institutions. However, this reference, although brief, is justified, since the next chapter will deal with the various alternatives to institutionalisation. The Special Rapporteur is aware of the importance of bringing fully to light the tragic situation obtaining in some psychiatric establishments and of the many and profound after-effects of confinement in them, so as to finally bring about a change of policy in this area.

197. It is an established fact that, while only a small minority of disabled persons are institutionalised, such confinement is ultimately one of the most severe and common forms of exclusion of such persons. Many facilities, by virtue of being located in unpopulated rural areas, are physically remote from the community, which only serves to increase this exclusion. Life within them bears little or no relation to the life of the community at large, or even that of other disabled persons living outside. In institutions, freedom to associate is usually limited by segregation of the sexes. It is very common for inmates to have their mail opened and be denied other means of communication with the outside world. They are generally prevented from marrying and having children and, in some cases, even from voting. Internment also tends to lead to excessive use of drugs and other forms of behaviour control. Even the most modern, well-equipped and well-staffed institutions have a somewhat dehumanising character since institutionalisation is based on the assumption that the persons concerned are incapable of leading an independent

life as members of the community, so that inmates tend to become passive and dependent. The very fact that they are segregated from society promotes this tendency and causes inmates to develop what has been called an "institutional mentality", itself a further disability in that it impedes their reintegration into the community.

198. In addition to horrible misuses of psychiatry of the kind frequently reported in the media, particularly when they have resulted in the death of an inmate, the ordinary routine of institutions can give rise to appalling situations which are usually unknown or inconceivable to anyone who has never visited an establishment of this type. For example, non-governmental organisations report that one typical aspect of life within institutions is the virtually total loss of privacy for inmates. They usually have to share their accommodation with one or more other persons, which is itself results in a complete lack of privacy. Moreover, visitors are received in communal areas, thus precluding any natural display of affection which is so necessary for such persons when they meet their loved ones. It is also not unusual for visits to become less frequent and less regular, particularly if the institution is far from the city. However modern and efficient the institution, the inmates will tend to lose any real concept of the outside world, their only contact with it being through television, or the visits of relatives or friends, if any. Even in developed countries, persons in institutions have been known to spend years, and sometimes the rest of their lives, without anyone claiming them, despite their being equipped to live as members of the community.

199. It may seem surprising, but some developing countries point out that, in present circumstances, extreme poverty, overpopulation and insanitary conditions as regards the family and the local environment prevent the authorities from adopting any approach other than committing disabled persons to institutions. In Thailand, for example, chronic patients who remain in hospital for more than five years usually occupy more than 30 per cent of hospital beds. Although in 1986 a mobile treatment programme was introduced, 22 per cent of chronic psychiatric patients continue to be confined in institutions. Despite this policy of treatment outside institutions, most mental health services continue to be overextended and patients do not participate actively in seeking solutions.

F. ELIMINATION OF ABUSES AND OF ACTS OF DISCRIMINATION

200. The existence of effective remedies to prevent this type of abuse (habeas corpus, for example) and the introduction of laws penalising discrimination is a question of the utmost importance which will be dealt with fully at the end of the following chapter. For the moment, it is worth noting that this is a question which is widely discussed in non-governmental circles but which, with a few exceptions, Governments have been very slow to take up.

201. One such exception is the United States Rehabilitation Act of 1973, section 504 of which provides that "No otherwise qualified handicapped individual...shall, solely by reason of his handicap, be excluded from participation in, be denied the benefits of or be subjected to discrimination under any programme or activity receiving Federal financial assistance". This prohibition was extended to the private sector in 1990 by the Americans with Disabilities Act (ADA'90). Another similar example is the Anti-Discrimination Act of New South Wales, Australia, which makes it unlawful to discriminate against an intellectually handicapped person on the basis of her or his intellectual impairment in six important areas of social life, namely, work, accommodation, public education, provision of goods and services, membership of trade unions and membership of clubs. In 1988, Argentina adopted Act No. 23, 592 under which various forms of discrimination, including those directed specifically against disabled persons, were made punishable offences. Sweden is currently preparing an anti-discrimination law and it has been agreed that an ombudsman will be appointed to supervise its implementation.

202. The special Rapporteur shares the view that anti-discrimination legislation, particularly when it refers specifically to disabled persons, is an appropriate way of combating certain reprehensible attitudes, particularly in so far as it affords the possibility of suing owners of bar, hotels and other public premises who have practised discrimination and to bring claims against national or local authorities whose officials have been guilty of discrimination. The Special Rapporteur nevertheless considers public information and education campaigns conducted by the public authorities, trade unions and organisations of disabled persons to be of vital importance in eradicating prejudices which continue to exist and in putting an end to discrimination.

203. Another decisive step in combating discrimination would be a systematic review of national laws and the incorporation in them of the principles and guidelines contained in the various international instruments which prohibit, with increasing specificity, any form of discrimination against disabled persons. An example of this is the application clause of the Principles for the Protection of Persons with Mental Illness, which states: "These Principles shall be applied without discrimination of any kind such as on grounds of *disability,* race, colour, sex, language, religion..." (emphasis added). More recently, General Assembly resolution 45/113 entitled "United Nations Rules for the Protection of Juveniles Deprived of Their Liberty", contains in paragraph 4 of its annex, the following statement:

The Rules should be applied impartially, without discrimination of any kind as to race, colour, sex, are, language, religion, nationality, political or other opinion, cultural beliefs or practices, property, birth or family status, ethnic or social origin, and *disability*...(emphasis added).

12

NATIONAL AND INTERNATIONAL POLICIES AND MEASURES DESIGNED TO ERADICATE DISCRIMINATORY PRACTICES AND GUARANTEE THE DISABLED THE FULL ENJOYMENT OF HUMAN RIGHTS.

A. PRELIMINARY CONSIDERATIONS

204. It seems appropriate to point out at the outset of this chapter that its content accords in essentials with the aims and strategies of the World Programme of Action, whose implementation, within the United Nations system, is the responsibility of the Centre for Social Development and Humanitarian Affairs, which has in this regard performed commendable and noteworthy work. We would therefore like to refer to the Centre's many documents and publications,[66] which give a comprehensive and detailed account of its numerous activities and efforts on the subject. In this context, the Special Rapporteur will confine himself to a bare summary of the information received, stressing only those issues which he feels essential in achieving the Programme's objectives.

205. Possibly one of the most striking aspects is the realisation of the joint responsibility of governments, the community and disabled persons themselves for achieving these aims. In this context, there is no doubt that one of the most notable features of the Decade has been the leading role played by non-governmental organisations headed by disabled people, and the acknowledgement of their status as experts in their own affairs. At the social level, there has also been an extremely positive development as increasing importance is

attached to the integration of disabled persons in the community. This has been suitably reflected in the conceptual transformation of rehabilitation, which has lost its strictly medical character and incorporated the social dimension previously lacking. Nevertheless, more than a few Governments, on the broad pretext of "economic crisis", have sent replies that often present a picture of a "hands off" State which believes itself exempt from any social function as a result of the prevailing economic situation.

206. It is therefore important to point out in this introduction that, while joint responsibility may be the dominant concept behind the World Programme of Action, the principal obligation to remove obstacles impeding or hindering the integration and full participation of disabled persons lies with Governments This means that they cannot be mere onlookers; they must act, sometimes with great vigour, and especially in difficult situations, in order to prevent marginalisation and to ensure that equalisation of the opportunities is not just rhetoric but real and effective.

B. COMMITTAL TO AN INSTITUTION OR REHABILITATION IN THE COMMUNITY

207. Experience has shown that therapy which involves the isolation of disabled persons not only prevents their full integration into their social milieu but in most cases aggravates existing disabilities or causes new ones. This is because rehabilitation is not a purely medical concept but a comprehensive process which covers the physical, mental, social and vocational rehabilitation of the individual. This statement in turn has numerous implications. On the one hand, it means that it is only within the community that a process of rehabilitation which aims to achieve the maximum participation of the individual can take place, and on the other hand that the individual must participate in the formulation, choice and evaluation of his or her own rehabilitation process. This last assertion might seem elementary and possibly superfluous, until we remember that for centuries and even now this possibility has been regularly denied to persons with mental disabilities.

208. The World Programme of Action concerning Disabled Persons specifically mentions the growing tendency to integrate rehabilitation services into general public services. It is clearly indicated

that this must take place in a natural environment and be supported by mechanisms based in the community itself and in specialised institutions. Furthermore, at the mid-point of the Decade, it was once more stressed that, wherever possible, services for disabled persons must be provided within the existing social, educational, health and labour structures in society and that procedures should be established to permit the effective participation of disabled persons in the decision-making process.

209. Subsequently, at the sixth annual inter-agency meeting on the United Nations Decade of Disabled Persons (Vienna, 5-7 December 1988) the World Health Organisation representative[67] pointed out that developing countries had an unfortunate shortage of specialists in every aspect of community-level services. Only 25 per cent of disabled persons were actively involved in rehabilitation programmes and in most developing countries the potential demand for rehabilitation services was far greater than could be met in the near future. It was also pointed out that rehabilitation activities should meet the care needs of all disabled persons, including those with locomotor, visual, hearing and mental disabilities.

210. At the same meeting, the representative of the International Labour Organisation[68] said that more needed to be done to integrate disabled persons in the community and that assistance should be offered to them where they lived. Indeed the comments made by this representative are of great importance in that they stressed the need for a critical evaluation of the various approaches taken and results achieved until now with the aim of improving the system and obtaining better results in rehabilitation in the community. The paper submitted by the ILO recommended that the term "community-based rehabilitation" should be changed to "community-integration programme" whenever a rehabilitation agency was setting up programmes geared to equalisation of opportunities in training and employment and the socio-economic integration of disabled persons. It further emphasised that as local conditions were very varied there was no single global approach to organising community-based rehabilitation.

211. The Food and Agriculture Organisation of the United Nations,[69] for its part, reported that it has not specifically worked on the reintegration of blind or partially sighted persons into society (Onchocerciasis Control Programme in Senegal, Mali and Guinea), as

they had never been excluded but were simply a burden on the society which supported them. With the improvement in their physical condition the "reintegration" occurred quite naturally, whether the community remained in its old area or move to the new onchocerciasis-freed areas.

212. At the International Meeting on Human Resources in the Field of Disability, which took place in Tallinn, Estonian Soviet Socialist Republic, from 14 to 22 August 1989,[70] it was pointed out that "the abilities of disabled persons and their families should be strengthened through community-based supplementary services provided by Governments and non-governmental organisations.... These services should promote self-determination and enable disabled persons to participate in the development of society." Many speakers considered that, while community-based rehabilitation was an approach best suited to rural areas, it was also appropriate for urban areas due to the severe deprivation experienced in them by disabled persons. It was agreed that the involvement of the family and the community as essential to such rehabilitation. Lastly, the importance of this approach was emphasised because even now disabled persons continue to be deprived of opportunities to develop their potential, their productive capabilities and their self-reliance and are thus cut off from the mainstream of national development.

213. At the seventh annual inter-agency meeting, which took place in Vienna from 6 to 8 December 1989,[71] it was acknowledged that the concept of community-based rehabilitation had received considerable attention over the past Decade and that it was extremely important to utilise and build on existing resources in disabled persons themselves, their families and their communities. The World Programme of Action was seen as the guiding principle in the evaluation of this concept and the participants recognised the need for a further clarification of the concept of community-based rehabilitation as a multidisciplinary and intersectoral approach. Lastly, it was pointed out that the preparatory work on the Principles for the Protection of Persons with Mental illness and for the Improvement of Mental Health Care had adopted this approach. Principle 3 states that "Every person with a mental illness shall have the right to live, as far as possible, in the community",[72] and principle 7 that "Every patient shall have the right to be treated and cared for, as far as possible, in the community in which he or she lives".[73]

C. MEASURES TAKEN TO LIMIT COMMITTAL TO INSTITUTIONS AND TO PREVENT ABUSES

214. An integrationist trend can also be discerned at the national level, at least judging by Government replies. Most Governments are clearly turning away from committal to institutions as a priority strategy. The stress is now on reintegration into the family and the community with a view to encouraging the maximum integration of disabled persons in social life. However, institutionalisation is still a last resort in situations provided for under the law which appear to be of extreme seriousness, for example when an individual suffering from serious mental illness is found guilty of a crime[74] or when medical and social reports indicate that the minimum welfare of the individual cannot be guaranteed outside of an institution.[75] In some replies abuses arising from committal, such as sterilisation or castration, were mentioned, in particular concerning persons with mental disabilities, and the replies indicated the intention to eliminate these abuses.

215. In order to prevent the institutional abuses often suffered by disabled persons, especially those with mental illnesses, some States have set up supervisory committees, or other relevant bodies, and have established standards to regulate admission to and retention in mental health-care services. For instance, the Mental Health Act of Alberta, Canada, protects the right of patients to be informed of the reason for admission or to be issued with certificates for renewal of detention. Throughout the committal period, the patients have the right to apply to a review panel for cancellation of the admission certificate or renewal certificate. The Act also protects the confidentiality of a patient's diagnosis and records and prohibits any disclosure that would be detrimental to the patient's personal interest, reputation or privacy.[76] Another set of national regulations worthy of mention is the Mental Health Act 1959 of the United Kingdom, which provides for the detention in psychiatric hospitals of mentally disordered patients. However, the compendium of national legislation contained in annex III tot he report of Mrs. Erica-Irene Daes is sufficiently illustrative and comprehensive on this subject, and the reader is therefore referred to it.

216. Going beyond legal remedies, which are in any case inadequate, non-governmental organisations emphasise the need for

genuine alternatives to allow disabled persons to integrate in society. The lack of community-based services is what often leads to disabled persons being confined to institutions. They have the right to normalise their lives through the provision of "alternative residential options" which do not impose restrictions on their freedom and enable them to integrate. These options include the possibility of allocating housing for the rehabilitation of persons recently discharged from institutions, and also apartments in cooperative or public housing specially adapted for them. If they are able to live with their families or on their own, there should be community services enabling them to live independently.

217. Certain of the support services offered by some European Governments to disabled persons living in their own homes show the way ahead in this field. These include, for instance, domestic and personal care arrangements which cover cooking, cleaning, laundry, ironing, personal hygiene, vocational and cultural activities, substitution of direct relative, psychological care, etc. In some cases these services are provided by the municipality and include occupational therapy, social workers, home helps and occasionally small grants to adapt accommodation or to buy electronics aids affording greater independence in the home.

218. Without denying the need to increase the economic aid given for such services, the non-governmental organisations maintain that, there public resources are in short supply, it is particularly important to mobilise the resources of the community and of disabled persons themselves. Especially in developing countries, primary health-care services must be used as much as possible for prevention and medical rehabilitation, the generation of local technical assistance, and the establishment of integrated schools. Furthermore, disabled persons' cooperatives should be encouraged and opportunities for self-employment should be created.

219. The non-governmental organisations have expressed scepticism concerning the effectiveness until now of the scarce legal resources to prevent institutional abuse, and indicated, as we shall see, that they need to be strengthened. Neither have they concealed their belief that the many cultural factors which lead individuals casually to abandon their close relatives in such places have also influenced the unscrupulous management of some institutions and the abuses regularly committed in them.

220. Finally, there is no common terminology in existence among the organisations to describe the exceptional cases in which committal is advisable. Some of them use the phrase "only as a last resort" or "in those cases in which there is no really valid alternative"; some, on the other hand, apply the criterion "where other methods of treatment have clearly failed".[77] However, it is indisputable that in those few cases in which committal is accepted it does not lose its restrictive nature and whatever formulation is used should always take into account " that the society has done everything in its power in order to avoid it". This is very important as it translates into words that are not only moral but legal, society's obligation to adjust to the needs of disabled persons. It is far more logical and just that society should adapt to the basic needs of disabled persons than that they should be required not only to overcome the objective impediments arising form their disability but also to adapt themselves to society's foolish excesses.

D. MEASURES TO FACILITATE THE ESTABLISHMENT AND ACTIVITIES OF ASSOCIATIONS OF DISABLED PERSONS

221. It should be recalled that the Pan of Action for the International Year of Disabled Persons (1981) urged the establishment of national committees to plan, coordinate and execute the activities of the Year. Although some countries had already established similar committees during the 1960s and 1970s, the great majority of Governments only set them up in response to this request. This is evidenced by the fact that during the International Year it was reported that national committees existed in 141 countries and territories. However, it seems that by the end of the year most of the national committees had been dissolved.[78]

222. The World Programme of Action, after pointing out the obligation of Governments to establish a focal point to look into and follow the activities of various ministries, other government agencies and non-governmental organisations, stated under the heading "Participation of disabled persons in decision-making" that Member States should increase their assistance to organisations of disabled persons and help them organise and coordinate the representation of the interests and concerns of disabled persons. It also said that Member States should actively seek out and encourage in every possible way—including through financial support—the development

of organisations composed of, or representing, disabled persons. It further recognised the importance of such organisations influencing government policies and decisions in all areas that concerned them. This means that the Programme of Action acknowledges that non-governmental organisations composed of disabled persons or representing their interests have one of the most important roles to play in implementing the Plan and achieving the objectives of the Decade.

223. The leading role achieved by these organistions is perhaps one of the most striking features of the Decade and the positive impact of their activities has yet to be adequately appreciated. What appears to be an issue at the present time is not the indisputable legitimacy of these associations' activities but rather the broadening of the legal base enabling disabled persons to participate as citizens with full rights in the decision-making process at all levels of the planning, implementation, monitoring and evaluation of policies and programmes. This was one of the main concerns of the Tallinn meeting and some of the guidelines formulated there are aimed at encouraging grass-roots initiatives. For instance, articles 14 and 16 contain the following provisions:

14. Local community initiatives should be especially promoted. Disabled persons and their families should be encouraged to form grass-roots organisations, with governmental recognition of their importance and governmental support in the form of financing and training.

15. Governmental and non-governmental organisations concerned with disability issues should allow disabled persons to participate as equal partners.

16. The efficient functioning of governmental and non-governmental organisations concerned with disability calls for training in organisational and management skills.

224. At the Global Meeting of Experts held in Stockholm in August 1987, the participants agreed on the importance of encouraging non-governmental organisations, especially as they often act as a vehicle for self-development and at the same time can effectively influence certain decisions made by Governments and other sectors of society. More recently, the International Meeting on the Roles and

Functions of National Coordinating Committees on Disability in Developing Countries (Beijing, China, 5-11 November 1990) adopted Guidelines for the Establishment and Development of National Coordinating Committees on Disability. Among the goals of those committees are those aimed at developing national policy and legislation on disability and related issues and at inspiring effective measures for the prevention of disability, for rehabilitation and for the realisation of goals of "full participation" of persons with disability in social life and development. Furthermore, on 20 February 1991, the Social Committee of the Economic and Social Council adopted a draft resolution urging the establishment and strengthening of national coordinating committees and similar bodies on disability. For this reason the Secretary-General was requested to distribute as widely as possible, with copies in Braille, the Guidelines adopted in Beijing.

225. The idea has gradually taken shape that if disabled persons have equal rights they should also have equal obligations, and that is why their involvement in the building of society is both a "right" and a "duty". The concept has given a new impulse and direction to the work of the relevant organisations, which do not confine themselves to merely defending rights but have also undertaken other activities such as promotion of equality of opportunity through the provision of certain services, for example leadership training, vocational training, the encouragement of job-creation schemes, etc. In Argentina, "PAR", which is an organisation made up of disabled persons, has done much valuable work in finding employment. Disabled Peoples' International is sponsoring self-help movements through regional seminars, congresses and its own newspaper. The World Blind Union not only sponsors conventions of the blind but alto helps them to create their own national organisations. The League of the Red Cross and the Red Crescent Societies has adopted first-aid training for the disabled and consults disabled persons about the planning, implementation and evaluation of programmes that are of concern to them. There are in fact many examples that could be given of such work which bear witness to the change in the approach to responsibility, and the results of this have been particularly encouraging, especially in developing countries, where basic needs are still not met and social security is virtually non-existent.

226. It is clear from the information received from Governments that in almost all States disabled persons have the right to associate in organisations, societies and federations.[79] Many replies specify that disabled persons have the right and means to influence the decision making process.[80] On the other hand, in other States, the power to make decisions is kept in the hands of governmental bodies[81] and some Governments appoint their own representatives in organisations of disabled persons.[82] On the whole Governments are clearly taking initiatives to encourage the activities of such organisations, especially in consultation and advice, while in some countries the authorities delegate extensive powers to voluntary associations in the application of policies for the disabled.[83] In addition, the replies highlighted the importance role played by trade unions with regard to the rehabilitation and vocational integration of the disabled and their access to equality of opportunity and treatment.

227. It has already been pointed out that, at the international level, the Centre for Social Development and Humanitarian Affairs is the United Nations body responsible for implementing the World Programme of Action and, through the department for the disabled, it maintains close relations with non-governmental organisations throughout the world. The annual inter-agency meetings on the Decade, organised by the United Nations office at Vienna, have been instrumental in establishing an important working link for cooperation between the United Nations system and the main non-governmental organisations concerned. In December 1985 a number of non-governmental organisations with offices in Vienna combined to form an NGO committee on disabled persons for the purpose of enhancing assistance to the United Nations in the Implementation of the World Programme of Action.

228. Finally, it must be stressed that it is largely due to the information activities carried out by these bodies, especially those of a transnational nature, such as Disabled Peoples' International, that it has been possible for the issue of disability to be looked at from the human rights point of view. Furthermore, what might seem obvious today was not so less than a decade ago, and to write a report on the violation of the human rights of disabled persons has been a very real achievement by these organisations and is further testimony to their determined struggle. In addition to this acknowledgement, the Special Rapporteur would like to express once more his deepest gratitude for the cooperation he has received from them.

E. RIGHTS OF DISABLED PERSONS IN THE MATTER OF EDUCATION, TRAINING AND VOCATIONAL GUIDANCE

1. Education and training

229. In this area, the basic idea of the World Programme of Action is to promote policies which recognise the right of disabled persons to equal educational opportunities. The Programme stipulates in this case that the education of the disabled should as far as possible be carried out within the general education system, pointing out that at least 10 per cent of the disabled population are children who have the right to education, even though this may necessitate special educational services. The Tallinn Guidelines contain recommendations for specific programmes and training materials, the provision of special education teachers as consultants to regular education teachers, the setting up of resource rooms with specialised personnel and materials, the running of special courses in regular schools, etc.

230. It is evident from the replies received that, in regard to education and training, considerable efforts are being made in most countries with three broad aims: to ensure the fullest possible integration of the disabled in ordinary school systems, to train specialised teachers and advisers, and to make sure that the necessary equipment is available to bring disabled persons up to the same level of education as other pupils and thus enable them to become self-sufficient and self-supporting rather than being ensnared in the social security system. The setting up of special education institutions is necessary, for example, when the nature or gravity of the disability prevents the persons concerned from attending normal classes.[84] The Government of Sweden has pointed out in its reply that qualified technical and teaching staff are available to assist in the education of those with a disability and that special educational conditions are provided for the mentally retarded, just as the deaf are taught by sign language.

231. In Belguim, where schooling is obligatory for 12 years, a juvenile court has the power to exempt disabled children from compulsory education. Courses and university studies are available for the training of special education teachers. Canada points out that current policy is tending towards abandonment of the principle that the disabled should be educated separately. Special services are run

by the Ministry of Education in Venezuela, providing education for disabled children from a very early age and job-related training for adolescents and adults. At the national level there are 16 public and private institutions operating at university level, which train teaching and technical staff in individual aspects of special education. In Cyprus, an act has been passed on special education and the Government assumes responsibility for the education of children with slight mental retardation and physical or sensory disabilities between the ages of 5 and 18. The general policy is not to separate such children from the others, although special schools are available where this is not possible. In the Philippines, special education is provided for blind and deaf children and children with orthopaedic disabilities and mental retardation, although in some schools they are integrated in the general education system. Qater reports that it provides special educational services for children with disabilities, with separate institutions for boys and for girls. If they cannot be educated in Qatar, they may be sent abroad, the expenses being borne by the State. Lastly, the replies received indicated that African countries have not set up separate special education facilities, but most make provision in specialised residential or day schools for students with visual, hearing or mental disabilities.

232. UNESCO's action in the educational field, as set out in the Medium-Term Plan (1990-1995) is very significant. It addresses the educational needs of children and young persons with disabilities by means of an integrated education approach and community-based programmes. Within this framework, UNESCO's aim is to establish a link with the facilities normally available within the education sector and with operational activities in Member States. During the first biennium, efforts will be concentrated on three main areas:

(a) Planning, organisation and management of special eduction provision;

(b) Teacher-training to meet special needs in the classroom;

(c) Early identification of disability in children, rapid remedial action and education of the parents. In this connection, UNESCO, in addition to drawing up manuals on special education, has published a number of works and is currently preparing a publication on education for disabled children and adolescents and on the use of Braille.

2. Vocational training and rehabilitation

233. At the start of this chapter (paras. 207-213) we referred at some length to the subject of rehabilitation in the broad sense. Accordingly, we can now confine ourselves to summarising the information received, especially from governmental sources, since non-governmental organisations generally agree that rehabilitation has to be considered as a whole and not subdivided between the various services and agencies responsible for training, on the one hand, and employment and health on the other. It is therefore of interest to know how Governments are incorporating these ideas in their policies and how they are gradually refining the machinery for cooperation between themselves on the one hand and non-governmental organisations and specialised agencies of the United Nations on the other.

234. Training for independent day-to-day living has become a focus in some countries. In others, reintegration and vocational rehabilitation programmes are being implemented as part of non-formal as well as formal education. Many States report on the implementation of community-based rehabilitation programmes. Twofold results can be achieved by this approach, namely expansion of the rehabilitation services and promotion of the integration of disabled persons. In this case, the community has a part to play in the planning, initiation and provision of the service, as has been done, for example, in some regions of Thailand for mentally disabled persons and in India for the blind. Nepal has also recently trained a number of instructors who are actively involved in the implementation of community-based rehabilitation programmes for persons with impaired vision.

235. Some Governments report that they have set up sheltered workshops in rural areas[85] and emphasise the importance of training persons with a disability for agricultural tasks or as craftsmen.[86] The USSR reported positive results from home-training and Sweden highlighted the results achieved by in-service training. Apprenticeships with craftsmen have also been mentioned by various sources as a useful means of reintegration in society. Other forms of preparatory training have been found necessary in the case of persons with a severe or multinle disability and the need for medical assessment and therapy to be carried out in parallel was frequently stressed. Other

replies emphasised the importance in local communities of making use of acquired skills, including those of disabled persons, for use in training programmes. Almost all replies stressed the importance of respect and confidence for the training and reintegration of disabled persons, as well as the encouragement of a feeling of self-esteem.

236. In regard to the training of professional and auxiliary staff, the replies indicated the efforts made by Governments to expand training facilities and training programmes for rehabilitation, counselling and skills training, in both community-and institution-based programmes. Pakistan reported an expansion of medical and paramedical facilities to enable them to be used both for training and for the provision of services. In Thailand, for example, rural health, workers, parents and those providing care to persons with mental disorders are being given special training. India has also been providing short-term training courses for teachers working in the regular school system, to enable them to educate and train disabled children. To remedy the shortage of trained professional and auxiliary staff in the Congo, bilateral agencies have been conducting courses for community workers. Some countries report a lack of rehabilitation specialists, physiotherapists and specialists in the education of persons with physical disabilities and mental disorders. Nigeria emphasised the training of personnel working in hospitals and rehabilitation centres, while indicating that it is also looking into ways of increasing the number of occupational and speech therapists. There is in general a tendency for the training of disabled persons to be directed toward self-employment activities, which provide more realistic opportunities for the disabled to use their skills and generate income.

237. As already pointed out, ILO as an intergovernmental organisation has been very actively engaged in vocational training and guidance. One of the paramount aims of its policy has been to ensure the right to participation of children by means of active vocational rehabilitation programmes. The adoption of ILO standards on vocational rehabilitation has greatly stimulated world-wide action in promoting and developing vocational rehabilitation and employment services for all categories of disabled persons. According to an ILO brochure entitled "Experiences and reflections on a new concept of service provision for disabled people", experience of providing services has shown that it is essential to maintain close contacts with local

sources, to give disabled persons adequate information about those services, to provide follow-up at each level of training and to undertake a general evaluation of what has been achieved.

238. In addition to what was said earlier regarding the training activities of UNHCR and those of the Centre for Social Development and Humanitarian Affairs—especially its role in coordinating the policies and programmes of different organisations actively engaged in this field—it is important to emphasise the work of WHO, which has published a useful manual entitled *Training in the community for people with disabilities* (1989), now available in all the working languages of the United Nations.

239. The African Rehabilitation Institute is also playing a key part in responding to the training needs of disabled people throughout the continent, ensuring the coordination of measures and programmes between the different African countries and channelling the contributions of the various international donor organisations. Lastly, the International Committee of the Red Cross and the Red Crescent has set up a special fund for the rehabilitation of disabled persons (mainly war victims) and its programmes concentrate on making the fullest use of local resources and on training craftsmen and disabled persons themselves in the production of prostheses and similar devices which are not manufactured in the country.

F. RIGHTS OF DISABLED PERSONS IN RESPECT OF EMPLOYMENT AND WORKING CONDITIONS

240. The World Programme of Action calls for Member States to adopt policies to ensure that disabled persons have equal opportunities for productive and gainful employment in the open labour market. Measures in support of the integration of the disabled in the labour market include employment quotas with corresponding incentives, reserved or earmarked employment, loans or grants to small businesses and cooperatives, exclusive contracts or priority production rights, tax exemptions, preferential purchasing and other forms of technical or financial aid to firms employing disabled workers.

241. Measures for providing work for disabled persons obviously depend largely on the condition of the individual, although such measures all have two distinct but often complementary aims. They should be directed, on the one hand, at alleviating the inevitable

disadvantages and often considerable suffering of disabled persons and at the same time facilitate their integration in the labour market, so as to make them financially independent and productive members of society, capable of paying their taxes and in a position to reduce their demands for services.[87] Particular emphasis has been placed on the need to give the workforce proper training as an important means of preventing disabilities caused by industrial accidents. This aspect is also a major concern of the ILO, as reflected in its occupational health and safety programme. If adopted and applied, the ILO Vocational Rehabilitation and Employment Convention will guarantee that disabled persons are not subjected to discrimination at work. The following provisions of existing ILO standards may be given by way of examples: (a) the ILO Vocational Rehabilitation and Employment Convention No. 159 (1983) emphasises that a national policy on the vocational rehabilitation and employment of disabled persons must be based on the principle of equal opportunity and treatment of disabled men and women workers; (b) the ILO Vocational Rehabilitation and Employment Recommendation No. 168 (1983) states that: "Disabled persons should enjoy equality of opportunity and treatment in respect of access to, retention of and advancement in employment which, wherever possible, corresponds to their own choice and takes account of their individual suitability for such employment".

242. The Tallinn Guidelines contain the following provisions on the promotion of employment:

Disabled persons have the right to be trained for and to work on equal terms in the regular labour force. Community-based rehabilitation programmes should be encouraged to provide better job opportunities in developing countries.

Employment opportunities can be promoted primarily by measures relating to employment and salary standards that apply to all workers and secondarily by measures offering special support and incentives. In addition to formal employment, opportunities should be broadened to include self-employment, cooperatives and other group income-generating schemes. Where special national employment drives have been launched for youth and unemployed persons, disabled persons should be included. Disabled persons should be actively recruited, and when a disabled candidate and a non-disabled candidate are equally qualified, the disabled candidate should be chosen.

Employers' and workers' organisations should adopt, in cooperation with organisations of disabled persons, policies that promote the training and employment of disabled and non-disabled persons on an equal basis, including disabled women.

Policies for affirmative action should be formulated and implemented to increase the employment of disabled women. Governments and non-governmental organisations should support the creation of income-generating projects involving disabled women.

243. According to the information given, many States have developed and introduced programmes to create jobs for persons with disabilities, preferential treatment being accorded to those persons.[88] The programmes also encourage or require the recruitment of a certain percentage of the labour force from persons with disabilities. Several countries have set minimum quotas of posts for disabled persons and also established special workshops and sections for persons with disabilities.[89] Financial incentives available to employers are another means of ensuring that preferential treatment is given to disabled persons. Although a number of countries have not provided information on this aspect,[90] others have mentioned subsidies or tax concessions which are granted to employers who comply with the requirements.[91] Some countries have also set up an incentives system for persons with disabilities to encourage them to take up gainful employment. In India, the granting of credits on very favourable conditions in order to encourage the launching of small-scale business ventures is an example of such incentives. In other countries, managers are required to notify social welfare services of vacancies suitable for disabled persons. Another two States report that there is an obligation on official services to assist disabled persons in finding work.[92]

244. In some countries, the authorities and the trade unions ensure close cooperation between training centres for the disabled, government services and firms with a view to guaranteeing maximum opportunities for employment of the disabled. In the developing countries, work in cooperatives has been found to be much more effective than other forms of assistance that have a charitable motive. Self-help cooperatives for disabled persons, for example, are a good way of promoting self-employment. Such bodies have also received the support of large international cooperative movements.

245. Reference has already been made to the important part played by ILO In regard to working conditions and work safety, and in particular to the currently valid standards issued by that Organisation. Non-governmental organisations have also attached great importance to working conditions and in particular to cases of failure to comply with regulations governing health and safety at work. Where a disability has occurred at the worksite, they demand that the person concerned should be reintegrated as soon as the rehabilitation process allows.[93] If the consequences of the disability prevent the resumption of previous activities, the disabled person should be offered employment suited to his capacities. Temporary wage subsidies should also be provided to compensate for the losses sustained and the distress suffered during a disabled persons's period of inactivity. It was stated that all countries should pay priority attention to employment, which is an important part of activities for the development of human resources at the national level. Many countries have received ILO assistance in this connection.

G. OTHER RIGHTS OF DISABLED PERSONS

246. As was stated previously, the physical barriers of architecture and building are among the main obstacles to the full integration of disabled persons into social, economic and cultural life. It should be noted, however, that this is one of the areas in which the greatest results have been achieved, at least in the course of the Decade. Available information reveals that significant progress has been made in the steps taken by Governments to facilitate the access of disabled persons to buildings and transport services particularly in the public sector.

247. Some States report that they have adopted measures intended to facilitate full access to buildings including levelling off pavement, laying paving, marking parking areas, installing automatic doors, widening lifts and installing toilet facilities for wheelchair users.[94] Other report the adoption of measures to facilitate access to such public places as stadiums, commercial centres and shops.[95] As regards the problem of suitable housing, some countries have given priority to improving housing[96] and to making it easier for disabled persons to move around inside. Steps have also been taken to grant interest-free loans for building and renovating housing.[97]

248. As regards transport services accessible to disabled persons, the steps taken and the regulations brought into force in many States give evidence of considerable improvements. Some Governments also supply free or low cost transport cards in cities and rural districts.[98] Others provide specially designed motor vehicles (cars with manual controls, etc.[99]) and many facilitate their import if they are not manufactured locally.[100]

249. At the request of the General Assembly, a study was carried out in 1981 by the Centre for Social Development and Humanitarian Affairs, entitled "Access to United Nations buildings, documents and information facilities for persons with sensorial disabilities". The three-part study was compiled by experts who were themselves disabled persons, and covered the United Nationals buildings in New York, Geneva and Vienna. It was observed that in all three cases considerable investments were required to facilitate full and equal access by disabled persons to the facilities and the meetings which took place in them. Recently a number of improvements have been introduced in the United Nations Industrial Development Organisations (UNIDO), the Economic and Social Commission for Western Asia (ESCWA), the United Nations Educational, Scientific and Cultural Organisation (UNESCO), the United Nations Environment Programme (UNEP), the Food and Agriculture Organisation of the United Nations (FAO) and the United Nations Children's Fund (UNICEF).

250. The World Programme of Action emphasises the great importance of leisure, sports and other recreational activities for disabled persons. It also lays down that States have an obligation to ensure that disabled persons have an opportunity to use their creative, artistic and intellectual capacities to the maximum, not only for their own benefit, but also for the enrichment of the community. Examples of this are the grants awarded in the United Kingdom and Northern Ireland by the Arts Council to a number of theatre companies, particularly the British Theatre of the Deaf, Graece and Strathcona. The Arts Council has also prepared a deontological code which includes the employment of disabled persons. The Carnegie Trust has sponsored the production of "Arts for Everyone", which is a practical guide to the arts for persons suffering from any form of disability. China has set up the Disabled Artists' Company.

251. The available information reveals considerable efforts by Governments and local communities to facilitate access by disabled persons to museums, art galleries, libraries, etc. A number of States earmark funds for the publication of journals and books in Braille and for recording cassettes.[101] In recreational activities, the Office of Tourism of the Canadian Government has sponsored research projects to identify hotels or tourist accommodation accessible to travellers with sight or hearing disabilities and particularly motor disabilities. The Canadian parks have introduced programmes to create itineraries for such persons.

252. The World Programme of Action rightly stresses the paramount importance of sport for disabled persons, since sports activities are one of the most efficient means of enabling such persons to fulfil themselves physically and mentally. Such activities also have a positive effect in that they assist the development of the personality and facilitate family and professional integration while encouraging social contacts. Another very important aspect of sport is as a means of treatment and therapy. Rehabilitation through sport is in the case of disabled persons a doubly beneficial resource.

253. Many government replies describe the various measures adopted for developing sport and permitting disabled persons to have access to it. To illustrate this, we consider it important to mention the case of Paraguay, the Government of which has made provision for the building in various parts of the country of sports complexes which in addition to their social function, carry out a very important role *vis-a-vis* disabled persons; first of all, they are accessible; secondly, they provide sports activities for disabled persons, thirdly, they serve as centres for meeting, contact and social integration; and, fourthly, they also perform rehabilitation.[102] It may be noted that Paraguay is one of the developing countries which has earmarked most funds for this type of activity, and has provided that all income from games and lotteries will be devoted to this purpose. This seems to us an example worthy of imitation.

254. Another noteworthy example can be found in the activities of the International Boy Scout Movement for the integration of disabled children. Its programme on scouting with the disabled has been shown to be an extremely efficient means of bringing together children with disabilities and children without. The importance of practices of

this nature for stimulating and developing feelings of solidarity while at the same time eliminating prejudices and other cultural barriers which generally have their roots in childhood, will be evident to all.

H. MEASURES TO GUARANTEE THE EXERCISE OF THE RIGHTS OF DISABLED PERSONS AND THE EFFECTIVENESS OF THE REMEDIES AVAILABLE TO THEM

255. This is certainly one of the favourite subjects of the non-governmental organisations, while its incomparable importance and topically make it one of the key points of this report. In order to deal with it appropriately, its various components need to be clearly delimited, namely: (a) the problem of punishing acts of discrimination against disabled persons; (b) the recognition of their specific rights and the effectiveness of legal remedies for their defence; (c) the problems of statutory guardianship in the event of the institutionalisation of persons suffering from mental disorders; and (d) the issue of the international monitoring or supervision of due respect for the human rights and fundamental freedoms of disabled persons.

256. The legal treatment of acts of discrimination against disabled persons is undergoing a process of complete transformation. Summarising the contents of paragraphs 200-203 of this report, we might say that domestic legislation initially only prohibited discrimination in specific areas of social life, for example, education laws prohibited it in education; labour conventions prohibited it in labour, and so on successively covering the whole field of the professions, social security, etc. Only recently, particularly in the last few decades, have Governments begun to promulgate anti-discrimination laws of a general nature. Disabled persons have, however, always encountered enormous difficulties in persuading Governments and courts to apply these general laws to their particular case. The present trend, which consists in the adoption of specific laws which not only prohibit all types of discrimination but also penalise discriminatory acts, is extremely encouraging.

257. The legal protection of the specific rights of disabled persons give rise to a series of problems relating to the dissimilarity of treatment accorded to them in the various domestic legal systems. Generally speaking, it is only in exceptional instances that substantive law recognises their existence (civil codes, procedural codes, etc.) and, where this is done, the regulations are usually vague or inadequate,

which contributes to the fact that courts and administrative tribunals are reluctant to recognise disabled persons as an "identifiable class" liable to be the particular victims of violations.[103] On other occasions courts have considered that the legal interest is too imprecise and have given priority to economic interests. An example of this is the case of *Blair and Ors v. Venture Stores Retailers Pty. Ltd.*, a 1984 decision of the Equal Opportunity Board, Victoria, Australia. As may be recalled, in May 1983 Venture Stores took over the premises and closed off a lift which formerly gave customers access to the first floor sales area. Three women used wheelchairs took the store to court on the grounds that they had been discriminated against under article 27 H (2) of the Equal Opportunity Act 1977. The Board stated that the closing off of access to the lift had nothing to do with the issue of access to the first floor by persons in wheelchairs, since the decision had been taken for motives of profitability, and the provision of the services required would have been excessive and onerous for Venture Stores.[104]

258. This why it is very important to reiterate yet again that the recognition of the specific rights of disabled persons is not a matter which is concluded by merely listing those rights which are clearly embodied in the various legal instruments or recognised by case-law in the courts, the basic elements of which have been set out in this chapter. From a legal point of view the problem is somewhat more complex, in that the specific rights of disabled persons exactly parallel their needs, the satisfaction of which is an indispensable condition for their enjoyment of human rights, on an equal basis with the rest of society. In short, "the needs" of disabled persons and their "specific rights" are simply who sides of the same coin.[105]

259. The installation of ramps for disabled persons in public buildings, schools, polling stations, etc., can in no sense be construed as the recognition of special privileges on their behalf, but merely as compliance by Governments with their legal obligation to guarantee education for all and the exercise of political rights, also for everyone, on an equal basis. In other words, we are faced with requirements which in themselves are rights, but which at the same time are means of implementing other rights. We have already said that in a criminal trial in which the accused is a deaf mute, the absence of an interpreter would not only means the negation of a specific right and the transgression of a procedural norm, but purely and simply the deprivation of the right of defence.

260. The definition of these specific rights of disabled persons as their actual needs, the satisfaction of which is an essential condition for them to be able to enjoy human rights on an equal basis with others, not only engenders obligations for Governments, as we have just seen, but also obligations for society. In the specific case of forced institutionalisation, we said that, over and above the interests of the individual, society must do whatever it can to avoid that institutionalisation. This entails, *inter alia*, the primary obligation of the community to adapt to the elementary needs of disabled persons. Apart from this, there is also the specific issue of abuse in institutionalisation and during institutionalisation in special establishments. This requires the domestic legislation of States to make clear provision for effective remedies capable of preventing or terminating an arbitrary or unnecessary institutionalisation. Moreover, the non-governmental organisations which are most active in this area propose that the right of disabled persons to receive care, even in special institutions, also includes the right to oppose institutionalisation.

261. The Special Rapporteur wishes to point out that in view of the sensitive and complex nature of the problem of institutionalisation, it will always be useful for the decisions of administrative bodies to be reviewed and assessed by a legal authority. With regard to habeas corpus, he considers that universal experience is sufficiently instructive for its adoption to be advisable in countries—the majority—which have not yet included it in their domestic legislation. Lastly, he would point out that this should be the proper remedy not only when a legal authority considers whether a case of institutionalisation is arbitrary, but also when ending it as it has ceased to be necessary, or when the conditions of the institutionalisation have deteriorated or been aggravated or when there is evidence of ill-treatment. The last-mentioned, indeed, is a decisive factor in checking and cutting down the abuses which still frequently occur.

262. The international protection of the rights of disabled persons is one of today's most topical issues, since the United Nations Decade of Disabled Persons will very soon come to an end and so far no provision has been made for any monitoring mechanism of this type. The discussions in the Economic and Social Council on drafting an international convention on the subject led to the conclusion that the immediate future was not the moment for undertaking this activity, for reasons of circumstance rather than

substance. In any case the lack of a specific convention like those adopted for other vulnerable groups—women, refugees, immigrants, etc.—does not means that there are no international standards to protect disabled persons. Throughout chapter 1 we had occasion to refer in detail to the extensive, although admittedly scattered, range of international standards in existence. However, the problem which still remains is the lack of an international monitoring body to supervise, in particular, compliance with the various regulations for the protection of the human rights of disabled persons. The proposal of an appropriate monitoring mechanism perhaps constitutes the most delicate aspect of the mandate entrusted to the Special Rapporteur, and it is this which has aroused the greatest expectations among the non-governmental organisations.

263. As will be seen, in the final part of this report the Special Rapporteur sums up the many consultations which he has conducted and puts forward the following alternatives: (a) the establishment of an international ombudsman for disabled persons—this solution is the one which seems to find most favour with the non-governmental organisations; and (b) entrusting the Committee on Economic, Social and Cultural Rights with the task of supervision, once the Economic and Social Council has broadened the terms of its mandate. The preferred solution of the Special Rapporteur, as will be seen in the final paragraphs of this report, is the latter, or (c) a combination of the two alternatives.

13

PUBLIC INFORMATION AND EDUCATION

264. It would be wrong to think that the problem of discrimination and prejudices frequently directed against disabled persons amounts to a strictly legal issue or one that can be resolved through appropriate legislation. This is obviously only one aspect of a much more complex question, resulting from sociological and cultural factors that have a decisive effect on the behaviour of individuals and society towards such persons. Thus it is crucial to undertake and develop activities for the entire community, aimed at a genuine raising of awareness that will produce profound changes in attitude.

265. This is the basic thought behind the World Programme of Action, when it urges Member States to "encourage a comprehensive public information programme about the rights, contributions and unmet needs of disabled persons that would reach all concerned, including the general public. In this connection, attitude change should be given special importance".

266. In other words, the following should be the content and target population of the information to be disseminated:

(a) Adequate information on the means and services available for persons with disabilities and on their specific rights, in order for them to make full use of them. Persons concerned should be understood as including the family, for example.

(b) The information for he general public should stress human needs, especially those that are as yet unmet, the specific rights that disabled persons should be recognised as having and the need to respect them.

(c) For both sections of the target population, i.e. the general public and the disabled persons themselves, the information should stress the objective contribution of disabled persons tct he community and the benefits, both spiritual and material, that the integration and full participation of disabled persons in social life will bring the community.

267. According to the information available to the Special Rapporteur, the activities conducted during the Decade in this sphere have helped achieve some changes in attitude in the general public, although the results cannot be termed fully satisfactory. The examples of public information programmes and campaigns undertaken by various Governments are extremely varied and in some cases extremely ingenious, especially when they have been conducted jointly with the organisations concerned, thus changing this modality into a genuine reference model.

268. Following the example of the Centre for Social Development and Humanitarian Affairs, which has set up an international data bank with information on disabled persons, some States have established national banks. Similarly, the United Nations Department of Public Information is continuing to publicise the objectives of the Decade and the World Programme of Action through the distribution of information materials. The World Programme of Action itself has also been translated into all the official United Nations languages and distributed in over 60 countries.

269. In the publications category, mention should be made of those circulated by the organisations themselves, such as *Vox Nosra,* published by the Disabled Peoples' International. It contains the texts of international instruments, an account of the work of International human rights bodies, etc. The Swis Foundation pour 1'Intégration Professionnelle des Personnes Handicapées also publishes a bulletin whose purpose is to facilitate access to jobs by disabled persons seeking employment.

270. Finally, from the information received the Special Rapporteur has observed that the information campaigns undertaken by Governments are aimed primarily at highlighting the needs of persons with disabilities, which is correct but insufficient. Greater emphasis should be placed on their rights and on their contribution to society. The Special Rapporteur believes that the time has come for becoming truly aware, not only of what disabled persons might contribute if major obstacles are not placed in their path, but also of all that theyare

in fact contributing to the world of labour, science, arts and, especially, what they bring us every day, in that intimate area of our spiritual life, which persisting prejudices cannot prevent us from calling love.

RECOMMENDATIONS AND PROPOSALS

271. As we have seen, the Special Rapport has adopted the method of making at the end of each chapter, and even when concluding an important topic, a brief summary of the most appropriate measures in each case. For this reason the Special Rapporteur will not formulate general conclusions but will simply outline the most important recommendations which, as stated earlier, have been discussed throughout the various chapters. Rather, in these last few pages, the Special Rapporteur will focus his attention on two or three specific proposals.

A. GENERAL RECOMMENDATIONS

272. Internal legislation should be adapted to international norms and guidelines concerning the treatment of disabled persons. It should be periodically reviewed and constantly improved, for the standard of national legislation is far below the requirements of proper treatment of disabled persons.

273. Without prejudice to the specific proposal below, it is very important for existing international monitoring bodies, such as the Human Rights Committee and, in the regional sphere, the Inter-American Commission on Human Rights to supervise the specific implementation of the International Covenant on Civil and Political Rights and the American Convention as they relate to persons with disabilities. This recommendation is doubly valid with respect to the monitoring bodies that supervise the implementation of certain international instruments intended to protect various particularly vulnerable groups or sectors, such as the Committee on Discrimination against Women and the forthcoming Committee on the Protection of the Rights of All Migrant Workers and Members of Their Families. This is because of the frequent occurrence of double or triple discrimination.[106]

274. After the Decade has ended, the question of human rights and disability should be kept on the agendas of the General Assembly, the Economic and Social Council, the Commission on Human Rights

and the Sub-Commission as an item of constant concern and ongoing attention.

275. Support and encouragement for the activities of the Centre for Social Development and Humanitarian Affairs in Vienna should be reflected in larger financial contributions and better integration of its arduous work with the rest of the United Nations bodies.

276. It is recommended that cooperation and advisory assistance programmes should be stepped up between the various United Nations bodies and Governments, and even national entities working in the field of disability. In this connection, the work being conducted by the Centre in Vienna is very positive, and the Centre for Human Rights in Geneva could also do some useful work under its advisory assistance programmes. The activities in this area of other specialised organisations such as ILO, WHO, UNICEF. FAO, etc. should also be stepped up.

277. The guidelines contained in the World Programme of Action should be put into effect, in particular by strengthening or establishing national committees for the coordination and implementation of the Programme.

278. The establishment of non-governmental organisations formed by disabled persons or defending their interests should be encouraged and their activities facilitated. This recommendation is crucial, since, as we said earlier, the leading role played by those organisations in decision-making, policy selection and defence of their own human rights is one of the most outstanding features of the Decade. The recognition of disabled persons as experts in their own affairs is relatively recent and coincides, not by accident, with the growing attention being paid to the topic by the international community. Needless to say, without the rigorous participation of organisation led by disabled persons, the link between disability and human rights would not have been stressed sufficiently to justify the appointment of a Special Rapporteur, who, in turn, has only been able to fulfil his mandate thanks to the contribution and cooperation he received from those organisations and the outstanding experts he met there.

B. SPECIFIC PROPOSALS

279. As was said earlier, the establishment of an international body or mechanism to supervise respect for the human rights of

disabled persons is one of the most cherished aims of the non-governmental organisations. The fact that the United Nations Decade of Disabled Persons is due to end shortly makes this a most topical and urgent question.

280. Despite the many actions undertaken throughout the Decade and the valuable results that have been achieved for disabled persons in many respects, it must be said that, at the end of this period, persons with disabilities are going to find themselves at a legal disadvantage in relation to other vulnerable groups such as refugees women, migrant workers, etc. The latter have the protection of a single body of binding norms, such as the Convention on the Elimination of All Forms of Discrimination Against Women, the International Convention on the Protection of the Rights of All Migrant Workers and Members of their Families, etc. In addition, those conventions have established specific protection mechanisms: the Committee on the Elimination of Discrimination Against Women and the Committee on the Protection of the Rights of all Migrant Workers and Members of Their Families are in charge of supervising compliance with the conventions.

281. It is a well-known fact that nothing of the sort has yet occurred with regard to disabled persons and that the discussions at the forty-second session of the General Assembly, in October 1987, concerning the elaboration of a convention on the human rights of disabled persons concluded with the postponement of that initiative.[107] The current situation may be summarised as follows:

(a) The Centre for Social Development and Humanitarian Affairs coordinates and supervises the implementation of the World Plan on the basis of the information provided in particular by Governments. The publications issued by the Centre on the basis of that information are extremely useful in indicating how the plan is developing and the progress being achieved in the various countries and fields (culture, employment, education, etc.).

(b) However, there is no specific body in charge of monitoring respect for the human rights of disabled persons and acting, whether confidentially or publicly, when particular violations occurs. It can be said that persons with disabilities are equally as protected as others by general norms, international covenants, regional conventions, etc. But although this is true, it is also true that unlike the other vulnerable groups, they do not have an international control body to provide them with particular and specific protection. Thus the most active non-governmental organisations are emphasising the need to establish a flexible mechanism that will adapt to the particular features of the problem that concerns them, such as an international ombudsman.

282. Regarding the ombudsman competence, mandate and sphere of action, there are a series of variants and possibilities that require thorough discussion, not only in the human rights bodies, but also with the Centre for Social Development and Humanitarian Affairs in Vienna. For that reason the Special Rapporteur will simply convey the general outline of this initiative, which should be discussed on a relatively urgent basis, with a view either to implementing it or to seeking alternatives.

283. The non-governmental organisations point out that the ombudsman has the main advantage of being able to act, that is to establish a dialogue, possibly confidential, with the Governments of countries where sensitive human rights situations exist; he would be able to perform some very productive preventive work through promotion activities and step up cooperation and advisory assistance activities. In particular, the ombudsman would have the assistance of experts on disability and would maintain close links with the non-governmental organisations and other sectors concerned.

284. The Special Rapporteur, for his part, feels that another possible alternative would be to entrust the supervisory task to the Committee on Economic, Social and Cultural Rights, which would receive a special mandate for that purpose. This proposal is based on the following considerations:

(a) It would meet the repeated recommendations being made in most organisations of the Unite Nations system not to increase the number of supervisory bodies but rather to entrust existing ones with new activities.

(b) The Committee of Economic, Social and Cultural Rights was not set up under the International Convenant on Economic, Social and Cultural Rights but was established by the

Economic and Social Council for the purpose of supervising implementation of the Convenant. It is therefore within the competence of the higher body to assign the Committee new powers, which may include supervisory powers of universal scope, that is, not limited to one particular treaty.

(c) In addition, developments in the field of international control have been so rich and dynamic as to have led to some surprising innovations, such as entrusting the supervision of two instruments to a single body. An example is the Inter-American Convention on Human Rights, which monitors compliance with the American Convention and the American Declaration, for those that have not ratified the Convention, and both instruments for those that have done so.

(d) In this event, the Committee could hold, in addition to the session it currently holds, a special session to deal with reports submitted by States and communications submitted by the non-governmental organisations, which can already present written communications to the Committee. Extending the functions of the Committee to the area of disability would be highly innovative and would achieve an adequate framework of protection and stimulate cooperation between Governments and concerned organisations in the national and international context.

(e) The normative framework of action would have to be specified, but, in addition to existing general and specific norms on the protection of disabled persons, other very valuable instruments are currently being drafted, such as: the standard rules on the equalisation of opportunities for disabled persons and the Set of Principles and Guarantees for the Protection of Mentally-ill Persons and the Improvement of Mental Health Care. In this connection, the relevance of incorporating this function is made clear by the lack of a reply to the question: If not the Committee on Economic, Social and Cultural Rights, what other United Nations body would be responsible for implementation and monitoring compliance?

(f) Finally, the Special Rapporteur has consulted non-governmental organisations and also the members of the

Committee on Economic, Social and Cultural Rights itself, at a public meeting to which he was invited, and noted that this proposal has the *prime facie* agreement of the sectors concerned, at least as a sound basis for discussion, to be elaborated upon by the contributions of, first, the experts of the Sub-Commission, and then the members of the Commission on Human Rights and the Economic and Social Council.

285. Lastly, as has been pointed out in paragraph 263, the establishment of an international ombudsman would not be incompatible with an extension of the mandate of the Committee on Economic, Social and Cultural Rights; on the contrary, the juxtapositioning of the two monitoring mechanisms is the alternative that best satisfies the outstanding aspirations.

REFERENCES

* Bantam Books, 1998.

1. Source: World Health Organisation (WHO).

2. *Human Rights—A Compilation of International Instruments* (United Nations publication, States NO. E. 88. XIV. 1).

3. See resolutions 31/123 and 34/54.

4. *World Programme of Action concerning Disabled Persons,* published by the Division of Economic and Social Information and the Centre for Social Development and Humanitarian Affairs (November 1983, DESI, S97).

5. E/CN.4/1985/SR. 23, para. 69; see also the background paper by the Branch for Equality of Men and Women for the fifth interagency meeting held in Viennna in February 1987.

6. E/CN.4/1985/SR. 23. para. 63.

7. Ibid., paras, 63 and 72

8. See E/CN.4/Sub.2/1985/SR.23, paras. 31, 37 and 40. See also note 50.

* See note 2.

9. *See Official Journal* No. L225/443 of 12 August 1986.

10. For the texts of the Conventions, see United Nations. *Treaty Series,* Vol. 75, Nos. 970-973. For the texts of the Protocols, see International Committee of the Red

Cross, *Protocols additional to the Geneva Conventions of 12 August 1949*, Geneva, 1977.

11. League of Nations, *Treaty Series*, vol. XCIV No. 2138, p. 65.

12. See also resolution 32/2 of 24 April 1991 of the Commission for Social Development in document E/1991/26-E/CN.5/1991/9.

13. E/CN.4/Sub.2/1985/32, paras. 8 and 9.

14. 9 November 1990.

15. *Disability prevention and rehabilitation Report of the WHO Expert Committee on Disability prevention and Rehabilitation.* (World Health Organisation, Technical Report Series No. 668, 1981) and ICIP/RHB/920,pp. 1-11.

16. Ibid.

17. Mary Chamie, "The status and use of the international classification of impairments, disabilities and handicaps (ICIDH)", *World Health Statistics Quarterly,* 43 (1990). p. 273.

18. Ibid.

19. See Summary document No. 1, *Concepts of Disability,* prepared by WHO, fifth inter-agency meeting (Vienna, February 1987) and documents E/CN.5/1987/7 and A/41/605 and Corr. 1.

20. See *Official Records of the Economic and Social Council, 1987, Supplement No. 7*, paras, 92-101, and draft resolution IX, and CSDHA/DDP/GME/7.

21. Belgium, Bulgaria, Canada, Chile Cyprus, Czech and Slovak Federal Republic, Finland, Netherlands, Paraguay.

22. Bangladesh, Belgium.

23. Ethiopia, USSR

24. China, Cyprus, Finland, Netherlands.

25. Chad, Jordan, Kenya, Singapore, Uruguay.

26. Norway.

27. Czech and Slovak Federal Republic, Finland, Romania.

28. China, Morocco.

29. Bangladesh, Trinidad and Tobago.

30. Norway, Trinidad and Tobago.

31. China, Ethiopia, Finland, Jordan, Mauritius, Norway, Poland, Singapore.

32. Czech and Slovak Federal Republic, Jordan, Kenya.

33. E/CN.4/Sub.2/1988/SR. 11, para. 29, SR. 12, para. 9.

34. See ST/ESA/STAT/SER.Y/4.

35. For a discussion of this matter see *Development of Statistics of Disabled Persons: Case Studies* (United Nations Publication, Sales No. E.86.XVII.17).

36. OMS, *La Voz*, Vol. 1, No. 2, Montevideo, June 1987.

37. Referred to in *Disabled Persons, Victims of Armed Conflicts and Civil Unrest,* Eighth inter-agency meeting on the United Nations Decade of Disabled Persons, 1983-1992, Vienna, 5-7 December 1990, agenda item 4, paper No. 1 (*The Case of Refugees*). Prepared by the United Nations High Commissioner for Refugees, Geneva, 1990, p. 1 (English only).

38. E/CN.4/Sub.2/1988/SR.11, para. 16.

39. E/CN.4/Sub.2/1985/SR.23, para. 11, 32 and 46, and E/CN.4/Sub.2/1988/SR.11, para. 42. and 61.

40. AWEPAA: *Conference Report on Child Survival on the Frontline,* Harare, Zimbabwe, 21-25 April 1990. See also note 37 above.

41. According to a WHO report, more than three quarters of the victims of organised violence are women and children. See also note 37 above.

42. See documents S/21363 and A/45/84, paras. 160-170, A/45/576, paras. 54-186, and A/45/726, paras. 15 and 16, and also *Disabled Persons, Victims of Armed Conflicts and Civil Unrest.* Eighth interagency meeting on the United Nations Decade of Disabled Persons, agenda item 4, paper No. 3, prepared by UNWRA, *op.cit.*, p. 143.

43. *Children and Armed Conflict.* Additional reading material from Part Six: *Children in Especially Difficult Circumstances,* a UNICEF Source book on Children and Development in the 1990s. Published on the occasion of the World Summit for Children, 29-30 September 1990, at the United Nations, New York, p. 12.

44. Ibid. p. 11.

45. *Relief and Rehabilitation of Traumatised Children in War Situations.* Eighth inter-agency meeting on the United Nations Decade of Disabled Persons, 1983-1992, Vienna, 5-7 December 1990, agenda item 4, paper No. 2. See note 37 above.

46. For more substantial information see: *Children Labour: A Threat to Health and Development.* Second (revised) addition, published by Defence for Children International, Geneva, Switzerland, 1985; and the report by Mr. Vitit Muntarbhorn, Special Rapporteur on the sale of children, child prostitution and child pornography (E/CN.4/1991/51).

47. *Activities on Women and Disability:* Division for the Advancement of Women/ Centre for Social Development and Humanitarian Affairs. Sixth inter-agency meeting on the United Nations Decade of Disabled Persons, 1983-1992, Vienna, 5-7 December 1988, agenda item 1, Background paper No. 9, p.p. 1-2.

48. B. Whitaker, "Revised and updated report on the question of the prevention and punishment of the crime of genocide", United Nations document E/CN.4/Sub.2/ 1985/6 and Corr. 1, paras. 40-41

49. J. A. Kruse, "The Inupiat and development How do they mix?" *United States Arctic Interests,* W. E. Westermeyer and K. M. Shusterich, eds. (New York, Springer Verlag, 1984), pp. 134-157

50. E/CN.4/Sub.2/1985/SR.23, para. 31, 40 and 41; E/CN.4/Sub.2/1988/SR.11, paras. 17, 22, 24, 30, 42; E/CN.4/Sub.2/1988/SR.12, para. 7,19, 20, 26, 34,. 55, 57.

51. See E/CN.4/Sub.2/1988/SR.12, para. 42.

52. Ibid., para. 26.

53. E/CN.4/Sub.2/1985/NGO/10; E/CN.4/Sub.2/1985/SR. 23, paras. 39, 47.

54. E/CN.4/Sub.2/1988/SR. 12, para. 28.

55. See E/CN.4/1986/42.

56. E/CN.4/Sub.2/1985/32, paras, 18, 27-29.

57. See, for example, document E/2087 and Economic and Social Council resolutions 305 (XI) and 386 (XIII).

58. *Human Organ Transplantation* (World Health Organisation, ED/87/12, 19 November 1990), p. 4.

59. See the end of para. 96.

60. Bengt Lindquist, "Handicapped rights", *Report of the International Expert Meeting on Legislation for Equalisation of Opportunities for People with Disabilities.* 2-6 June 1986, Vienna, p. 69.

61. Canada, Chad, China, Ethiopia, Germany, Ghana, Jamaica.

62. *Rehabilitation International,* No. 3, 1985.

63. E/CN.4/Sub.2/1983/17/Rev.1.

64. See the Canadian Immigration Act, art, 19.2, clause 2(2).

65. E/CN.4/Sub.2/1983/17/Rev.1, paras. 145-147

66. See, for example, *Manual on equalisation of opportunity for disabled persons* (ST/ESA/177). The Centre for Social Development and Humanitarian Affairs has an occasional publication *Disabled Persons Bulletin.* Document ST/ESA/176, *Study on disability: situation, strategies and policies,* was published in 1986.

67. *Rehabilitation in the Community: the Basis for a National Delivery System for Rehabilitation and Related Materials.* Sixth interagency meeting on the United Nations Decade of Disabled Persons, Vienna, 5-7 December 1988, agenda item 3, Summary paper No. 2, prepared by WHO.

68. *Vocational Rehabilitation of Disabled Persons: Current Programme and Future Plans (progress report as of July 1989).* Seventh inter-agency meeting on the United Nations Decade of Disabled Persons, Vienna, 6-8 December 1989, agenda item 1, Summary paper No. 7 prepared by ILO (English only).

69. Ibid. Progress report No. 14 prepared by FAO. p. 2.

70. See General Assembly resolution 44/70 of 8 December 1989.

71. See ACC/1988/PG/15, pp. 6, 7.

72. E/CN.4/1991/39.

73. Ibid.

74. Denmark.

75. Bulgaria, Canada, China, Cuba, Czech and Slovak Federal Republic, Ghana, Kenya, Norway, Turkey, Ukrainian Soviet Socialist Republic, USSR.

76. See the Mental Health Act of Alberta, art. 37, para. 4, and art. 24, paras. 1, 2, 3.

77. Statement by Disabled Peoples' International. See E/CN.4/Sub.2/1984/SR. 24.

78. See ACC/1988/PG/15, para. 19.

79. Canada, Cuba, China, Dominican Republic, Ghana, Mali, Norway, Philippines, Senegal, Sweden, Trinidad and Tobago, Ukrainian Soviet Socialist Republic, USSR.

80. Bahrain, Canada, Finland, Norway, Senegal, Sweden, USSR.

81. Canada, Cuba, Ghana, Philippine, Saudi Arabia.

82. Philippines, Trinidad and Tobago.

83. Singapore, United Kingdom.

84. Bahrain, Bangladesh, China, Finland, India, Nepal, Pakistan, Swaziland, Thailand, Ukrainian Soviet Socialist Republic USSR.

85. Canada, China, Jamica, Ukrainian Soviet Socialist Republic, USSR.

86. Jamaica, Poland.

87. United Nations Development Programme.

88. Bahrain, Belgium, Canada, Ghana, India, Jamaica, Japan, Mexico, Philippines, Poland, Switzerland, Ukrainian Soviet Socialist Republic, USSR.

89. Germany, Ghana, Jamaica, Japan Ukrainian Soviet Socialist Republic, USSR.

90. Germany, Uruguay.

91. Australia, China, Finland, Malta, Pakistan, Philippines, Sweden, USSR.

92. Australia, Jordan.

93. Rehabilitation International.

94. Canada, China, Ecuador, Germany, Greece, Jamaica, Malta, Norway, Portugal, Sweden.

95. China, Ecuador, Germany, New Zealand.

96. Ukrainian Soviet Socialist Republic, USSR.

97. Bahrain, Ukrainian Soviet Socialist Republic, USSR.

98. China, Germany, Greece, Sweden, Ukrainian Soviet Socialist Republic, USSR.

99. Bulgaria, Ukrainian Soviet Socialist Republic, USSR.

100. Argentina.

101. Canada, China, Finland, Sweden, United Kingdom.

102. Work programmes of the Paraguayan Directorate of Public Welfare and Social Assistance (DIBEN), which is doing important work on disability prevention, rehabilitation of the disabled and equalisation of opportunities.

103. E/CN.4/Sub.2/1985/SR.23, para. 43.

104. See Quentin E. Angus. "Is there a need for special 'Disabled Legislation'?", *Report of the International Expert Meeting on Legislation for Equalisation of Opportunities for People with Disabilities,* Vienna, 2-6 June 1986, pp. 70, 71.

105. The idea of need as a source of law is relatively new and has gradually been supplementing and in some areas replacing the idea of interest. (It will be recalled that learing recently defined a right as "a legally protected interest".) Nevertheless, the concept of need, in its social content, it currently gaining ground and it is undoubtedly the case that human rights have been a decisive factor in this gradual change of direction.

106. In a letter to the Special Rapporteur, the International Movement ATD Fourth World gives an encapsulated account of the dramatic nature of this phenomenon by describing the situation of a woman, a single parent wit two very young children, who is an immigrant and who, apart from existing under conditions of extreme poverty, suffers from multiple disabilities.

107. ST/ESA/177.

Annex

REPLIES RECEIVED

1. The Special Rapporteur received replies from the following member States: Argentina, Australia, Bahrain, Bangladesh, Barbados, Belgium, Brunei Darussalam, Bulgeria, Canada, Chile, China, Congo, Cuba, Cyprus, Czesh and Slovak Federal Republic, Denmark, Dominican Republic, Ecuador, El Salvador, Ethiopia, Finland, Gabon, Garmany, Ghana, Greece, Haiti, Iceland, India, Israel, Jamaica, Jordan, Kenya, Luxembourg, Mali, Malta, Mexico, Netherlands, Nigeria, Norway, Oman, Panama, Paraguay, Peru, Philippines, Poland, Portugal, Qatar, Romania, Rwanda, Saudi Arabia, Spain, Sri Lanka, Singapore, Sweden, Trinidad and Tobago, Turkey, Ukrainian Soviet Socaialist Republic, United Kingdom, USSR Venezuela, Yugoslavia and Zambia.

2. Reports were also received from the following United Nations bodies and specialised agencies: United Nations Centre for Social Development and Humanitarian Affairs; United Nations Economic and Social Commission for Asia and the Pacific; United Nations Economic Commission for Latin America and the Caribbean; Division for the Advancement of Women; Department of Public Information; Office of the United Nations Disaster Relief Coordinator; Office of the United Nations High Commissioner for Refugees; United Nations Centre for Human Settlements; United Nations Development Programme; United Nations Children's Fund; United Nations Relief and Works Agency for Palestine Refugees in the Near East: International Labour Organisation; United Nations Educational, Scientific and Cultural Organisation; World Health Organisation; and International Fund for Agricultural Development.

3. Reports were also received from the following organisations representing the disabled and from other non-governmental organisations: Disabled People' International (DPI); International Council on Disability; International League of Societies for Persons with Mental Handicap; International Committee of the Red Cross; World Federation for Mental Health: International Movement ATD Fourth World: World Veterans Federation; Four Directions Council; organisations in Italy, Pakistan, Portugal and Sri Lanka; Council of Europe; Lutheran World Federation; Rehabilitation International; World Federation for Mental Health and World Health Federation.

PART—3

WORLD PROGRAMME OF ACTION CONCERNING DISABLED PERSONS

14

OBJECTIVES, BACKGROUND AND CONCEPTS

A. OBJECTIVES

1. The purpose of the World Programme of Action concerning Disabled Persons is to promote effective measures for prevention of disability, rehabilitation and the realisation of the goals of "full participation" of disabled persons in social life and development, and of "equality". This means opportunities equal to those of the whole population and an equal share in the improvement in living conditions resulting from social and economic development. These concepts should apply with the same scope and with the same urgency to all countries, regardless of their level of development.

B. BACKGROUND

2. More than 500 million people in the world are disabled as a consequence of mental, physical or sensory impairment. They are entitled to the same rights as all other human begins and to equal opportunities. Too often their lives are handicapped by physical and social barriers in society which hamper their full participation. Because of this, millions of children and adults in all parts of the world often face a life that is segregated and debased.

3. An analysis of the situation of disabled persons has to be carried out within the context of different levels of economic and social development and different cultures. Everywhere, however, the ultimate responsibility for remedying the conditions that lead to impairment and for dealing with the consequences of disability rest with Governments. This does not weaken the responsibility of society in

general, or of individuals, or of organisations. Governments should take the lead in awakening the consciousness of populations regarding the gains to be derived by individuals and society from the inclusion of disabled persons in every area of social, economic and political life. Governments must also ensure that people who are made dependent by severe disability have an opportunity to achieve a standard of living equal to that of their fellow citizens. Non-governmental organisations can, in different ways, assist Governments by formulating needs suggesting suitable solutions and providing services complementary to those provided by Governments, Sharing of financial and material resources by all sections of the population, not omitting the rural areas of developing countries, could be of major significance to disabled persons by resulting in expanded community services and improved economic opportunities.

4. Much disability could be prevented through measures taken against malnutrition, environmental pollution, poor hygiene, inadequate pre-natal and post-natal care, water-borne diseases and accidents of all types. The international community could make a major breakthrough against disabilities caused by poliomyelitis, tetanus, whooping-cough and diphtheria, and to a lesser extent tuberculosis, through a worldwide expansion of programmes of immunisation.

5. In many countries, the prerequisites for achieving the purposes of the Programme are economic and social development, extended services provided to the whole population in the humanitarian area, the redistribution of resources and income and an improvement in the living standards of the population. It is necessary to use every effort to prevent wars leading to devastation, castastrophe and poverty, hunger, suffering, diseases and mass disability of people, and therefore to adopt measures at all levels to strengthen international peace and security, to settle all international disputes by peaceful means and to eliminate all forms of racism and racial discrimination in countries where they still exist. It would also be desirable to recommend to all States Members of the United Nations, that they maximise the use of their resources for peaceful purposes, including prevention of disability and satisfaction of the needs of disabled persons. All forms of technical assistance that help developing countries to move towards these objectives can support the implementation of the Programme. The realisation of these objectives will, however, require extended periods of effort, during which the

number of disabled persons is likely to increase. Without effective remedial action, the consequences of disability will add to the obstacles to development. Hence, it is essential that all nations should include in their general development plans immediate measures for the prevention of disability, for the rehabilitation of disabled persons and for the equalisation of opportunities.

C. DEFINITIONS

6. The following distinction is made by the World Health Organisation, in the context of health experience, between impairment, disability and handicap:

"*Impairment*: Any loss or abnormality of psychological, physiological, or anatomical structure or function. *Disability*: Any restriction or lack (resulting from an impairment) of ability to perform an activity in the manner or within the range considered normal for a human being. *Handicap:* A disadvantage for a given individual, resulting from an impairment or disability, that limits or prevents the fulfilment of a role that is normal, depending on age, sex, social and cultural factors, for that individual."[a]

7. Handicap is therefore a function of the relationship between disabled persons and their environment. It occurs when they encounter cultural, physical or social barriers which prevent their access to the various systems of society that are available to other citizens. Thus, handicap is the loss or limitation of opportunities to take part in the life of the community on an equal level with others.

8. Disabled people do not form a homogeneous group. For example, the mentally ill and the mentally retarded, the visually, hearing and speech impaired, those with restricted mobility or with so-called "medical disabilities" all encounter different barriers, of different kinds, which have to be overcome in different ways.

9. The following definitions are developed from that perspective. The relevant terms of action proposed in the World Programme are defined as prevention, rehabilitation and equalisation of opportunities.

10. *Prevention* means measures aimed at preventing the onset of mental, physical and sensory impairments (primary prevention) or at preventing impairment, when it has occurred, from having negative physical, psychological and social consequences.

11. *Rehabilitation* means a goal-oriented and time-limited process aimed at enabling an impaired person to reach an optimum mental, physical and/or social functional level, thus providing her or him with the tools to change her or his own life. It can involve measures intended to compensate for a loss of function or a functional limitation (for example by technical aids) and other measures intended to facilitate social adjustment or readjustment.

12. *Equalisation of opportunities* means the process through which the general system of society, such as the physical and cultural environment, housing and transportation, social and health services, educational and work opportunities, cultural and social life, including sports and recreational facilities, are made accessible to all.

D. PREVENTION

13. A strategy of prevention is essential for reducing the incidence of impairment and disability. The main elements of such a strategy would vary according to country's state of development, and are as follows:

(a) The most important measures for prevention of impairment are: avoidance of war; improvement of the educational, economic and social status of the least privileged groups; identification of types of impairment and their causes within defined geographical areas; introduction of specific intervention measures through better nutritional practices; improvement of health services, early detection and diagnosis; pre-natal and post-natal care; proper health care instruction, including patient and physician education; family planning; legislation and regulations; modification of life-style; selective placement services; education regarding environmental hazards; the fostering of better informed and strengthened families and communities.

(b) To the extent that development takes place, old hazards are reduced and new ones arise. These changing circumstances require a shift in strategy, such as nutrition intervention programmes directed at specific population groups most at risk owing to vitamin A deficiency; improved medical care for the aging; training and regulations to reduced accidents in industry, in agriculture, on the roads and in the home;

the control of environmental pollution and of the use and abuse of drugs and alcohol. In this connection, the WHO strategy for Health for All by the Year 2000 through primary health care should be given proper attention.

14. Measures should be taken for the earliest possible detection of the symptoms and signs of impairment, to be followed immediately by the necessary curative or remedial action, which can prevent disability or at least lead to significant reductions in the severity of disability and can often prevent its becoming a lasting condition. For early detection it is important to ensure adequate education and orientation of families and technical assistance to them by medical social services.

E. REHABILITATION

15. Rehabilitation usually includes the following types of services;

(a) Early detection, diagnosis and intervention;

(b) Medical care and treatment;

(c) Social, psychological and other types of counselling and assistance;

(d) Training in self-care activities, including mobility, communication and daily living skills, with special provisions as needed, e.g., for the hearing impaired, the visually impaired and the mentally retarded;

(e) Provision of technical and mobility aids and other devices;

(f) Specialised education services;

(g) Vocational rehabilitation services (including vocational guidance), vocational training, placement in open or sheltered employment.

(h) Follow-up

16. In all rehabilitation efforts, emphasis should be placed on the abilities of the individual, whose integrity and dignity must be respected. The normal development and maturation process of disabled children should be given the maximum attention. The capacities of disabled adults to perform work and other activities should be utilised.

17. Important resources for rehabilitation exist in the families of disabled persons and in their communities. In helping disabled persons, every effort should be made to keep their families together, to enable them to live in their own communities and to support family and community groups who are working with this objective. In planning rehabilitation and supportive programmes, it is essential to take into account the customs and structures of the family and community and to promote their abilities to respond to the needs of the disabled individual.

18. Services for disabled persons should be provided, whenever possible, within the exiting social, health, education and labour structures of society. These include all levels of health care; primary, secondary and higher education; general programmes of vocational training and placement in employment; and measures of social security and social services. Rehabilitation services are aimed at facilitating the participation of disabled persons in regular community services and activities. Rehabilitation should take place in the natural environment, supported by community-based services and specialised institutions. Large institutions should be avoided. Specialised institutions, where they are necessary, should be organised so as to ensure an early and lasting integration of disabled persons into society.

19. Rehabilitation programmes should make it possible for disabled persons to take part in designing and organising the services that they and their families consider necessary. Procedures for the participation of disabled persons in the decision-making relating to their rehabilitation should be provided for within the system. When people such as the severely mentally disabled may not be able to represent themselves adequately in decisions affecting their lives, family members or legally-designated agents should take part in planning and decision-making.

20. Efforts should be increased to develop rehabilitation services integrated in other services and make them more readily available. These should not rely on imported costly equipment, raw material and technology. The transfer of technology among nations should be enhanced and should concentrate on methods that are functional and relate to prevailing conditions.

F. EQUALISATIONS OF OPPORTUNITIES

21. To achieve the goals of "full participation and equality", rehabilitation measures aimed at the disabled individual are not sufficient. Experience shows that it is largely the environment which determines the effect of an impairment or a disability on a person's daily life. A person is handicapped when he or she is denied the opportunities generally available in the community that are necessary for the fundamental elements of living, including family life, education, employment, housing, financial and personal security, participation in social and political groups, religious activity, intimate and sexual relationships, access to public facilities, freedom of movement and the general style of daily living.

22. Societies sometimes cater only to people who are in full possession of all their physical and mental faculties. They have to recognise the fact that, despite preventive efforts, there will always be a number of people with impairments and disabilities, and that societies have to identify and remove obstacles to their full participation. Thus, whenever pedagogically possible, education should take place in the ordinary school system, work be provided through open employment and housing be made available as to the population in general. It is the duty of every Government to ensure that the benefits of development programmes also reach disabled citizens. Measures to this effect should be incorporated into the general planning process and the administrative structure of every society. Extra services which disabled persons might need should, as far as possible, be part of the general services of a country.

23. The above does not apply merely to Governments. Anyone in charge of any kind of enterprise should make it accessible to people with disabilities. This applies to public agencies at various levels, to non-governmental organisations, to firms and to private individuals. It also applies to the international level.

24. People with permanent disabilities who are in need of community support services, aids and equipment to enable them to live as normally as possible both at home and in the community should have access to such services. Those who live with such disabled persons and help them in their daily activities should themselves receive support to enable them to have adequate rest and relaxation and an opportunity to take care of their own needs.

25. The principle of equal rights for the disabled and non-disabled implies that the needs of each and every individual are of equal importance, that these needs must be made the basis for the planning of societies, and that all resources must be employed in such a way as to ensure, for every individual, equal opportunity for participation. Disability policies should ensure the access of the disabled to all community services.

26. As disabled persons have equal rights, they also have equal obligations. It is their duty to take part in the building of society. Societies must raise the level of expectation as far as disabled persons are concerned, and in so doing mobilise their full resources for social change. This means, among other things, that young disabled persons should be provided with career and vocational opportunities—not early retirement pensions or public assistance.

27. Persons with disabilities should be expected to fulfil their role in society and meet their obligations as adults. The image of disabled persons depends on social attitudes based on different factors that may be the greatest barrier to participation and equality. We see the disability, shown by the white cane, crutches, hearing aids and wheelchairs, but not the persons. What is required is to focus on the ability, not on the disability of disabled persons.

28. All over the world, disabled persons have started to unite in organisations as advocates for their own rights to influence decision-makers in Governments and all sectors of society. The role of these organisations includes providing a voice of their own, identifying needs, expressing views on priorities, evaluating services and advocating change and public awareness. As a vehicle of self-development, these organisations provide the opportunity to develop skills in the negotiation process, organisational abilities, mutual support, information-sharing and often vocational skills and opportunities. In view of their vital importance in the process of participation, it is imperative that their development be encouraged.

29. Mentally handicapped people are now beginning to demand a voice of their own and insisting on their right to take part in decision-making and discussion. Even those with limited communication skills have shown themselves able to express their point of view. In this respect, they have much to learn from the self advocacy movement of persons with other disabilities. This development should be encouraged.

30. Information should be prepared and disseminated to improve the situation of disabled persons. The co-operation of all public media should be sought to bring about presentations that will promote an understanding of the rights of disabled persons aimed at the public and the persons with disabilities themselves, and that will avoid reinforcing traditional stereotypes and prejudices.

G. CONCEPTS ADOPTED WITHIN THE UNITED NATIONS SYSTEM

31. In the Charter of the United Nations, the reaffirmation of the principles of peace, the faith in human rights and fundamental freedoms, the dignity and worth of the human person and the promotion of social justice, are given primary importance.

32. The Universal Declaration of Human Rights affirms the right of all people, without distinction of any kind, to marriage; property ownership; equal access to public services; social security; and the realisation of economic, social and cultural rights. The International Covenants on Human Rights,[b] the Declaration on the Rights of Mentally Retarded Persons,[c] and the Declaration on the Rights of Disabled Persons[d] give specific expression to the principles contained in the Universal Declaration of Human Rights.

33. The Declaration on Social Progress and Development[e] proclaims the necessity of protecting the rights of physically and mentally disadvantaged persons and assuring their welfare and rehabilitation. It guarantees everyone the right to and opportunity for useful and productive labour.

34. Within the United Nations Secretariat, a number of offices carry out activities related to the above concepts as well as to the World Programme of Action. They include: the Division of Human Right; the Department of International Economic and Social Affairs; the Department of Technical Co-operation for Development; the Department of Public Information; the Division of Narcotic Drugs and the United Nations Conference on Trade and Development. The regional commissions also have an important role: the Economic Commission for Africa in Addis Ababa (Ethiopia), the Economic Commission for Europe in Geneva (Switzerland), the Economic Commission for Latin America in Santiago (Chile), the Economic and Social Commissions for Asia and the Pacific in Bangkok (Thailand), the Economic Commission for Western Asia in Baghdad (Iraq).

35. Other organisations and programmes of the United Nations have adopted approaches related to development that will be significant in implementing the World Programme of Action concerning Disabled Persons. These include:

(a) The mandate contained in General Assembly resolution 3405 (XXX) on New Dimensions in Technical Co-operation, which directs the United Nations Development Programme, *inter alia,* to take into account the importance of reaching the poorest and most vulnerable sections of society when responding to Governments' requests for help in meeting their most urgent and critical needs and which encompasses the concepts of technical co-operation among developing countries;

(b) The concept adopted by the United Nations Children's Fund (UNICEF) of basic services for all children and the strategy adopted by it in 1980 to emphasise strengthening family and community resources to assist disabled children in their natural environments;

(c) The Office of the United Nations High Commissioner for Refugees (UNHCR) with its programme for disabled refugees;

d) The United Nations Relief and Works Agency for Palestine Refugees in the Near East (UNRWA), which is concerned, among other things, with the prevention of impairments among Palestine refugees and the lowering of social and physical barriers which confront disabled members of the refugee population;

(e) The concepts of specific measures of disaster preparedness and prevention for those already disabled, and of the prevention of permanent disability as a result of injury or treatment received at the time of a disaster, advanced by the Office of the United Nations Disaster Relief Co-ordinator (UNDRO);

(f) The United Nations Centre for Human Settlements (UNCHS) with its concern about physical barriers and general access to the physical environment;

(g) The United Nations Industrial Development Organisation (UNIDO); the activities of UNIDO cover the production of drugs essential for the prevention of disability as well as of technical devices for the disabled.

36. The specialised agencies of the United Nations system, which are involved in promoting, supporting and carrying out field activities, have a long record of work related to disability. Programmes of disability prevention, nutrition, hygiene, education of disabled children and adults, vocational training, job placement and others, represent a store of experience and know-how which opens up opportunities for further accomplishments and, at the same time, makes it possible to share these experiences with governmental and non-governmental organisations concerned with disability matters. They include:

(a) The basic needs strategy of the International Labour Organisation (ILO) and the principles set forth in the ILO recommendation No. 99 concerning vocational rehabilitation of the disabled, 1955;

(b) The Food and Agriculture Organisation of the United Nations (FAO) with its emphasis on the relation between nutrition and disability;

(c) The concept of adapted education recommended by an expert group of the United Nations Educational, Scientific and Cultural Organisation (UNESCO) on education of disabled persons has been reinforced by two guiding principles of the Sundberg Declaration:[f]

— Disabled persons shall receive from the community services adapted to their specific personal needs;

— Through decentralisation and sectorisation of services, the needs of disabled persons shall be taken into account and satisfied within the framework of the community to which they belong;

(d) The World Health Organisation's programme of health for all by the year 2000 and the related primary health care approach, through which the member States of the World Health Organisation have already committed themselves to preventing diseases and impairments leading to disabilities. The concept of primary health care, as elaborated by the International Conference on Primary Health Care held at Alma-Ata in 1978, and the application of this concept to the health aspects of disability, are described in the World Health Organisation's policy on this subject, approved by the World Health Assembly in 1978;

(e) The International Civil Aviation Organisation (ICAO) has approved recommendations to contracting States concerning facilities of movement and provision of facilities for disabled passengers;

(f) The Executive Committee of the Universal Postal Union (UPU) has adopted a recommendation inviting all national postal administrations to improve access to their facilities for disabled persons.

15

CURRENT SITUATION

A. GENERAL DESCRIPTION

37. There is a large and growing number of persons with disabilities in the world today. The estimated figure of 500 million is confirmed by the results of surveys of segments of population, coupled with the observations of experienced investigators. In most countries, at least one person out of 10 is disabled by physical, mental or sensory impairment, and at least 25 per cent of any population is adversely affected by the presence of disability.

38. The causes of impairments vary throughout the world, as do the prevalence and consequences of disability. These variations are the result of different socio-economic circumstances and of the different provisions that each society makes for the well-being of its members.

39. A survey carried out by experts has produced the estimate of at least 350 million disabled persons living in areas where the services needed to assist them in overcoming their limitations are not available. To a large extent, disabled persons are exposed to physical, cultural and social barriers which handicap their lives even if rehabilitation assistance is available.

40. Many factors are responsible for the rising numbers of disabled persons and the relegation of disabled persons to the margin of society. These include:

(a) Wars and the consequences of wars; and other forms of violence, destruction, poverty, hunger, epidemics, major shifts in population;

(b) A high proportion of overburdened and impoverished families; overcrowded and unhealthy housing and living conditions;

(c) Populations with a high proportion of illiteracy and little awareness of basic social services or of health and eduction measures;

(d) An absence of accurate knowledge about disability, its causes, prevention and treatment; this includes stigma, discrimination and misconceived ideas on disability;

(e) Inadequate programmes of primary health care and services;

(f) Constraints, including a lack of resources, geographical distance, physical and social barriers, that make it impossible for many people to take advantage of available services;

(g) The channelling of resources to highly specialised services that are not relevant to the needs of the majority of people who need help;

(h) The absence or weakness of an infrastructure of related services for social assistance, health, education, vocational training and placement;

(i) Low priority in social and economic development for activities related to equalisation of opportunities, disability prevention and rehabilitation;

(j) Industrial, agricultural and transportation-related accidents;

(k) Natural disaster and earthquake;

(l) Pollution of the physical environment;

(m) Stress and other psycho-social problems associated with the transition from a traditional to a modern society;

(n) The imprudent use of medication, the misuse of therapeutic substances and the illicit use of drugs and stimulants;

(o) The faulty treatment of injured persons at the time of a disaster, which can be the cause of avoidable disability;

(p) Urbanisation and population growth and other indirect factors.

41. The relationship between disability and poverty has been clearly established. While the risk of impairment is much greater for the poverty-stricken, the converse is also true. The birth of an impaired child, or the occurrence of disability in the family, often places heavy demands on the limited resources of the family and strains on its morale, thus thrusting it deeper into poverty. The combined effect of these factors results in higher proportions of disabled persons among the poorest strata of society. For this reason, the number of affected families living at the poverty level steadily increases in absolute terms. The negative impact of these trends seriously hinders the development process.

42. Existing knowledge and skills could prevent the onset of many impairments and disabilities, could assist affected people in overcoming or minimising their disabilities, and could enable nations to remove barriers which exclude disabled persons from everyday life.

1. Disabilities in the developing countries

43. The problems of disability in developing countries need to be specially highlighted. As many as 80 per cent of all disabled persons live in isolated rural areas in the developing countries. In some of these countries, the percentage of the disabled population is estimated to be as high as 20 per cent and, thus, if families and relatives are included, 50 per cent, of the population could be adversely affected by disability. The problem is made more complex by the fact that, for the most part, disabled persons are also usually extremely poor people. They often live in areas where medical and other related services are scarce, or even totally absent and where disabilities are not and cannot be detected in time. When they do receive medical attention, if they receive it at all, the impairment may have become irreversible. In many countries, resources are not sufficient to detect and prevent disability and to meet the need for the rehabilitation and supportive services of the disabled population. Trained personnel, research into newer and more effective strategies and approaches to rehabilitation and the manufacturing and provision of aids and equipment for disabled persons are quite inadequate.

44. In such countries, the disability problem is further compounded by the population explosion, which inexorably pushes

up the number of disabled persons both in proportional and absolute terms. There is, thus, an urgent need, as the first priority, to help such countries to develop demographic policies to prevent an increase in the disabled population and to rehabilitate and provide services to the already disabled.

2. Special groups

45. The consequences of deficiencies and disablement are particularly serious for women. There are a great many countries where women are subjected to social, cultural and economic disadvantages which impede their access to, for example, health care, eduction, vocational training and employment. If, in addition, they are physically or mentally disabled their chances of overcoming their disablement are diminished, which makes it all the more difficult for them to take part in community life. In families, the responsibility for caring for a disabled parent often lies with women, which considerably limits their freedom and their possibilities of taking part in other activities.

46. For many children, the presence of an impairment leads to rejection or isolation from experiences that are part of normal development. This situation may be exacerbated by faulty family and community attitudes and behaviour during the critical years when children's personalities and self-images are developing.

47. In most countries the number of elderly people is increasing, and already in some as many as two thirds of disabled people are also elderly. Most of the conditions which cause their disability (for example, arthritis, strokes, heart disease and deterioration in hearing and vision) are not common among younger disabled people and may require different forms of prevention, treatment, rehabilitation and support services.

48. With the emergence of "victimology" as a branch of criminology, the true extent of injuries inflicted upon the victims of crime, causing permanent or temporary disablement, is only now becoming generally known.

49. Victims of torture who have been disabled physically or mentally, not by accident of birth or normal activity, but by the deliberate infliction of injury, form another group of disabled persons.

50. There are over 10 million refugees and displaced persons in the world today as a result of man-made disasters. Many of the them are disabled physically and psychologically as a result of their sufferings from persecution, violence and hazards. Most are in third-world countries, where services and facilities are extremely limited. Being a refugee is in itself a handicap, and a disabled refugee is doubly handicapped.

51. Workers employed abroad often find themselves in a difficult situation associated with a series of handicaps resulting from differences in environment, lack or inadequate knowledge of the language of the country of immigration, prejudice and discrimination, lack of deficiency of vocational training, and inadequate living conditions. The special position of migrant workers in the country of employment exposes them and their families to health hazards and increased risk of occupational accidents which frequently lead to impairment or disability. The situation of disabled migrant workers may be further aggravated by the necessity for them to return to the country of origin, where, in most cases, special services and facilities for the disabled are very limited.

B. PREVENTION

52. There is a steady growth of activities to prevent impairment, such as the improvement of hygiene, education, nutrition, better access to food and health care through primary health care approaches with special attention to mother and child care; counselling parents on genetic and pre-natal care factors; immunisation and control of diseases and infections; accident prevention; and improving the quality of the environment. In some parts of the world, such measures have a significant impact on the incidence of physical and mental impairment.

53. For a majority of the world's population, especially those living in countries in the early stages of economic development, these preventive measures effectively reach only a small proportion of the people in need. Most developing countries have yet to establish a system for the early detection and prevention of impairment through periodic health examinations, particularly for pregnant women, infants and young children.

54. In the Leeds Castle Declaration on the Prevention of Disablement of 12 November 1981, an international group of scientists, doctors, health administrator and politicians calls attention, among others, to the following practical measures to prevent disablement:

"3. Impairment arising from malnutrition, infection and neglect could be prevented by inexpensive improvement in primary health care...

4. ...Many disabilities of later life can be postponed or averted. There are promising lines of research for the control of hereditary and degenerative conditions...

5. ...Disability need not give rise to handicap. Failure to apply simple remedies very often increase disability, and the attitudes and institutional arrangements of society increase the chance of disability placing people at a disadvantage. Sustained education of the public and of professionals is urgently needed.

6. Avoidable disability is a prime cause of economic waste and human deprivation in all countries, industrialised and developing. This loss can be reduced rapidly.

The technology which will prevent or control most disablement is available and is improving. What is needed is commitment by society to overcome the problems. The priority of existing national and international health programmes must be shifted to ensure the dissemination of knowledge and technology...

7. Although technology for preventive and remedial control of most disabilities exists, the remarkable recent progress in bio-medical research promises revolutionary new tools which could greatly strengthen all interventions. Both basic and applied research deserve support over the coming years."

55. It is becoming increasingly recognised that programmes to prevent impairment or to ensure that impairment do not escalate into more limiting disabilities are less costly to society in the long run than having to care later for disabled persons. This applies, for instance, not least to occupational safety programmes, a still neglected field of concern in many countries.

C. REHABILITATION

56. Rehabilitation services are often provided by specialised institutions. However, there exists a growing trend towards placing greater emphasis on the integration of services in general public facilities.

57. There has been an evolution in both the content and the spirit of the activities described as rehabilitation. Traditional practice viewed rehabilitation as a pattern of therapies and services provided to disabled persons in an institutional setting, often under medical authority. This is gradually being replaced by programmes which, while still providing qualified medical, social and pedagogical services, also involve communities and families and help them to support the efforts of their disabled members to over-come the disabling effects of impairment within a normal social environment. Increasingly it is being recognised that even severely disabled persons can, to a great extent, live independently if the necessary support services are provided. The number requiring care in institutions is much smaller than had previously been assumed and even they can, to a great extent, live a life that is independent in its essential elements.

58. Many disabled persons require technical aids. In some countries the technology needed to produce such items is well developed, and highly sophisticated deviçes are manufactured to assist the mobility, communication and daily living of disabled individuals. The costs of such items are high, however, and only a few countries are able to provide such equipment.

59. Many people need simple equipment to facilitate mobility, communication and daily living. Such aids are produced and available in some countries. In Many other Countries, however, they cannot be obtained because of a lack of their availability and/or of high cost. Increasing attention is being given to the design of simpler, less expensive devices, with local methods of production which are more easily adapted to the country concerned, more appropriate to the needs of most disabled persons and more readily available to them.

D. EQUALISATION OF OPPORTUNITIES

60. The rights of persons with disabilities to participate in their societies can be achieved primarily through political and social actions.

61. Many countries have taken important steps to eliminate or reduce barriers to full participation. Legislation has in many cases been enacted to guarantee to disabled persons the rights to, and opportunities for, schooling, employment and access to community facilities, to remove cultural and physical barriers and to proscribe discrimination against disabled persons. There has been a movement away from institutions to community-based living. In some developed and developing countries, the emphasis in schooling is increasingly on "open education", with a corresponding decrease in institutions and special schools. Methods of making public transport systems accessible have been devised, as well as methods of making information accessible for sensory-disabled persons. Awareness of the need for such measures has increased. In many cases, public education and awareness campaigns have been launched to educate the public to alter its attitudes and actions towards disabled persons.

62. Often, disabled persons have taken the lead in bringing about an improved understanding of the process of equalisation of opportunities. In this context, they have advocated their own integration into the mainstream of society.

63. Despite such efforts, disabled persons are yet far from having achieved equal opportunities and the degree of integration of disabled persons into society is yet far from satisfactory in most countries.

1. Education

64. At least 10 per cent of children are disabled. They have the same right to education as non-disabled persons and they require active intervention and specialised services. But most disabled children in developing countries receive neither specialised services nor compulsory education.

65. There is a great variation from some countries with a high educational level for disabled persons to countries where such facilities are limited or non-existent.

66. There is a lack in existing knowledge of the potential of disabled persons. Furthermore, there is often no legislation which deals with their needs and a shortage of teaching staff and facilities. Disabled persons have is most countries so far not benefited from a life-long education.

67. Significant advances in teaching techniques and important innovative developments have taken place in the field of special education and much more can be achieved in the education of disabled persons. But the progress is mostly limited to a few countries or only a few urban centres.

68. The advances concern early detection, assessment and intervention, special education programmes in a variety of settings, with many disabled children able to participate in a regular school setting, while others require very intensive programmes.

2. Employment

69. Many persons with disabilities are denied employment or given only menial and poorly remunerated jobs. This is true even though it can be demonstrated that with proper assessment, training and placement, the great majority of disabled persons can perform a large range of tasks in accordance with prevailing work norms. In times of unemployment and economic distress, disabled persons are usually the first to be discharged and the last to be hired. In some industrialised countries experiencing the effects of economic recession, the rate of unemployment among disabled job-seekers is double that of able-bodies applicants for jobs. In many countries various programmes have been developed and measures taken to create jobs for disabled persons. These include sheltered and production workshops, sheltered enclaves, designated positions, quota schemes, subsidies for employers who train and subsequently engage disabled workers, co-operatives of and for the disabled, etc. The actual number of disabled workers employed in either regular or special establishments is far below the number of employable disabled workers. The wider application of ergonomic principles leads to adaptation of the work place, tools, machinery and equipment at relatively little cost and helps widen employment opportunities for the disabled.

70. Many disabled persons, particularly in the developing countries, live in rural areas. When the family economy is based on agriculture or other rural occupations and when the traditional extended family exists, it may be possible for most disabled persons to be given some useful tasks to perform. As more families move from rural areas to urban centres, as agriculture becomes more mechanised and commercialised, as money transactions replace

barter systems and as the institution of the extended family disintegrates, the vocational plight of disabled persons becomes more severe. For those living in urban slums, competition for employment is heavy, and other economically productive activity is scarce. Many disabled persons in such areas suffer from enforced inactivity and become dependent; others must resort to begging.

3. Social questions

71. Full participation in the basic units of society—family, social groups and community—is the essence of human experience. The right to equality of opportunity for such participation is set forth in the Universal Declaration of Human Rights and should apply to all people, including those with disabilities. In reality, however, disabled persons are often denied the opportunities of full participation in the activities of the socio-cultural system of which they are a part. This deprivation comes about through physical and social barriers that have evolved from ignorance, indifference and fear.

72. Attitudes and behaviour often lead to the exclusion of disabled persons from social and cultural life. People tend to avoid contact and personal relationships with those who are disabled. The pervasiveness of the prejudice and discrimination affecting disabled persons and the degree to which they are excluded from normal social intercourse produce psychological and social problems for many of them.

73. Too often, the professional and other service personnel with whom disabled persons come into contact fail to appreciate the potential for participation by disabled persons in normal social experiences and thus do not contribute to the integration of disabled individuals and other social groups.

74. Because of these barriers, it is often difficult or impossible for disabled persons to have close and intimate relationships with others. Marriage and parenthood are often unattainable for people who are identified as "disabled", even when here is no functional limitation to preclude them. The needs of mentally handicapped people for personal and social relationship, including sexual partnership, are now increasingly recognised.

75. Many persons with disabilities are not only excluded from the normal social life of their communities but in fact confined in

institutions. While the leper colonies of the past have been partly done away with and large institutions are not as numerous as they once were, far too many people are today institutionalised when there is nothing in their condition to justify it.

76. Many disabled persons are excluded from active participation in society because of doorways that are too narrow for wheelchairs; steps that cannot be mounted leading to buildings, buses, trains and aircraft; telephones and light switches that cannot be reached; sanitary facilities that cannot be used. Similarly they can be excluded by other types of barriers, for example oral communication which ignores the need of the hearing impaired and written information which ignores the needs of the visually impaired. ?such barriers are the result of ignorance and lack of concern; they exist despite the fact that most of them could be avoided at no great cost by careful planning. Although some countries have enacted legislation and launched campaigns of public education to eliminate such obstacles, the problem remains a crucial one.

77. Generally, existing, services, facilities and social actions for the prevention of impairment, the rehabilitation of disabled persons and their integration into society are closely linked to the Governments' and society's willingness and ability to allocate resources, income and services to disadvantaged population groups.

E. DISABILITY AND A NEW INTERNATIONAL ECONOMIC ORDER

78. The transfer of resources and technology from developed to developing countries as envisaged within the framework of the new international economic order, as well as other provisions for strengthening the economies of developing nations, would, if implemented, be of benefit to the people of these countries, including the disabled. Improvement of economic conditions in the developing countries particularly their rural areas, would provide new employment opportunities for disabled persons and needed resources to support measures for prevention, rehabilitation and the equalisation of opportunities. The transfer of appropriate technology, if properly managed, could lead to the development of industries specialising in the mass production of devices and aids for dealing with the effects of physical, mental or sensory impairments.

79. The International Development Strategy for the Third United Nations Development Decade[g] states that particular efforts should be made to integrate the disabled in the development process and that effective measures for prevention, rehabilitation and equalisation of opportunities are therefore essential. Positive action to this end would be part of the more general effort to mobilise all human resources for development. Changes in the international economic order will have to go hand in hand with domestic changes aimed at achieving full participation by disadvantaged population groups.

F. CONSEQUENCES OF ECONOMIC AND SOCIAL DEVELOPMENT

80. To the extent that development efforts are successful in bringing about better nutrition, education, housing, improved sanitary conditions and adequate primary health care, the prospects of preventing impairment and treating disability greatly improve. Progress along these lines may also be especially facilitated in such areas as:

(a) The training of personnel in general fields such as social assistance, public health, medicine, education and vocational rehabilitation;

(b) Enhanced capacities for the local production of the appliances and equipment needed by disabled persons;

(c) The establishment of social services, social security systems, co-operatives and programmes for mutual assistance at the national and community levels;

(d) Appropriate vocational guidance and work preparation services as well as increased employment opportunities for disabled persons.

81. Since economic development leads to alterations in the size and distribution of the population, to modifications in life-styles and to changes in social structures and relationships, the services needed to deal with human problems are generally not being improved and expanded rapidly enough. Such imbalances between economic and social development add to the difficulties of integrating disabled persons into their communities.

16

PROPOSALS FOR THE IMPLEMENTATION OF THE WORLD PROGRAMME OF ACTION CONCERNING DISABLED PERSONS

A. INTRODUCTION

82. The objectives of the World Programme of Action concerning Disabled Persons are to promote effective measures for prevention of disability, rehabilitation and the realisation of the goals of "full participation" of disabled persons in social life and development, and of "equality". In implementing the World Programme due regard has to be paid to the special situation of developing countries and, in particular, of the least developed countries. The immensity of the task of improving living conditions for the whole population and the general scarcity of resources make the attainment of the objectives of the Programme much more difficult in these countries. At the same time, it should be recognised that the implementation of the World Programme of Action in itself will make a contribution to the development process through the mobilisation of all human resources and the full participation of the entire population. Though some countries may already have initiated or carried out some of the actions recommended in this Programme, more needs to be done. This applies also to countries with a high general standard of living.

83. Since the situation of the disabled is closely connected with the overall development at the national level, the solution of problems of developing countries depends to a very large extent on the creation of adequate international conditions for the faster social and economic

development. Accordingly, the establishment of a new international economic order is of direct relevance to the implementation of the objectives of the Programme. It is particularly essential that the flow of resources to developing countries be substantially increased, as agreed upon in the International Development Strategy for the Third United Nations Development Decade.

84. The realisation of these goals will require a multisectoral and multidisciplinary global strategy for combined and co-ordinated policies and action relevant to the equalisation of opportunities of disabled persons, effective rehabilitation services and measures for prevention.

85. Disabled persons and their organisations should be consulted in the further development of the World Programme of Action and in its implementation. To this end, every effort should be made to encourage the formation of organisations of disabled persons at the local, national, regional and international levels. Their unique expertise, derived from their experience, can make significant contributions to the planning of programmes and services for disabled persons. Through their discussion of issues they present points of view most widely representative of all concerns of disabled persons. Their impact on public attitudes warrants consultation with them and as a force for change they have significant influence on making disability issues a great priority. The disabled themselves should have a substantive influence in deciding the effectiveness of policies, programmes and services designed for their benefit. Special efforts should be made to involve mentally handicapped persons in this process.

B. NATIONAL ACTION

86. The World Programme of Action is designed for all nations. The time-span for its implementation and the choice of items to be implemented as a priority will, however, vary from nation to nation depending on the existing situation and their resource constraints, levels of socio-economic development, cultural traditions, and their capacity to formulate and implement the actions envisaged in the Programme.

87. National Governments bear the ultimate responsibility for the implementation of the measures recommended in the present

section. Owing, however, to constitutional differences between countries, both local authorities and other bodies within the public and private sector will be called upon to implement the national measures contained in the World Programme of Action.

88. Member States should urgently initiate national long-term programmes to achieve the objectives of the World Programme of Action; such programmes should be an integral component of the nation's general policy for socio-economic development.

89. Matters concerning disabled persons should be treated within the appropriate general context and not separately. Each ministry or other body within the public or private sector responsible for, or working within, a specific sector should be responsible for those matters related to disabled persons which fall within its area of competence. Governments should establish a focal point (for example, a national commission, committee or similar body) to look into and follow the activities related to the World Programme of Action of various ministries, of other government agencies and of non-governmental organisations. Any mechanism set up should involve all parties concerned, including organisations of disabled persons. The body should have access to decision-makers at the highest level.

90. To implement the World Programme of Action, it is necessary for Member States:

(a) To plan, organise and finance activities at each level;

(b) To create, through legislation, the necessary legal bases and authority for measures to achieve the objectives;

(c) To ensure opportunities by eliminating barriers to full participation;

(d) To provide rehabilitation services by giving social, nutritional, medical, educational and vocational assistance and technical aids to disabled persons;

(e) To establish or mobilise relevant public and private organisations;

(f) To support the establishment and growth of organisations of disabled persons;

(g) To prepare and disseminate information relevant to the issues of the World Programme of Action among all elements of the population, including persons with disabilities and their families;

(h) To promote public education to ensure a broad understanding of the key issues of the World Programme of Action and its implementation;

(i) To facilitate research on matters related to the World Programme of Action;

(j) To promote technical assistance and co-operation related to the World Programme of Action;

(k) To facilitate the participation of disabled persons and their organisations in decisions related to the World Programme of Action.

1. Participation of disabled persons in decision-making

91. Member States should increase their assistance to organisations of disabled persons and help them organise and co-ordinate the representation of the interests and concerns of disabled persons.

92. Member States should actively seek out and encourage in every possible way the development of organisations composed of or representing disabled persons. Such organisations, in whose membership and governing bodies disabled persons, or in some cases relatives, have a decisive influence, exist in many countries. Many of them have not the means to assert themselves and fight for their rights.

93. Member States should establish direct contacts with such organisations and provide channels for them to influence government policies and decisions in all areas that concern them. Member States should give the necessary financial support to organisations of disabled persons for this purpose.

94. Organisations and other bodies at all levels should ensure that disabled persons can participate in their activities to the fullest extent possible.

2. Prevention of impairment, disability and handicap

95. The technology to prevent and control most disablement is available and improving but is not always fully utilised. Member States should take appropriate measures for the prevention of impairment and disability and ensure the dissemination of relevant knowledge and technology.

96. Co-ordinated programmes of prevention at all levels of society are needed. They should include:

(a) Community-based primary health care systems that reach all segments of the population, particularly in rural areas and urban slums;

(b) Effective maternal and child health care and counselling, as well as counselling for family planning and family life;

(c) Education in nutrition and assistance in obtaining a proper diet, especially for mothers and children, including the production and utilisation of foods rich in vitamins and other nutrients;

(d) Immunisation against communicable diseases, in line with the objectives of the Expanded Programme of Immunisation of the World Health Organisation;

(e) A system for early detection and early intervention;

(f) Safety regulations and training programmes for the prevention of accidents in the home, in the work place, on the road and in leisure-related activities;

(g) Adaptation of jobs, equipment and the working environment and the provision of occupational health programmes to prevent the generation of occupational disabilities or diseases and their exacerbation;

(h) Measures to control the imprudent use of medication, drugs, alcohol, tobacco and other stimulants or depressants in order to prevent drug-related disability, particularly among school children and elderly people. Of particular concern also is the effect upon unborn children of imprudent consumption of these substances by pregnant women;

(i) Educational and public health activities that will assist people in attaining life-styles that will provide the maximum defence against the causes of impairment;

(j) Sustained education of the public and of professionals as well as public information campaigns related to disability prevention programmes;

(k) Adequate training for medical, para-medical and other persons who may be called upon to deal with casualties in emergencies;

(l) Preventive measures incorporated in the training of rural extension workers to assist in reducing incidence of disabilities;

(m) Well-organised vocational training and practical on-the-job training of workers with a view to preventing accidents at work and disabilities of different degrees. Attention should be paid to the fact that outdated technology is often used in developing countries. In many cases, old technology is transferred from industrial countries to developing countries. The old technology, inappropriate for the conditions in developing countries together with insufficient training and deficient labour protection, contributes to an increased number of accidents at work and to disabilities.

3. Rehabilitation

97. Member States should develop and ensure the provision of rehabilitation services necessary for achieving the objectives of the World Programme of Action.

98. Member States are encouraged to provide for all people the health care and related services needed to eliminate or reduce the disabling effects of impairment.

99. This includes the provision of social, nutritional, health and vocational services needed to enable disabled individuals to reach optimum levels of functioning. Depending on such factors as population distribution, geography and stages of development, services can be delivered through the following channels:

(a) Community-based workers;

(b) General facilities providing health, education, welfare and vocational services;

(c) Other specialised services where the general facilities are unable to provide the necessary services.

100. Member States should ensure the availability of aids and equipment appropriate to the local situation for all those to whose functioning and independence they are essential. It is necessary to ensure the provision of technical aids during and after the rehabilitation process. Follow-up repair services and replacement of aids that are obsolete are also needed.

101. It is necessary to make certain that disabled persons who need such equipment have the financial resources as well as the practical opportunities for obtaining them and learning to use them. Import taxes or other procedures that block the ready availability of aids and materials which cannot be manufactured in the country and must be obtained from other countries should be eliminated. It is important to support local production of aids that are suited to the technological, social and economic conditions under which they will be used. Development and production of technical aids should follow the overall technological development of a specific country.

102. To stimulate local production and development of technical aids, Member States should consider establishing national centres with a responsibility to support such local development. In many cases existing special schools, institutes of technology, etc., could serve as a basis for this. Regional co-operation in this connection should be considered.

103. Member States are encouraged to include within the general system of social services personnel competent to provide counselling and other assistance needed to deal with the problems of disabled persons and their families.

104. When the resources of the general social service system are inadequate to meet these needs, special services may be offered until the quality of the general system has been improved.

105. Within the context of available resources, Member States are encouraged to initiate whatever special measures may be

necessary to ensure the provision and full use of services needed by disabled persons living in rural areas, urban slums and shanty towns.

106. Disabled persons should not be separated from their families and communities. The system of services must take into account problems of transportation and communication; the need for supporting social, health and education services; the existence of primitive and often hazardous living conditions; and, especially in some urban slums, social barriers that may inhibit people's readiness to seek or accept services. Member States should assure an equitable distribution of these services to all population groups and geographical areas according to need.

107. Health and social services for mentally ill persons have been particularly neglected in many countries. The psychiatric care of persons with mental illness should be supplemented by the provision of social support and guidance to these persons and their families, who are often under particular strain. Where such services rea available, the length of stay and the probability of renewed referral to institutions are lessened. In cases where mentally retarded persons are additionally afflicted with problems of mental illness, provisions are necessary to ensure that health care personnel are aware of the distinct needs related to retardation.

4. Equalisation of opportunities

(a) Legislation

108. Member States should assume responsibility for ensuring that disabled persons are granted equal opportunities with other citizens.

109. Member States should undertake the necessary measures to eliminate any discriminatory practice with respect to disability.

110. In drafting national human rights legislation, and with respect to national committees or similar co-ordinating national bodies dealing with the problems of disability, particular attention should be given to conditions which may adversely affect the ability of disabled persons to exercise the rights and freedoms guaranteed to their fellow citizens.

111. Member States should give attention to specific rights, such as the rights to education, work, social security and protection from inhuman or degrading treatment, and should examine these rights from the perspective of disabled persons.

(b) Physical environment

112. Member States should work towards making the physical environment accessible to all, including persons with various types of disability, as specified in paragraph 8 of this document.

113. Member States should adopt a policy of observing accessibility aspects in the planning of human settlements, including programmes in the rural areas of developing countries.

114. Member States are encouraged to adopt a policy ensuring disabled persons access to all new public buildings and facilities, pubic housing and public transport systems. Furthermore, measures should be adopted that would encourage access to existing public buildings and facilities, housing and transport wherever feasible, especially by taking advantage of renovation.

115. Member States should encourage the provision of support services to enable disabled persons to live as independently as possible in the community. In so doing, they should ensure that persons with a disability have the opportunity to develop and manage these services for themselves, as is now being done in some countries.

(c) Income maintenance and social security

116. Every Member State should work towards the inclusion, within its systems of laws and regulations, of provisions covering the general and supporting objectives of the World Programme of Action referring to social security.

117. Member States should ensure that disabled persons have equal opportunities to obtain all forms of income, maintenance thereof, and social security. Such a process should take place in forms adjusted to the economic system and degree of development of the Member State.

118. Where social security, social insurance and other such systems exist for the general population, they should be reviewed to make certain that adequate benefits and services for prevention,

rehabilitation and the equalisation of opportunities are provided for disabled persons and their families and that regulations under these systems, whether applicable to services providers or the services recipients, should not exclude or discriminate against such persons. The establishment and the development of a public system of social care and of industrial safety and health protection constitute essential prerequisites for achieving the aims set.

119. Easily asscessible arrangements should be made by which disabled persons and their families can appeal, through impartial hearing, against decisions concerning their rights and benefits in this field.

(d) Education and training

120. Member States should adopt policies which recognise the rights of disabled persons to equal educational opportunities with others. The education of disabled persons should as fare as possible take place in the general school system. Responsibility for their education should be placed upon the educational authorities and laws regarding compulsory education should include children with all ranges of disabilities, including the most severely disabled.

121. Member States should allow for increased flexibility in the application to disabled persons of any regulation concerning admission age, promotion from class to class and, when appropriate, in examination procedures.

122. Basic criteria are to be met when developing educational services for disabled children and adults. These services should be:

(a) *Individualised,* i.e., based on the assessed needs mutually agreed upon by authorities, administrators, parents and disabled students and leading to clearly stated curriculum goals and short-term objectives which are regularly reviewed and where necessary revised;

(b) *Locally accessible,* i.e., within reasonable travelling distance of the pupil's home or residence except in special circumstances;

(c) *Comprehensive,* i.e., serving all persons with special needs irrespective of age or degree of disability, and such that no child of school age is excluded from educational provision on grounds of severity of disability or receives educational services significantly inferior to those enjoyed by any other students;

(d) *Offering a range of choices* commensurate with the range of special needs in any given community.

123. Integration of disabled children into the general educational system requires planning by all parties concerned.

124. If, for some reasons, the facilities of the general school system are inadequate for some disabled children, schooling for these children should then be provided for an appropriate period of time in special facilities. The quality of this special schooling should be equal to that of the general school system and closely linked to it.

125. The involvement of parents at all levels of the educational process is vital. Parents should be given the necessary support to provide as normal a family environment for the disabled child as is possible. Personnel should be trained to work with the parents of disabled children.

126. Member States should provide for the participation of disabled persons in adult education programmes, with special attention to rural areas.

127. If the facilities of regular adult education courses are inadequate to meet the needs of some disabled persons, special courses or training centres may be needed until the regular programmes have been modified. Member States should grant disabled persons possibilities for education at the university level.

(e) Employment

128. Member States should adopt a policy and supporting structure of services to ensure that disabled persons in both urban and rural areas have equal opportunities for productive and gainful employment in the open labour market. Rural employment and the development of appropriate tools and equipment should be given particular attention.

129. Member States can support the integration of disabled persons into open employment through a variety of measures, such as incentive-oriented quota schemes, reserved or designated

employment, loans or grants for small business and co-operatives, exclusive contracts or priority production rights, tax concessions, contract compliance or other technical or financial assistance to enterprises employing disabled workers. Member States should support the development of technical aids and facilitate access for disabled persons to aids and assistance, which they need to do their work.

130. The policy and supporting structures, however, should not limit the opportunities for employment and should not hinder the vitality of the private sector of the economy. Member States should remain able to take a variety of measures in response to their domestic situations.

131. There should be mutual co-operation at the central and local level between government and employers' and workers' organisations in order to develop a joint strategy and joint action with a view to ensuring more and better employment opportunities for disabled persons. Such co-operation could concern recruitment policies, measures to improve the work environment in order to prevent handicapping injuries and impairments, measures for rehabilitation of employees impaired in the job, e.g. by adjusting work places and work contents to their requirements.

132. The services should include vocational assessment and guidance, vocational training (including that in training work-shops), placements and follow-up. Sheltered employment should be made available for those who, because of their special needs or particularly severe disabilities, may not be able to cope with the demands of competitive employment. Such provisions could be in the form of production workshops, home working, and self-employment schemes, and small groups of severely disabled people employed in sheltered conditions within competitive industry.

133. When acting as employees, central and local governments should promote employment of disabled persons in the public sector. Laws and regulations should not raise obstacles to the employment of disabled persons.

(f) Recreation

134. Member States should ensure that disabled persons have the same opportunities for recreational activities as other citizens. This involves the possibility of using restaurants, cinemas, theatres,

libraries, etc., as well as holiday resorts, sport arenas, hotels, beaches and other places for recreation. Member States should take action to remove all obstacles to this effect. Tourist authorities, travel agencies, hotels voluntary organisations and others involved in organising recreational activities or travel opportunities should offer their services to all and not discriminate against disabled persons. This involves, for instance, incorporating information on accessibility into their regular information to the public.

(g) Culture

135. Member States should ensure that disabled persons have the opportunity to utilise their creative, artistic and intellectual potential to the full, not only for their own benefit but also for the enrichment of the community. To this end, access to cultural activities should be ensured. If necessary, special arrangements should be made to meet the needs of individuals with mental or sensory impairments. These could include communication aids for the deaf, literature in braille and/or cassettes for the visually impaired and reading material adapted to the individual's mental capacity. The domain of cultural activities includes dance, music, literature, theatre and plastic arts.

(h) Religion

136. Measures should be undertaken to ensure that disabled persons have the opportunity to benefit fully from the religious activities available to the community. In this way, the full participation by disabled persons in these activities will be made possible.

(i) Sports

137. The importance of sports for disabled persons is becoming increasingly recognised. Member States should therefore encourage all forms of sports activities of disabled persons, *inter alia,* through the provision of adequate facilities and the proper organisation of these activities.

5. Community action

138. Member States should give high priority to the provision of information, training and financial assistance to local communities for the development of programmes that achieve the objectives of the World Programme of Action.

139. Arrangements should be made to encourage and facilitate co-operation among local communities and the exchange of information and experience. A Government, benefiting from international technical assistance or technical co-operation disability-related matters, should ensure that the benefits and results of the assistance reach the communities in greatest need.

140. It is important to enlist the active participation of local government bodies, agencies and community organisations, such as citizen's groups, trade unions, women's organisations, consumer organisations, service clubs, religious bodies, political parties and parent's associations. Each community could designate an appropriate body, where organisations of disabled persons could have an influence, to serve as a focal point of communication and co-ordination to mobilise resources and initiate action.

6. Staff training

141. All authorities responsible for the development and provision of services for disabled persons should give attention to staff matters, particularly to recruitment and training.

142. The training of community-based workers in the early detection of impairment, the provision of primary assistance and referral to appropriate facilities, and follow-up, are vital, as well as the training of medical teams and other personnel at referral centres. Whenever possible, these should be integrated into such related services as primary health care, schools and community development programmes. Member States should develop and intensify training for doctors which emphasises the disabilities that can be produced by the indiscriminate use of some pharmaceutical products. Sale of proprietary/patent drugs whose unsupervised use could, in the long term, pose personal and public health hazards should be restricted.

143. If services related to mental and physical disabilities are to reach a growing number of disabled persons who receive none at present, it is necessary to provide them through various types of health and social workers in the local communities. Some of their activities are already related to prevention and to services for disabled persons. They will need special guidance and instruction, for instance, on simple rehabilitation measures and techniques to be used by disabled persons and their families. Guidance might be given by rehabilitation professionals at the community or district level, according

to the area covered. Special training will be necessary for the professionals at the peripheral level who would be responsible for the supervision of local programmes for persons with disability and for contact with rehabilitation and other services available in the region.

144. Member States should ensure that community workers receive, in addition to specialised knowledge and skills, comprehensive information concerning the social, nutritional, medical, educational and vocational needs of disabled persons. Community workers, with adequate training and supervision, can provide most services needed by disabled persons and can be a valuable asset in overcoming personnel shortages. Their training should include appropriate information on contraceptive technology and planned parenthood. Volunteers can also provide very useful services and other forms of support. Greater emphasis should be placed on expanding the knowledge, capabilities and responsibilities of providers of other services who are already at work in the community in related fields, such as teachers, social workers, professional auxiliary health service personnel, administrators, government planners, community leaders, clergy and family counsellors. Individuals working in service programmes for disabled persons should be trained to understand the reasons for, and importance of, seeking, stimulating and assisting the full participation of disabled persons and their families in decisions concerning care, treatment, rehabilitation and subsequent living employment arrangements.

145. Special teacher training is a dynamic field, and wherever possible it should take place in the country in which the education is to be used, or at least in a place where the cultural background and level of development are not too different.

146. A prerequisite for successful integration is the provision of appropriate teacher-training programmes, both for ordinary teachers and special teachers. The concept of integrated education should be reflected in teacher-training programmes.

147. When training special teachers, it is important to cover as wide a spectrum as possible, since in many developing countries the special teacher will be a multidisciplinary team on his own. It should be noted that a high level of training is not always necessary or desirable, and that the vast majority of personnel come from the middle and lower levels of training.

7. Information and public education

148. Member States should encourage a comprehensive public information programme about the rights, contributions and unmet needs of disabled persons that would reach all concerned, including the general public. In this connection, attitude change should be given special importance.

149. Guidelines should be developed in consultation with organisations of disabled persons to encourage the news media to give a sensitive and accurate portrayal of, as well as fair representation of, and reporting on, disabilities and disabled persons in radio, television, film, photography and print. An essential element in such guidelines would be that disabled persons should be able to present their problems to the public themselves and to suggest how they might be solved. The inclusion of information on the realities of disabilities in the curricula of journalists' training should be encouraged.

150. Pubic authorities are responsible for adapting their information so that it reaches everybody, including disabled persons. This does not apply only to the information mentioned above, but also to information concerning civil rights and obligations.

151. A public information programme should be designed to ensure that the most pertinent information reaches all appropriate segments of the population. In addition to the regular media and other normal channels of communication, attention should be given to:

(a) The preparation of special materials to inform disabled persons and their families of the rights, benefits and services available to them and of the steps to be taken to correct failures and abuses in the system. Such materials should be available in forms that can be used and understood by people with visual, hearing or other communication limitations;

(b) The preparation of special materials for groups within the population who are not easily reached by the normal channels of communication. Such groups may be separated by language, culture, levels of literacy, geographical distance and other factors;

(c) The preparation of pictorial material, audio-visual presentations and guidelines for use by community workers in remote areas and other situations where normal forms of communication may be less effective.

152. Member States should ensure that current information is available to disabled persons, their families and professionals regarding programmes and services, legislation, institutions, expertise, aids and devices etc.

153. The authorities responsible for public education should ensure the presentation of systematic information about the realities of disability and its consequences and about prevention, rehabilitation and the equalisation of opportunities for disabled persons.

154. Disabled persons and their organisations should be given equal access, employment, adequate resources and professional training with regard to public information, so they may express themselves freely through the media and communicate their points of view and experiences to the general public.

C. INTERNATIONAL ACTION

1. General aspects

155. The World Programme of Action, as adopted by the General Assembly, constitutes an international long-term plan based on extensive consultations with Governments, organs and bodies within the United Nations system and intergovernmental and non-governmental organisations, including organisations of and for disabled persons. Progress in reaching the goals of the Programme could be achieved more quickly, efficiently and economically if close co-operation were maintained at every level.

156. In view of the role that the Centre for Social Development and Humanitarian Affairs of the Department of International Economic and Social Affairs has been playing within the United Nations in the field of disability prevention, rehabilitation and equalisation of opportunities for disabled persons, the Centre should be designated as the focal point for co-ordinating and monitoring the implementation of the World Programme of Action, including its review and appraisal.

157. The Trust Fund established by the General Assembly for the International Year of Disabled Persons should be used to meet requests for assistance from developing countries and organisations of disabled persons and to further the implementation of the World Programme of Action.

158. In general, there is a need to increase the flow of resources to developing countries to implement the objectives of the World Programme of Action. Therefore, the Secretary-General should explore new ways and means of raising funds and take the necessary follow-up measures for mobilising resources. Voluntary contributions from Governments and from private sources should be encouraged.

159. The Administrative Committee on Co-ordination should consider the implications of the World Programme of Action for the organisations within the United Nations system and should use the existing mechanisms for continuing liaison and co-ordination of policy and action, including overall approaches on technical co-operation.

160. International non-governmental organisations should join in the co-operative effort to accomplish the objectives of the World Programme of Action. Existing relationships between such organisations and the United Nations system should be used for this purpose.

161. All international organisations and bodies are urged to cooperate with, and assist, organisations composed of, or representing, disabled persons and to ensure that they have opportunities to make their views known when subjects related to the World Programme of Action are discussed.

2. Human rights

162. In order to achieve the theme of the International Year of Disabled Persons, "Full participation and equality", it is strongly urged that the United Nations system makes all its facilities totally barrier-free, ensures that communication is fully available to sensory impaired persons, and adopts an affirmative action plan that includes administrative policies and practices to encourage the employment of disabled persons in the entire United Nations system.

163. In considering the status of disabled persons with respect to human rights, priority should be placed on the use of United Nations

covenants and other instruments, as well as those of other international organisations within the United Nations system that protect the rights of all persons. This principle is consistent with the theme of the International Year of Disabled Persons, "Full participation and equality".

164. Specifically, organisations and bodies involved in the United Nations system responsible for the preparation and administration of international agreements, covenants and other instruments that might have a direct or indirect impact on disabled people should ensure that such instruments fully take into account the situation of persons who are disabled.

165. The States parties to the International Covenants on Human Rights should pay due attention, in their reports, to the application of the Covenants to the situation of disabled persons. The working group of the Economic and Social Council entrusted with the examination of reports under the International Covenant of Economic, social and Cultural Rights and the Commission on Human Rights, which has the function of examining reports under the International Covenant on Civil and Political Rights, should pay due attention to this aspect of the reports.

166. Particular conditions may exist which inhibit the ability of disabled persons to exercise the human rights and freedoms recognised as universal to all mankind. Consideration should be given by the United Nations Commission on Human Rights to such conditions.

167. National Committees or similar co-ordinating bodies dealing with problems of disability should also pay attention to such conditions.

168. Incidences of gross violation of basic human rights, including torture, can be a cause of mental and physical disability. The Commission on Human Rights should give consideration, *inter alia,* to such violations for the purpose of taking appropriate ameliorative action.

169. The Commission on Human Rights should continue to consider method of achieving international co-operation for the implementation of internationally recognised basic rights for all, including disabled persons.

3. Technical and economic co-operation

(a) Interregional assistance

170. The developing countries are experiencing increasing difficulties in mobilising adequate resources for meeting the pressing needs of disabled persons and the millions of disadvantaged persons in these countries in the face of the pressing demands from high priority sectors such as agriculture, rural and industrial development, population control, etc., concerned with basic needs. Their efforts should therefore be supported by the international community, in line with paragraphs 82 and 83 above, and the flow of resources to developing countries should be substantially increased, as stated in the International Development Strategy for the Third United Nations Development Decade.

171. Inasmuch at most international technical co-operation and donor agencies can undertake to collaborate with national endeavours only on the basis of official requests from Governments, increased efforts should be made by all parties concerned with the establishment of programmes related to disabled persons to apprise Governments of the exact nature of the support that can be sought from these agencies.

172. The Vienna Affirmative Action Plan[h] prepared by the World Symposium of Experts on Technical Co-operation among Developing Countries and Technical Assistance for Prevention of Disability and Rehabilitation of Disabled Persons, could serve as guidelines for the implementation of technical co-operation activities within the World Programme of Action.

173. Those organisations within the United Nations system that have a mandate, resources and experience in areas related to the World Programme should explore, with the Governments to which they are accredited, ways of adding to existing or planned projects in different sectors components that would respond to the specific needs of disabled persons and the prevention of disability.

174. All international organisations whose activities have a bearing on financial and technical co-operation should be encouraged to ensure that priority is accorded to requests from Member States for assistance in the prevention of disability, rehabilitation and the equalisation of opportunities which are in accordance with their

natural priorities. Such measures will ensure the allocation of increased resources for both capital investment and recurrent expenditure for services related to prevention, rehabilitation and equalisation of opportunities. This action should be reflected in the programmes for economic and social development of all multilateral and bilateral aid agencies, including technical co-operation among developing countries.

175. In seeking to collaborate with Governments to serve better the needs of disabled persons, the various United Nations organisations, as well as bilateral and private institutions, should closely co-ordinate their inputs in order to contribute more efficiently to the attainment of established goals.

176. As most of the United Nations organisations involved already have the specific responsibility of promoting the establishment of projects or the addition of project components directed towards disabled persons, a clearer division of responsibilities, as set out below, should be established among them in order to improve the response of the United Nations system to the challenge of the International Year of Disabled Persons and the World Programme of Action:

(a) The United Nations and, in particular, the Department of Technical Co-operation for Development should, together with the specialised agencies and other intergovernmental and non-governmental organisations, carry out technical co-operation activities in support of the implementation of the World Programme of Action; in this connection, the Centre for Social Development and Humanitarian Affairs of the Department of International Economic and Social Affairs should continue to give substantive support, in the implementation of the World Programme of Action, to technical co-operation, projects and activities;

(b) The United Nations Development Programme should continue to use its field establishment to give considerable attention, within its normal programmes and procedures, to project requests from Governments that specially respond to the needs of disabled persons and to prevention of disability. It should particularly encourage technical co-operation in the field of disability prevention, rehabilitation and equalisation of opportunities by using its various programmes and services, such as technical co-operation among developing countries, global and interregional projects and the Interim Fund for Science and Technology:

(c) The main efforts of UNICEF would continue to be directed towards better preventive measures involving greater support for maternal and child health services, health education, disease control and the improvement of nutrition; for those who are already disabled, UNICEF encourages the development of integrated education projects and supports rehabilitation activities at the community level, using inexpensive local resources;

(d) The specialised agencies, within their mandate and sectoral responsibilities, should give, on the basis of requests from Governments, still greater emphasis to efforts to help meet the needs of disabled persons by using the chances offered to them through the programming processes of individual countries and the establishment of regional, interregional and global projects, as well as through the use of their own resources, when feasible. Their different spheres of responsibility in this respect should be as follows: ILO—vocational rehabilitation and occupational safety and health; UNESCO—education of disabled children and adults; WHO—prevention of disability and medical rehabilitation; FAO—improvement of nutrition;

(e) In their lending activities, multilateral financial institutions should take into serious consideration the objectives and proposals of the World Programme of Action.

(b) Regional and bilateral assistance

177. The regional commissions of the United Nations and other regional bodies should encourage regional and subregional cooperation in the area of prevention of disability, rehabilitation of disabled persons and equalisation of opportunities. They should monitor progress in their regions, identify needs, collect and analyse information, sponsor action-oriented research, supply advisory services and engage in technical co-operation activities. They should include in their action plans research and development, preparation of information materials and the training of personnel; and they should,

as an interim measure, facilitate activities in the field of technical co-operation among developing countries which are related to the objectives of the World Programme of Action. They should promote the development of organisations of disabled persons as an essential resource in developing the activities referred to earlier in this paragraph.

178. Member States, in co-operation with regional bodies and commissions, should be encouraged to establish regional (or sub-regional) institutes or offices to promote the interests of persons with a disability, in consultation with organisations of disabled persons and the appropriate international organisations. Other functions should be to promote the activities mentioned above. It is important to understand that the function of the institutes is not to provide direct services but to promote innovative concepts like community based rehabilitation, co-ordination, information training and advice in organisational development of disabled persons.

179. Donor countries should attempt to find the means within their bilateral and multilateral technical assistance programmes to respond to requests for assistance from Member States relating to national or regional measures in the area of prevention, rehabilitation and the equalisation of opportunities. These measures should include assistance to appropriate agencies and/or organisations to expand co-operative arrangements within and between regions. Technical co-operation agencies should actively recruit disabled persons at all levels and functions, including field positions.

4. Information and public education

180. The United Nations should carry out and continue activities to increase public awareness of the objectives of the World Programme of Action. To this end the substantive offices should regularly and automatically furnish the Department of Public Information (DPI) with information on their activities so as to enable it to publicise these activities through press releases, features, newsletters, fact sheets, booklets, radio and television interviews and in any other appropriate forms.

181. All agencies involved in projects and programmes that are connected with the World Programme of Action should continue in their endeavours to inform the public. Research should be undertaken by those agencies whose fields of specialisation require involvement in such activity.

182. The United Nations, in collaboration with the specialised agencies concerned, should develop innovative approaches using a variety of media for conveying information, including the principles and objectives of the World Programme of Action, to audiences not regularly reached by conventional media or which are unaccustomed to using such media.

183. International organisations should assist national and community bodies in the preparation of public education programmes by suggesting curricula and providing teaching materials and background information about the objectives of the World Programme of Action.

D. RESEARCH

184. In view of the little knowledge that is available as to the place of the disabled person within different cultures, which in turn determine attitudes and behaviour patterns, there is a need to undertake studies focusing on the socio-cultural aspects of disability. This will give a more perceptive understanding of the relations between non-disabled and disabled persons in different cultures. The results of such studies will make it possible to propose approaches suited to the realities of the human environment. Furthermore, an effort should be made to develop social indicators relating to the education of disabled persons so as to analyse the problems involved and plan programmes accordingly.

185. Member States should develop a programme of research on the causes, types and incidence of impairment and disability, the economic and social conditions of disabled persons, and the availability and efficacy of existing resources to deal with these matters.

186. Research into the social, economic and participation issues that affect the lives of disabled persons and their families, and the ways these matters are dealt with by society, is of particular importance. Research data may be obtained through national statistical offices and census bureaux; however, it should be noted that a household survey programme designed to collect information about disability issues is more likely to produce useful results than a general census of the population.

187. There is also a need to encourage research with a view to developing better aids and equipment for disabled persons. Particular efforts should be devoted to find solutions which are suited to the technological and economic conditions in developing countries.

188. The United Nations and its specialised agencies should follow the trends of international research into disability and related research issues to identify existing needs and priorities, while emphasizing innovative approaches to all forms of action recommended in the World Programme of Action.

189. The United Nations should encourage and assist in research projects designed to increase knowledge about the issues covered in the World Programme of Action. It is necessary for the United Nations to be familiar with research findings from various countries and to be aware of research proposals now pending approval. The United Nations also needs to give increased attention to research results and to stress their use and their dissemination. A permanent link with bibliographical retrieval systems is highly recommended.

190. The regional commissions of the United Nations and other regional bodies should include in their action plans research activities to assist Governments in implementing the proposals contained in the World Programme of Action. The key to maximising the effectiveness of research expenditure for the disabled is the dissemination and sharing of information on the results of research. International governmental and non-governmental agencies should play an active role in establishing collaborative mechanisms between regional and local institutions for joint studies and for the exchange of information.

191. Research at the medical, psychological and social levels offers the promise of reducing physical, mental and social disability. There is a need to develop programmes which include the identification of areas where the probability of progress through research is high. The difference between industrialised countries and developing countries should not prevent the development of fruitful collaboration since many problems are of universal concern.

192. Studies in the following fields are of value to both developing and developed countries:

(a) Clinical research into the containment of those events which cause disability; evaluation of the individual's functional capacity from the medical, psychological and social aspects, evaluation of rehabilitation programmes, including information aspects;

(b) Studies into the prevalence of disability, the functional limitations of the disabled, the conditions under which they live and the problems they face;

(c) Health and social service research, including research into the gains and costs of different rehabilitation and care policies, ways of making programmes as effective as possible and a search for alternative approaches. Studies on community care of disabled persons would be particularly relevant to developing countries, and the study and evaluation of experiments, as well as comprehensive demonstration programmes, would be of value to all. Much information is available which could be productive for secondary analysis.

193. Health and social science research institutions should be encouraged to undertake research and to collect information on disabled persons. Applied research activities are of particular value in the development of new techniques for the delivery of services, the preparation of information materials appropriate for different language and culture groups, and the training of personnel under conditions relevant to the region.

E. MONITORING AND EVALUATION

194. It is essential that assessment of the situation relating to disabled persons should be carried out periodically and that a baseline should be established to measure developments. The most important criteria for evaluating the World Programme of Action are suggested by the theme of the International Year of Disabled Persons, "Full participation and equality". Monitoring and evaluation should be carried out at periodic intervals at the international and regional levels, as well as at the national level. Evaluation indicators should be selected by the United Nations Department of International Economic and Social Affairs in consultation with Member States and relevant United Nations agencies and other organisations.

195. The United Nations system should carry out a critical periodic evaluation of progress made in implementing the World Programme of Action and to that end should select appropriate indicators for evaluation in consultation with Member States. The Commission for Social Development should play an important role in this respect. The United Nations, together with the specialised agencies, should develop, on a continuing basis, suitable systems for the collection and dissemination of information so as to ensure the improvement of programmes at all levels on the basis of evaluation results. In this connection, the Centre for Social Development and Humanitarian Affairs should have an important role of play.

196. The regional commissions should be requested to carry out monitoring and evaluation functions that would contribute to the global assessments carried out at the international level. Other regional and intergovernmental bodies should be encouraged to take part in this process.

197. At the national levels, an evaluation of programmes relating to disabled persons should be carried out periodically.

198. The Statistical Office is urged, together with other units of the Secretariat, the specialised agencies and regional commissions, to co-operate with the developing countries in evolving a realistic and practical system of data collection based either on total enumeration or on representative samples, as may be appropriate, in regard to various disabilities, and in particular, to prepare technical manuals/ documents on how to use household surveys for the collection of such statistics, to be used as essential tools and frames of reference for launching action programmes in the post-IYDP years to ameliorate the condition of disabled persons.

199. In this extensive exercise the United Nations Centre for Social Development and Humanitarian Affairs should play a major role, supported by the United Nations Statistical Office.

200. The Secretary-General should report periodically on efforts by the United Nations and the specialised agencies to hire more disabled persons and to make their facilities and information more assessible to disabled persons.

201. On the basis of the results of the periodic evaluation and of developments in the world economic and social situation, it may be necessary periodically to revise the World Programme of Action. These revisions should take place every five years, the first being in 1987, based upon a report of the Secretary-General to the General Assembly at its forty-second session. The review should also constitute an input to the process of review and appraisal of the International Development Strategy for the Third United Nations Development Decade.

NOTES

a. International Classification of Impairments, Disabilities and Handicaps (ICIDH), World Health Organisation, Geneva, 1980

b. General Assembly resolution 2200 A (XXI)

c. General Assembly resolution 2856 (XXVI)

d. General Assembly resolution 3447 (XXX)

e. General Assembly resolution 2542 (XXIV)

f. United Nations document A/36/766

g. General Assembly resolution 35/56

h. General Nations document IYDP/SYMP/L.2/Rev.1 of 16 March 1982

PART—4
LEGISLATION PERTAINING TO SPECIAL NEEDS EDUCATION

INTRODUCTION

The present day study presents information from fifty-two Member States collected by UNESCO during the course of its second investigation into the state of legislation on special needs education. (The first study appeared in 1969). The information was gathered in 1992-93, when a first compilation and analysis was done in 1993 by Professor Maria Rita Saulle, the findings of which were shared at the World Conference on Special Needs Education, Salamanca Spain, 1994. Following this first attempt, countries were invited to re-examine the initial information, for any corrections or modifications.

This document represent the final work compiled in 1994-95. This last phase of the work was carried out by Jonathan Robinson. The study was conducted in response to the requests of Member States for information on legislative provision related to special needs education. Such a study was very timely as the last two decades witnessed important landmarks in national developments in this domain. We recall here some of the major ones—the International Year of Disabled Persons (1981), the Decade of Disabled Persons (1983-1992), the World Programme of Action in Favour of Disabled Persons (1983), the Convention on the Rights of the Child (1989) and more recently the Standard Rules on Equalisation of Opportunities for Disabled Persons (1993).

Legislation is needed to ensure the rights of disabled persons to equal rights and opportunities; it can further help in securing the resources needed to translate abstract rights into practical entitlements. It can also enhance the integration of special needs education within more general frameworks. Many changes in legislation have been made in the last ten years, particularly in relation to compulsory education, and the inclusion of special needs education within general education.

UNESCO received information from 52 Member States as to legislation pertaining to special needs education. This Study is an analysis and synthesis of these country entries. The Study has relied upon the country entries as the only source of information, and the findings are subject to the vital provisos that (i) the country entries should be referred to for their detailed terms, and (ii) the country entries do not purport to be verbatim extracts from the legislation. To that extent, the sources are (in purely technical terms) secondary. For the study, 'Financing of Education' and 'Teacher Training' were excluded from the country entries and 'Parents' has been included. The world 'Orientation' has been used to mean placement.

Much of the data contains direct reference to primary or subordinate legislation in the strict sense. Frequently, however, the data is expressed more generally. Accordingly, where entries refer to Departments, Ministries or other official bodies, it has been assumed that their powers and duties as stated in the country entries have been derived from legislation. Government or Ministerial Resolutions or Orders and (in the case of one country) executive Circulars are also mentioned in the country entries and, on the same assumption, have been taken into account and noted in the Study.

Furthermore, where relevant, information which has been included by a country under one heading has been incorporated in the Study also under a different heading. The information in the Study may not always appear, therefore, to correspond precisely with the country entries. This is solely due to a desire to use the available information fully and in a constructive manner. Every effort has been made to interpret the country entries objectively and accurately, but with a wealth of information there is an element of discretion, as to the extent to which reference should be made to any one country's entry. Because the Study is to a large extent a fusion of the country entries, quotation marks have not been used rigorously; in the interest of a lucid analysis they appear only where is has been considered that a country entry should be seen tc have been quoted verbatim.

A statistical approach has been incorporated, with the objective to place in relative context each issue raised by the country entries. The statistics are accurate to one decimal pcint, except for two exceptions where total percentages have been rounded down rather than up, in order to achieve the total figure of 100.0 per cent without distorting its individual components. That said, the statistics should not be taken as anything more than what is intended to be a useful indicator of emphasis, and it is essential to note the various occasions where information has been unavailable to any significant extent.

The study is presented in two parts. Part I presents an analysis and synthesis of the country entries. This part is based on the information submitted by countries as the only source of information, and the country entries do not all purport to be verbatim extracts from the legislation. Every effort has been made to interpret the country entries objectively and accurately, but there is always an element of caution in the interpretation of the text. A statistical approach has been incorporated with the aim of placing in relative context issues raised by the country entries.

Part II of the study, the country entries, follows a uniform plan, corresponding as closely as possible with that of Part I, excluding "financing of education" and "teacher training".

17

THE NATURE AND EXTENT OF THE LEGISLATION PERTAINING TO SPECIAL NEEDS EDUCATION

1. THE NATURE OF THE LEGISLATION

The first section of this Study examines the nature of the legislation pertaining to special needs education in terms of special education as a constitutional right (in the sense of a general right which is contained within a body of fundamental and broad principles according to which a country is to be governed); the relationships between special eduction and the universal right to education, and disability as a basis for the right to education; and the extent to which the legislation is prescriptive (i.e. mandatory) or permissive (i.e. discretionary). It then analyses the extent of the legislation in terms of broad classifications of special needs as expressed in the legislation.

Although in a number of cases the legislation sets out requirements which must be met as to delivery of special educational provision, section I of this Study does not consider such matters, which will be covered later under other headings (e.g. responsibility for and the organisation of special education).

Special needs education is expressed as an explicit constitutional right in 3 countries, and it is a right arising from disability in 5 other countries. The constitutional references, therefore, amount to 8 in all (15.4 per cent of countries). Even then, legislation by way of Acts, Laws etc. is required to give practical effect to the general principle, and such legislation may contain or refer to other provisions as to general rights, such as protection against discrimination. As to the

Constitutional rights

Table 17.1 : Special needs education expressed as a constitutional right

Classification	*Countries*	
Educational and special education as separate rights	3	5.8%
Education generally[1] as a right	4	7.7%
Education generally[2] and disability as a right	5	9.6%
Total	12	23.1%

imperative nature of the legislation, arising in this and other sections of the Study, legislation is treated as mandatory when expressing special education as a right which 'shall' be observed or when specifying the provisions for special education as a duty or a responsibility which the State has assumed, and permissive if conferring a mere discretion.

Acts, Laws, Regulations etc.

Table 17.2 : The elements and volume of legislation[3] pertaining to special needs education

Classification	*Countries*	
Countries with special needs education legislation	48	92.3%
No special needs education legislation[4]	4	7.7%
Special education allied with anti-discrimination[5] rights	10	19.2%
Mandatory nature of the legislation[6]	47	90.4%
No total is shown because of overlapping classifications		

The mandatory nature of the legislation in 47 countries out of the 48 countries with special needs education legislation is consistent with the broad theme of the State accepting responsibility for the disadvantaged, and in 10 countries (19.2%) giving further explicit support by way of legislation prohibiting discrimination.

Integration

Two concepts of integration recur. The first sense is pedagogic, in that it involves the admission of children with special educational needs in 'ordinary' or 'regular' schools and may be described as 'pedagogic integration'. This may be mandatory under legislation or it may take the form of statements of policy which aim to encourage such integration. There is also a broader concept of what may be described as 'socio-economic' integration into the community and the world of work and leisure, expressed in the legislation as a goal or an objective of special needs education. Integration is analysed in detail later (section V, *infra*).

The Extent of Legislation

Again, this section of the Study does not consider matters which are covered under other headings. The sole objective of the following analysis is to answer the single question as to the extent to which 'special needs education' is defined and categorised in the relevant legislation of the 52 Member States.

Table 17.3 : Classifications of special needs expressed in the legislation

Classification		*Countries*	
Class A	Disability, handicap or deficiency alone	31	59.6%
Class B	Disability, and learning difficulties combined	9	17.3%
Class C	Learning,[7] pedagogic, intellectual difficulties alone	5	9.6%
Class D	General reference[8] to special needs	3	5.8%
Class E	Information unavailable	4	7.7%
	Total	52	100.0%
Classes A and B combined		40	76.9%

There are divergent views as to categorisation. In France the assessment is an estimate 'rate' of disability (established with respect to national standards). Romania has specific categories of disability in the legislation, while in Portugal classification and diagnosis are based on pedagogical rather than medical criteria.

By contrast, Denmark takes the view that the "traditional division of handicap into groups" is considered "invalid and superfluous". The number of countries which express special needs in terms of learning, pedagogic, or intellectual difficulties alone is modest (5 countries, 9.6% of total). From these, it should be noted that in one case (Belgium) the legislation has two basic principles. First, the Act gives only a pedagogical definition of 'handicap' and not a medical, psychological or psychometric one and stresses an educational rather than a therapeutic approach for ameliorating disability, also defining 'handicap' in terms of extra educational and didactic needs. Second, the legislation also provides for special needs education to be divided into eight types or pedagogical settings in order to meet the needs of the individual student (and these, described in a decree, include physical and mental handicap, emotional and behavioural problems and serious learning difficulties). Each type of special education has its own didactic content, teaching methods and organisation, adapted to the educational needs of the pupils. The central emphasis is, none the less, on pedagogical needs. Overall, however, the predominant definition of special needs in the legislation is 'disability' or 'handicap', whether standing alone (class A, 59.6 per cent of countries) or in combination with learning, pedagogic and other difficulties (class B, 17.3 per cent). As a result, in 40 countries (76.9 per cent) 'disability' or 'handicap' are a constituent of the classification. A breakdown of the elements of 'disability' and 'handicap', and of references to needs and/or objectives expressed in socio-economic terms, demonstrates the extent to which special needs are categorised.

Table 17.4 : Disability expressed as physical, mental or sensory difficulties

Classification		*Countries*	
Class A	Disability, handicap, or deficiency alone	20	38.5%
Class B	Disability and learning difficulties combined	7	13.5%
	Total	27	52.0%

Table 17.5 : Disability expressed as emotional, behavioural or psychological difficulties

Classification		*Countries*	
Class A	Disability, handicap, or deficiency alone	9	17.3%
Class B	Disability and learning difficulties combined	3	5.8%
	Total	12	23.1%

Table 17.6 : Socio-economic factors or integration into the community expressed as a goal

Classification		*Countries*	
Class A	Disability, handicap, or deficiency alone	12	23.1%
Class B	Disability and learning difficulties combined	2	3.9%
	Total	14	26.9%

Gifted children

The spectrum of special needs education has been widened by 3 countries (5.8 per cent) in which gifted children have special educational needs. Columbia refers to "exceptional capacities", and Brazil to "gifted students". Costa Rica has also been included under this heading, because the legislation refers to "maximising the development of the person", a Department in the Ministry of Education having among its responsibilities "Giftedness". In addition, the publication *Basic Education in Namibia* (1992) proposes that children with special needs shall include the "highly gifted".

Summary

1. Provision for special needs education is either an explicit constitutional right, or such a right arising from disability, in 8 countries (15.4 per cent of total).

2. 48 countries (92.3 per cent) have enacted legislation pertaining to special needs education. The remaining 4 countries (7.7 per cent) have active proposals; 3 of those countries have existing

special education provision, which is being introduced in the other country.

3. The legislation in 45 countries (86.5 per cent) defines special needs in terms either of a disability or a learning difficulty. In 40 countries (76.9 per cent) the legislation refers to disability, handicap or other deficiency, either as a single definition or in combination with learning, pedagogic or intellectual difficulties.

4. In 31 countries (59.6 per cent) the definition of special needs is expressed solely in terms of disability, handicap or other deficiency. By contrast, in 5 countries (9.6 per cent) that definition is expressed solely in terms of learning, pedagogic or intellectual difficulties. Gifted children are treated as having special educational needs in the legislation of 3 countries (5.8 per cent).

5. 27 countries (52.0 per cent) express disability and learning difficulties in terms of physical, mental or sensory difficulties. 12 countries (23.1 per cent) also express disability and learning difficulties in terms of emotional behavioural or psychological difficulties. 14 countries (26.9 per cent) do not break down the constituent elements of disability, handicap or learning difficulties.

18

SPECIAL NEEDS EDUCATION—RESPONSIBILITY AND ORGANISATION

1. THE RESPONSIBILITY FOR SPECIAL NEEDS EDUCATION

Section II of this Study analyses the manner in which responsibility for special needs education is imposed by legislation. It then focuses on the question of organisation, in the sense of identifying how policy as to special needs education is administered. The manner and extent to which special needs education is integrated in ordinary/regular schools or delivered in special schools is considered in section V (*infra*).

Table 18.1 : Responsibility expressed in the legislation as either a central or local function

Classification	*Countries*	
Central or Federal Government responsible for special needs education[9]		
Function of Government in general terms	1	1.9%
Ministry of Education or Minister	14	26.9%
Ministry of Education with a Special Needs Department[10]	23	44.2%
Education, Social Welfare/Affairs, Health, jointly[11]	7	13.5%
National Council or Commission[12] without any Special Needs Department	2	3.9%
Local Authority, State,[13] or others responsible for special needs education	4	7.7%
Information unavailable	1	1.9%
Total	52	100.0%

In 47 countries (90.4 per cent) central or federal government is responsible for special needs education. In 37 countries (71.2 per cent), Ministries of Education are charged explicitly with the responsibility for special needs education, and 23 of these (62.2 per cent of the 37 countries, 44.2 per cent of total) have a Special Needs Department in the Ministry of Education.

The complexity of the issues is illustrated by the fact that in 7 countries (13.5 per cent) responsibility for special needs education is shared jointly with one or more separate Ministries, and in 2 countries (3.9 per cent) the responsibility is assumed by a National Council or Commission. As a result, in 9 countries (17.3 per cent) the Ministry of Education shares responsibility for, or is only party to, decisions as to special needs education.

There are only 4 countries (7.7 per cent) where the Local Authority or State (as defined in Table 18.1) is responsible for special needs education, 2 of which (Canada and Australia) are large geographical federations.

2. THE ORGANISATION OF SPECIAL NEEDS EDUCATION

The position is different in respect of the organisation of special needs education.

Table 18.2 : Organisation (administration) of special needs education legislation

Classification	*Countries*	
Central or Federal Government implements legislation		
Government Ministry	31	59.6%
Specified Officer within Ministry	3	5.8%
Local Authority, State or others (per table 18.1) implements legislation		
Where Central or Federal Government responsible for legislation	11	21.2%
Where Local Authority or State responsible for legislation[14]	5	9.6%
Specified Officer	1	1.9%
Information unavailable	1	1.9%
Total	52	100.0%

When it comes to the organisation of special needs education, the administrative function is exercised centrally in 34 countries (65.4 per cent). In 17 countries (32.7 per cent) special needs education is administered locally. This is a significant contrast to the number of countries (4, constituting 7.7 per cent) in which overall responsibility, especially in terms of policy, has been allocated locally (Table 18.1)

There are various national or local bodies with co-ordinating or advisory functions. Those which make a pedagogic contribution should be distinguished from others which are concerned generally with the disabled and (for example) their social integration.

Table 18.3 : Other bodies making a pedagogic contribution to special needs education

Classification	*Countries*	
National[15] advisory function as to policy and/or training	5	6%
National and Local[16] functions	1	9%
Local[17] co-ordination of special needs pupils into schools	1	9%
Total	7	13.4%

Summary

1. In 47 countries (90.4 per cent) responsibility for special needs education rests with central or federal government. In 4 countries (7.7 per cent) special needs education is the responsibility of a local authority, state or province (with no information in 1 case).

2. The Ministry of Education is responsible for special needs education in 37 countries (71.2 per cent), and 23 countries (44.2 per cent) have a Special Needs Department. In 7 countries (13.4 per cent) the responsibility for special needs education is shared jointly with one or more other Ministries. Because a National Council or Commission is responsible in 2 countries (3.9 per cent), the Ministry of Education shares responsibility for, or is only party to decisions as to special needs education in 9 countries (17.3 per cent).

3. Special needs education is organised (i.e. administered) centrally in 34 countries (65.4 per cent), and by local authorities in 17 countries (32.7 per cent). This is in contrast to the allocation of responsibility set out in paragraph 1 (90.4 per cent and 7.7 per cent respectively).

4. Other bodies make a pedagogic contribution to special needs education centrally in 6 countries (11.5 per cent) and locally in 1 country (1.9 per cent).

19

IDENTIFICATION, ASSESSMENT AND ORIENTATION (PLACEMENT)

INTRODUCTION

The data on which the following analysis is based offers an interesting variety of approaches to the manner in which pupils and students with special needs are identified and assessed, and to the consequential decision as to the appropriate type of educational provision, 'orientation' being interpreted to mean 'placement'.

As background information, 21 countries (40.4 per cent) express the responsibility in terms of a duty imposed on a body specified in the legislation, in most cases the Ministries of Education or Health. Some of the information from the 21 countries referred to is brief and general, although it has been incorporated into the detailed anaylsis. The statistics are, however, based mainly upon 22 countries (42.3 per cent). These provide a considerable variety of approaches, and raise significant issues. It is probable, therefore, that the analysis of various aspects of identification, assessment and orientation is an understatement, especially because of the lack of information in respect of 11 countries (21.2 per cent).

Identification, assessment and orientation

The dominant theme is assessment, the spirit of the legislation to a considerable extent appearing to be based on the pragmatic assumption that parents, schools, individual teachers and/or organisations concerned with disabled people will in effect identify pupils with special needs.

The processes of assessment and subsequent decision-making are so linked in the legislation that they are treated for the purposes of this section of the Study as essentially one exercise. Because integration and curriculum entitlement are dealt with respectively in sections V and VI of this Study, for present purposes the issues of assessment and orientation are analysed with the specific objective to ascertain who are parties to the processes and decisions.

In 14 countries (26.9 per cent) there are bodies with particular responsibility for assessment and/or orientation. They are described as Commissions, Medical and Pedagogical Boards, Centres, Committees or other generic, terms, the common feature of all of which is expertise both in health and special needs education, their functions being divided as follows.

Table 19.1 : Functions of Special Needs Boards, Committees etc.

Classification	*Countries*	
Bodies with responsibility for evaluation (i.e. assessment) alone	6	11.5%
Bodies making decisions[18] as to orientation	6	11.5%
Bodies with responsibility for evaluation and orientation[19]	2	3.9%
Total	14	26.9%

The assessment process emphasises the importance of inter-disciplinary professional co-operation and the express involvement of teachers, parents and (in 4 cases) pupils.

Table 19.2 : Express involvement in and consultation as to assessments

Classification	*Countries*	
Assessment expressed as an inter-disciplinary professional function	22	42.3%
Bodies with responsibility for evaluation, alone or jointly (Table 19.1)	8	15.4%
Teachers expressly involved in the process of assessment	11	21.2%
Parents' right to be consulted in identification, assessment[20] and orientation	24	46.2%
Pupils[21] and parents both entitled to be consulted during assessment		7.7%
No total is shown because of the different and overlapping functions		

Orientation

The emphasis is different as to orientation, for which fewer persons or bodies are given express powers to make decisions. This is because assessment and orientation are two stages of one exercise.

Table 19.3 : Express involvement in decisions as to orientation

Classification	*Countries*	
Bodies making decisions as to orientation alone or jointly (Table 19.2)	8	15.4%
Decision made by parents[22]	5	9.6%
Decision made by school	3	5.8%
Decision made by school inspector or adviser	3	5.8%
Total	19	36.6%

Documentation

There is a reference to documentation in the legislation of 4 countries (7.7 per cent). For a child in Belgium to be enrolled in a special school, two documents have to be obtained. The first states that the child is not able to benefit from a regular classroom and indicates the level and type (and, if applicable, the form) of special teaching within special education. The second document justifies the certificate with a synthesis of the professional assessments. Admission to integrated education also requires a certificate of acceptance, with an agreed education plan. In France, a confidential document records the interventions of all relevant specialists, so as to form an individualised record of the student's progress at school and the frequency of medical appointments. When a special school in Holland is deciding whether to admit a child, it is advised by a committee of experts and the parents have access to the committee's report. By Regulation in Iceland, parents have the right of access to all information pertaining to their child's schooling. The question of documentation recurs in connection with the curriculum (section V of this Study), in the form of records for monitoring and reviewing a child's progress.

Reviews

Reviews are specified in 5 countries (9.6 per cent). Formal plans for education in Belgium are regularly evaluated and updated. If a child in Holland enters a special school, he or she is re-assessed after two years to determine whether the child is at the right school or should be moved to another special or to an ordinary school. The child's results are reviewed twice a year in Italy. In the Philippines, periodic evaluation is one of the five stages of identification and admission of children. Monitoring student development, progress and ensuring the quality of education are among the objectives of a Law Decree in Portugal. The question of reviews arises also in connection with the curriculum (section VI of this Study).

Permissive or mandatory legislation

On assessment and orientation, the legislation is permissive in 5 countries (9.6 per cent). In Belgium "special education is a right and never an obligation". The tenor is discretionary in a Canadian Province (New Brunswick), where the Minister "may" provide special education at a child's home or an approved (i.e. not an ordinary/regular) institution, with emphasis on consultation and partnership with parents. Parents in Malta consent "in most cases...to their children being posted in a special school". All recommendations of special education are to be discussed with parents in Norway, where it is necessary to obtain parents' written approval before any measure is put into action. In the Philippines there are "no requirements nor time limitation imposed for attendance to a non-formal education programme".

There is a mandatory element in the case of 3 countries (5.8 per cent). Although parents in Austria "decide if they wish to send their children to an elementary school adapted to the child's needs or a special school", in the event that a suitable elementary school cannot be found to meet the child's needs, the child is "required" to attend a special school. In Hungary, although the parents may choose the educational institution for their child's special education, an Act provides that in the interest of a child or student the notary of the local authority can "oblige" parents to take the child for examination by an expert, as a pre-requisite for enrolment at an appropriate institution. A student may be admitted at any time of year in Sri Lanka, but all schools are "required to admit children with special needs", emphasis also being placed on parents as partners in special education.

These comments on the permissive or mandatory nature of the legislation are made subject to an important proviso. The country entries are not necessarily verbatim translations, and the samples in this Study, especially those above, tare merely indicative and not exhaustive.

Summary

1. In 21 countries (40.4 per cent) responsibility for identification, assessment and orientation is stated in general terms as that of a specified body, in most cases the Ministries of Education or Health. There is no information for 11 countries (21.2 per cent). The following statistics are based mainly upon 22 countries (42.3 per cent).

2. There are bodies (described as Commissions, Medical and Pedagogical Boards etc.) with particular responsibility for assessment and/or orientation in 14 countries (26.9 per cent).

3. Assessment is expressed as an inter-disciplinary function in 22 countries (42.3 per cent), and in 8 countries (15.4 per cent) bodies described in paragraph 2 (above) are involved, alone or jointly. Teachers are expressly involved in assessment in 11 countries (21.2 per cent). Parents are involved in identification, assessment and orientation as of right in 24 countries (46.2 per cent) and both parents and pupils in 4 countries (7.7 per cent).

4. Decisions as to orientation are made by bodies described in para 1 (above), alone or jointly, in 8 countries (15.4 per cent). Such decisions are made by parents in 5 countries (9.6 per cent), the school in 3 countries (5.8 per cent), or by a school inspector or adviser in 3 countries (5.8 per cent).

5. There is reference to formal documentation in the case of 4 countries (7.7 per cent) Reviews are specified in 5 countries (9.6 per cent). Both of these matters arise in the subsequent context of the curriculum (Part VI of this Study).

6. The legislation is permissive in 5 countries (9.6 per cent), while there is a mandatory element in the case of 3 countries (5.8 per cent). These statistics are merely indicative and are not exhaustive.

20

AGE RANGE COVERED BY THE LEGISLATION

INTRODUCTION

In this section of the Study, the data is analysed by reference to the extent to which particular ages for pupils and students with special needs are specified in the legislation, first by age ranges and stages in the education system, and then special education in terms of the number of school years which are states to be compulsory. Thereafter, the category of school is identified. Individual countries may fall into more than one classification, and for this reason countries are named wherever necessary, in order to clarify the statistics.

Specification by age

Table 20.1 : Specification by age ranges

Age range	Country
0 - 18	Zimbabwe[23]
3 - 18	Greece
3 - 19	Norway
3 - 21	Canada (Province, New Brunswick)
5 - 12	Pakistan
6 - 13	Uganda
6 - 15	Ireland
6 - 16	Malta, Namibia, Spain[24]
6 - 18	Finland
7 - 14	Tanzania

Table 20.2 : Specification by stages of education expressed as age ranges

Age ranges	*Country*
0 - 4, 4 - 16	Venezuela[25]
0 - 6, 6 - 16, 16 - 29	Iceland
0 - 6, 7 - 20	Sweden
2 - 6, 6 - 13, 13 - 21	Belgium[26]
3 - 6, 6 - 20	Holland
3 - 5, 6 - 12, 13 - 18	Zaire

Compulsory school education

The requirement to provide special education is expressed solely in terms of an obligation which lasts during compulsory school education in 10 countries (19.2 per cent) and has been taken to include secondary education unless there is an express statement to the contrary. Three countries (5.8 per cent) express this requirement in terms of a minimum number of years at school (Germany 9-10, Japan and Sweden 9 years).

Special needs provision according to school stages

Table 20.3 : Breakdown of special needs provision according to schools

Classification	*Countries*	
Pre-Primary[27] special needs provision	22	42.3%
Primary school special needs provision	44	84.6%
Secondary school[28] special needs provision	42	80.8%
No legislation as to school age	2	3.9%
Information not available	6	11.5%
No total is shown because of overlapping classifications.		

It is arguable that inclusion of countries where there is no information (6) or no legislation (2) results in a distortion, because those who classifications (8 countries) amount to 15.4 per cent of all countries. For that reason, Table 20.4 excludes the 8 countries in respect of which there is no express legislation as to age.

Table 20.4 : Special provision according to schools, excluding countries without legislation

Classification	*Countries (44)*	
Pre-Primary special needs provision	22	50.0%
Primary school special needs provision	44	100.0%
Secondary school special needs provision	42	95.5%

Pre-Primary pupils-a definition

'Pre-Primary' pupils can be defined as under the age of 6 years (matching the ages in Tables 20.1 and 20.2). A feature of both Tables 20.3 and 20.4 is the extent to which Pre-Primary pupils with special needs are included in the education systems of their respective countries. It is significant that 22 countries (representing 42.3 per cent of all countries, and 50.0 per cent of those which have provided positive information as to the age range covered by the legislation) make provision at the Pre-Primary stage. This is a major indicator of the commitment by Member States to identify and to take appropriate action in respect of a disability, handicap or learning difficulty (as defined in section I of this Study) at an early stage in a child's life.

Higher and other "post-school" education

The legislation in 9 of the countries (17.3 per cent) includes references to university, tertiary, higher or "post-studies" education, and to adult education (Belgium and Sweden). The vocational aspect is analysed in section VII of this Study.

Summary

1. In 12 countries (23.1 per cent) specific age ranges are stated for provision of special needs education, and in a further 6 countries (11.5 per cent) stages of education are expressed in terms of ages. Thus, in 17 countries (32.7 per cent) an age or ages are specified in the legislation.

2. Taking the provision of special needs eduction expressed according to provision by schools, 22 countries (42.3 per cent) make express provision at the Pre-Primary stage (taken, for the purposes of this Study, to mean pupils under the age of 6).

3. On the same basis as paragraph 2 (above), 44 countries (84.6 per cent) make express special educational provision at primary level, and 42 countries (80.8 per cent) make express provision at secondary level.

4. Excluding countries without legislation specifying any age, 22 countries (50.0 per cent) provide Pre-Primary special needs education. Of the same grouping of countries, all (44) provide such education at primary level, and 42 (95.5 per cent) also provide such education at secondary level, taken to mean (for the purposes of this Study) up to the age of 16 years.

5. University, tertiary or higher education is expressly referred to by 9 countries (17.3 per cent).

21

INTEGRATION

INTRODUCTION

While the concept of 'integration' is familiar, this Study does not assume that there is a universal agreement as to what it involves. Indeed, two possible forms of integration have been identified in section I (*supra*), namely integration in the sense of the provision of education (described in this Study as 'pedagogic integration'), in contrast to integration more generally into the community and the world of work and leisure (described as 'socio-economic integration'). A distinction is draw, therefore, between the two approaches to integration, justified by reference to the legislation. Account is taken also of countries which have a policy on integration, the Study treating such policy as quasi-legislation, in that it has been formulated by the government of the country and is put into effect on a basis that is enforceable.

INTEGRATION IN THE PEDAGOGIC SENSE

An explanation of 'integration' in the pedagogic sense must be derived solely from within the legislation analysed in this Study. A recurring alternative to the notion of 'special' needs is the expression 'exceptional' needs. Because special needs are 'exceptional', they are not 'ordinary'. The issue, therefore, is whether all children (with and without exceptional needs) should, in principle, be educated in an 'ordinary' (or 'regular' or 'mainstream') school thereby integrating the learning experience of exceptional children into a mainstream framework. It follows that exceptional educational provision is blended into an ordinary school's range of provision. Where integration applies, there remains still the practical question as to the extent to which in ordinary schools it is possible to provide facilities (i.e. adapted accommodation, specialist teachers, equipment, and multi-disciplinary professional support) which are suitable for each child's special needs. The principle of integration (described in this Study as 'mandatory pedagogic integration') acknowledges, accordingly, that some children have such disabilities and/or learning difficulties (from those classified in Table 17.3, *supra*) that education in a special school is necessary. There are countries (Table 21.1, *infra*) where there is a definite policy favouring integration in the pedagogic sense, but this has not been classified as truly mandatory.

PRINCIPLES UNDERLYING PEDAGOGIC INTEGRATION

The majority of country entries express pedagogic integration in succinct terms with two elements - (i) the *prima facie* right of a child with special needs to be educated in an ordinary school, subject to (ii) an ordinary school having the capacity to meet those needs. It is possible, however, to extract from a modest number of detailed country entries more specific principles underlying integration, based on legislation (including circulars stating policy).

A 1984 review in the State of Victoria, Australia, offers a useful focus by setting out the principles as the right of every child to be educated in a regular school; provision to be organised according to student needs rather than disability; resources and school services should be school based; decision-making should be collaborative; all children can learn and be taught; and integration is a curriculum issue.

Student needs are expressed elsewhere in terms of partial or full integration as judged appropriate. Thus, in a circular letter (1994) the Minister of Education of the Flemish Community in Belgium accepted the 'equivalence' principle, meaning that although some pupils cannot follow all the lessons of the regular programme due to their disability, they can graduate with approved replacement lessons. One of main points of a 1990 Law in Spain is the attention to the diversity of interests, abilities and aptitudes of students, foreseeing measures to adjust the curriculum and organisation of schools to the needs of all students, special education only being authorised if the student's needs are not met in a regular school.

An organisational strategy for integration may be seen, alternatively, as having a locational approach, according to the student's needs and disability, and integration may be accomplished by a phased method. Chile achieves integration of children with mental, sensory or motor deficiencies either in special education courses in parallel to regular classes or by integration workshops, in each case with the assistance of special educators, while children with mild or moderate disabilities follow common courses at every level. In 1983, France adopted a very similar approach to that of Chile, and then in 1991 a French circular established "classes of school integration", designed to promote the transition of disabled students into regular classes. A variation of that approach is seen in The Philippines, where the concept of a "school-within-a-school" has been developed, by way of a special educational centre as part of a regular school, preparing disabled children, physically and psychologically, to shift into the regular class in the school, either partially or totally.

Collaboration has been amplified in particular in Germany, Italy and Namibia. The functions of the German "Resource Centres" include co-ordinating expertise and remedial programmes, assisting teachers with special need competence, advising parents, and generally co-ordinating in a multi-disciplinary way all of the disabled child's classroom provision. Italy provides for support from specialised personnel from the psycho-pedagogical services, while an Observatory Committee (which includes representatives from a number of relevant Ministries) evaluates current integration practices and makes proposals for future integration projects. Namibia has devised the Committee for Assistance in Remedial Teaching System (CART System)., by which selected class teachers are to be trained at certain schools in the rudiments of diagnosing learning problems, discussion with parents and principals, advising other teachers of children with learning difficulties, referring students with serious problems and conducting weekly meetings with colleagues and the principal for case studies.

INTEGRATION IN THE SOCIO-ECONOMIC SENSE

The legislation in a significant number of countries provides for integration into society or the community as a wider goal than education alone. This expresses integration frequently in terms of rehabilitations, based upon the right of the disabled to education, health, labour and leisure (including sport). As shown in Table 17.2 (*supra*), the special education legislation may also be linked with anti-discrimination rights. The concept of 'normalisation' and living conditions is also expressed in terms which are relative to persons who are not handicapped. It is important, therefore, to recognise that 'integration' is referred to in the legislation in this socio-economic sense, together with the fact that there are countries which include in their legislation both the pedagogic and the socio-economic approaches.

THE ROLE OF POLICY

Various countries state a formal policy of integration. Specific reference has been made above to a formal review (Victoria, Australia) and a circular letter (Belgium). Policy alone has not been treated in this Study as equivalent to legislation. Table 21 summarises the position.

Table 21.1 : References to 'integration' in the special needs education legislation

Classification	*Countries*	
Mandatory pedagogic integration	23	44.2%
Partial integration (pedagogic)[29]	4	7.7%
Socio-economic integration as an objective	20	38.5%
Legislation which refers to both concepts of integration	15	28.8%
Legislation as to integration (pedagogic) in draft/process[30]	5	9.6%
No legislation[31]	15	28.8%
Information unavailable	5	9.6%
No total is shown because of overlapping classifications		

Table 21.2 : Reconciliation of classifications of integration in the legislation

Classification	*Countries*	
Pedagogic integration - mandatory (23), partial (4)	27	51.9%
Socio-economic integration (20), less references including pedagogic (15)	5	9.6%
No legislation	15	28.8%
Information unavailable	5	9.6%
Total	52	100.0%

From Table 21.1 it can be seen that there is integration in the pedagogic sense through legislation in 23 countries (44.2 per cent), and that when partial integration is taken into account there is a formal element of pedagogic integration in 27 countries (51.9 per cent). The manner in which successful pedagogic integration is maximised in practice is illustrated by an executive Circular in France (1976), to the effect that it will be most successful if it is supported by the child, teachers and the administration. Section VIII of this Study enlarges upon the role of parents generally.

The Philippines provides for both full and partial integration, which is referred to as the "zero reject model". The extent to which integration is carried into effect in any country, nonetheless, depends ultimately on the nature and scale of the child's needs and the capacity of an ordinary school to meet them, an issue which is analysed also in terms of curriculum entitlement in Chap. 22.

In 5 countries (9.6 per cent) there are proposals to legislate. On the other hand, Denmark considers that integration cannot be promoted directly through legislation, taking the view that it may impede the process, and so "normalisation and decentralisation are embodied in laws which pave the way of integration."

The emphasis on socio-economic integration in 20 countries (38 per cent) is consistent with the predominant emphasis on disability or handicap, which has been shown to be a constituent of the classification of special needs in the legislation of 40 countries (Table 17.3 *supra*). The tenor of the legislation on socio-economic integration is mandatory when dealing with anti-discrimination issues, but while in other respects it is not permissive (i.e. discretionary), it constitutes wideranging goals or objectives (for example, integration into the community and the world of work, leisure, and/or raising the individual's self-esteem) rather than imposing a measurable outcome. These latter aspects of socio-economic integration (goals or objectives) may be described as mandatory guidelines—i.e. guidelines that are regarded as statutory obligation.

Summary

1. There are two substantive concepts of integration throughout the legislation, namely the provision of education for children in ordinary/regular schools (described in this Study as pedagogic integration), and a broader type of integration which is expressed in terms of anti-discrimination and/or integration into society, the world of work and leisure etc. (described as socio-economic integration).
2. Of the principles underlying pedagogic integration, the fundamental consideration is the individual pupil's needs. In some instances a phased process is used to meet the pupil's immediate needs by locating special education programmes within a regular school, aiming ultimately to achieve the maximum possible degree of integration in the same school.
3. Pedagogic integration is mandatory under the legislation in 23 countries (44.2 per cent). Formal pedagogic integration is partial in 4 countries (7.7 per cent). When partial integration is included, there is a formal element of pedagogic integration in 27 countries (51.9 per cent). In 3 other countries (5.8 per cent), partial integration exists on an informal basis.
4. Legislation as to pedagogic integration is in draft/process in 5 countries (9.6 per cent).
5. Socio-economic integration is an objective in the legislation of 20 countries (38.5 per cent). This reflects the predominance of disability or handicap as a constituent of the classification of special needs in 40 countries (76.9 per cent). It is mandatory to

the extent that it is expressed as being anti-discrimination. By contrast, much socio-economic integration is expressed in terms of goals or objectives, which do not have measurable outcomes and therefore can be described as mandatory guidelines.

6. In 15 countries (28.8 per cent) the legislation refers both pedagogic integration and to socio-economic integration. 'Integration', expressed either in terms of education or more broad social objectives, is referred to in the legislation pertaining to special needs education in 41 countries (78.8 per cent).

22
CURRICULUM ENTITLEMENT

THE FUNDAMENTAL BASIS FOR THE CURRICULUM

The first issue in this section of the Study is the extent to which the curriculum for children with special needs is based on a country's regular curriculum at any stage or on a special curriculum. The notes from 32 to 35 demonstrate variations in terminology and emphasis.

Table 22.1 : Curriculum entitlement based on regular or special curricula

Classification	*Countries*	
Curriculum based on regular[32] curriculum, adapted for special needs[33]	22	42.3%
Special curriculum for special needs children[34]	12	23.1%
No provision for special needs curriculum[35]	5	9.6%
Information unavailable	13	25.0%
Total	52	100.0%

At first sight, it may appear curious that, whereas the total of all forms of pedagogic integration in Tables 21.1 and 21.2 (*supra*) is 35 countries (67.3 per cent), the total number of countries which have an entitlement based on a regular curriculum, adapted for special needs, is 22 (42.3 per cent) (Table 22.1, *supra*). The data underlying this Study has been extensively analysed in statistical as well as qualitative terms. The apparent discrepancy between the statistics on integration and entitlement to an adapted regular curriculum is due (briefly) to two factors. First, information as to curriculum entitlement was unavailable in 13 cases (25 per cent), but in 8 of those countries there was positive information as to pedagogic integration, bringing the regular curriculum total of 22 up to a notional figure of 20. Second, a number of country entries (many of them set out in the notes from 32 to 35 quite properly focus on the entitlement to a special educational curriculum. This is not at all inconsistent with the principle of integration, in connection with which this Study has observed that there may be an equivalence principle (Belgium), and organisational strategies within schools (Spain) which may also have a locational approach (Chile, France, and The Philippines-*supra*). There can be a heavy reliance on statistics to analyse issues such as integration and the curriculum, both of which involve varieties and combinations of approaches, and for the reasons given it can be seen that there is no real discrepancy between two statistics viewing related issues from different aspects.

THE CURRICULUM—OBJECTIVES AND PROCEDURES

Some country entries make points which indicate that there are broad curricula objectives for children with special needs, and also (to some extent) procedures for monitoring progress and assessing outcomes. Though the numbers of country entries are relatively few, one can express these curricula objectives in the form of Table 22.2, although the stated goals are not always quantifiable.

Table 22.2 : Express special curricula objectives

Classification	*Countries*	
Meeting individual needs, or aptitudes, or disabilities	17	32.7%
Vocational training (including preparation), personal, social development	12	23.1%
No total is shown because of overlapping classifications		

Because 6 countries are included in both classifications, the total number of countries which have express special curricula objectives is 23 (44.2 per cent). When it comes to precise statements as to how these objectives are to be met, the number falls significantly, as follows.

PROGRESS, COUNSELING, RECORDS AND REVIEWS

There is express mention of monitoring progress by way of special individual teaching plans (3), counseling (3), provision for records (3), and formal review (3). Allowing for overlaps, the total number of countries making up these entries is 6 (11.5 per cent). These figures are no more than one method of illustrating certain practical aspects of delivering a curriculum. They are in line with the relatively low numbers of countries which mention formal documentation and reviews in connection with assessment and orientation (Chap. 19, *surpa*). The most likely explanation for the low numbers is that countries regard these as matters of practice rather than appropriate for formal expression in legislation.

Summary

1. The curriculum for children with special needs is based on a regular curriculum, adapted for those needs, in 22 countries (42.3 per cent).
2. There is express provision for a special curriculum for special needs children in 12 countries (23.1 per cent).
3. In 5 countries (9.6 per cent) there is no provision for a special needs curriculum.
4. Express special curricula objectives are stated in general terms, either as meeting individual needs or aptitudes or abilities in 17 countries (32.7 per cent), or educating children through vocational training (or preparing them for such training), or providing personal and/or social development in 12 countries (23.1 per cent). Because 6 countries have both types of special curricula objectives, the total number of countries which have express special curricula objectives is 23 (44.2 per cent).
5. 6 countries (11.5 per cent) have express provision for monitoring progress, and/or special individual teaching plans, and/or counseling, reports and/or reviews.
6. Because of the relatively high number of countries (13) in respect of which information is not available (25.0 per cent), the figures given the illustrative of trends and emphasis, and have been incorporated on that basis.

23

POST 16 YEARS—VOCATIONAL EDUCATION

References by the country entries under this heading include preparation for vocational education and provision of such training for pupils and students with special needs in schools, institutes and other centres. Where country entries have identified a Department or other responsible body or the actual provider of vocational education, it has been assumed that there is a legislative basis for that information. This Study identifies the objective of vocational education. The extent to which such education is available is analysed according to the age ranges of the students and the type of institution in which it is delivered.

THE OBJECTIVES OF VOCATIONAL EDUCATION

A total of 15 countries (28.8 per cent) state some form of objective. Integration into work and the acquisition of skills are the major objectives of vocational education in 12 countries (23.1 per cent). This is variously expressed in terms also of the acquisition of self-sufficiency, developing a professional attitude, creating equal opportunities, as part of social integration into the community, an aspect of citizenship, and as personal development. In Jordan, the result of vocational education should include support for protected workshop projects, an approach to be found also in Belgium. Two countries refer specifically to the wishes or preferences of the individual student as a major factor in decisions regarding vocational education.

In a number of countries there is, therefore, a stated purpose which considers vocational *education* as more than simply training to acquire skills. Although the primary objective is preparation for the world of work, an explicit commitment to education rather than a narrower view of training is demonstrated by an emphasis on the ability to adapt to and play a constructive role at work and in society, as well as on personal development.

AGE RANGES FOR VOCATIONAL EDUCATION

The ages include generalisations such as upper secondary, or secondary level, and specific ranges between the ages of 15-16 to 18-19 in 8 countries, the minimum age being stated as the end of compulsory education by 2 countries, 10 in all (19.2 per cent). The length of vocational education is specified by 2 countries (3.9 per cent) as 3 and 3-4 years respectively. Costa Rica implements vocational-based programmes both at high schools and, for persons aged 14-18 years with mild and moderate disabilities, in community educational institutions. In Mexico, apart from the right to a technical secondary education, there is an entitlement at the post-primary stage to enter into a special education training centre.

INSTITUTIONAL PROVISION OF SPECIAL NEEDS VOCATIONAL EDUCATION

There is a wide variety among the types of institutions which provide vocational education, as shown in the following table.

Table 23.1 : Institutions providing special needs vocational education

Classification	*Countries*	
Professional or vocational training institutes, centres or training schools[36]	11	21.2%
Upper secondary or secondary schools[37]	6	11.5%
Special or special vocational schools[38]	7	13.5%
Vocational education available, but no institution specified[39]	9	17.3%
Information unavailable	19	36.5%
Total	52	100.0%

From this table it can be seen that 24 countries (46.2 per cent) have specified the type of institution in which vocational education is delivered, and that 33 countries (63.5 per cent) state that they provide this education, albeit without specifying to what extent or in what manner.

Summary

1. Some form of objective for special vocational education is stated by 15 countries (28.8 per cent). The major objectives are integration into work and the acquisition of skills in 12 countries (23.1 per cent). Nonetheless, there are statements of wider objectives, expressed in socio-economic terms, based upon the personal development of the individual with special needs, equal opportunities, and citizenship. It is reasonable to observe that special vocational education is seen, therefore, as more than simply training to acquire skills.
2. There are relatively few references to ages, but special vocational education appears to be concentrated within the age ranges 15-16 to 18-19, during secondary or upper secondary education, also expressed as after the end of compulsory education, from the entries of 10 countries in all (19.2 per cent). The length of special vocational education is stated as 3 and 3-4 years by 2 countries (3.9 per cent). There is alternative provision in 2 countries (3.9 per cent), from 14-18, and post-primary, respectively.
3. Special vocational education is delivered by professional or vocational training institutes, centres or training schools in 11 countries (21.2 per cent); in upper secondary or secondary schools in 6 countries (11.5 per cent); and in special or special vocational schools in 7 countries (17.3 per cent). Special vocational education is available in 9 countries (17.3 per cent), which do not specify any type of institution.
4. Taking these sub-totals, it can be seen that 24 countries (46.2 per cent) have specified the type of institution in which special vocational education is delivered, and that this provision exists in 33 countries (63.5 per cent). There is no available information as to 19 countries (36.5 per cent).

24

PARENTS

THE CENTRAL EMPHASIS IN THE LEGISLATION

Parents (which includes 'the family' and guardians) of children with special needs are referred to in the legislation primarily in the context of identification, assessment, orientation and integration. This is not surprising, in view of the fact that the assessment of the needs of a child who has not reached the age of majority, and decisions which have to be made as to his or her future, are central to any scheme for special educational provision. Where there is legislation, in general terms it sets out rights and duties, emphasising consultation and collaboration with parents, in some cases with counseling/ orientation, in a spirit of partnership.

Consultation with parents and their involvement in decisions occurs also in the wider context of participation in the governance of schools and membership of Parent-Teacher or Parent Associations.

The Table 24.1 illustrates the nature and extent of the legal status which is conferred on parents under the special needs legislation pertaining to education.

One method of identifying and measuring the extent to which parents have rights and duties under the legislation is to deduct the number of countries (i) in which there is no reference to parents (21), and (ii) where there is only a general recognition of parental rights in respect of special needs education (4). These two classifications (26) account for 50.0 per cent of all countries.

Table 24.1 : References to rights and duties of parents, guardians or families

Classification	Countries	
General recognition of rights and duties[40] alone[41]	5	9.6%
Rights and duties in identification, assessment,[42] orientation,[43], integration[44]	24	46.2%
Involvement in school's responsibility for policy and/or management[45]	4	7.7%
Formal right of appeal against decisions[46]	2	3.8%
No reference to parents in the legislation	21	40.4%
No total is shown due to overlapping classifications		

APPEALS

Two countries provide for the resolution of disputes by specifying a formal procedure for an appeal. In Chile, if there is a dispute between the professional team and the parents or guardians, the school principal will decide the matter. In China, parents may appeal to the school authorities if their child is not admitted to a regular primary or secondary school, all such schools being obliged to admit disabled students who are able to participate in regular classes. There is no corresponding provision in any country for a public authority to appeal if it considers that a parent's refusal to agree to a particular form of special educational provision is contrary to the interests of the child.

It is, however, reasonable to assume that in most (if not all) countries which confer mandatory rights, parents (and/or children) will be able, at least in theory, to apply to the courts for an order to enforce, or to prohibit infringement of those rights, and also that public authorities will have a similar remedy which enables them to discharge their statutory obligations. It is, of course, questionable in many jurisdictions whether in practice parents or children are able to take proceedings, due to the cost and risk involved.

Summary

1. There are references to rights, and to duties, of parents throughout the legislation. The primary emphasis is on parental involvement in identification, assessment, orientation and integration in 24 countries (46.2 per cent).

2. There is an express right of appeal under certain circumstances in 2 countries (3.8 per cent). That said, it is reasonable to assume that in most (if not all) countries which confer mandatory rights, parents (and/or children) will be able to apply, at least in theory, to the courts for an order to enforce their rights, and that public authorities may also have a similar remedy.

3. Parents are involved in a less personal manner by way of school governance and policy in 5 countries (9.6 per cent).

4. In 21 countries there is no legislation (40.4 per cent). Taking those 21 countries together with the 5 countries where the legislation makes only a general reference to parents, in all 26 countries (50.0 per cent) make either no, or only a very general reference to parents.

25
SUMMARY AND CONCLUSIONS

The *nature and extent of the legislation* is illustrated by the fact that 48 countries have enacted legislation (which is mandatory in 47 countries) pertaining to special needs education, and the remaining 4 countries have active proposal (with provision already existing in 3 of those countries). The definition of special needs is according to categories of disability, handicap or other deficiency alone in 31 countries. In 5 countries that definition is expressed solely in terms of learning, pedagogic or intellectual difficulties. In 40 countries the legislation refers to a combination of disabilities and learning difficulties. There is, therefore, a clear pattern of categorisation, and in the case of disabilities there is a distinction between physical, mental or sensory difficulties and emotional, behavioural or psychological difficulties. Gifted children are treated as having special education needs in 3 countries.

Responsibility for special needs education is predominantly the function of central (or federal) government (47 countries). It is the function of a local authority in 4 countries (no information being available in 1_case). The Ministry of Education is responsible in 37 countries and 23 countries have a Special Needs Department. The Ministry shares responsibility in 9 other countries. Special needs education is *organised* (i.e. administered) centrally in 34 countries, and by local authorities in 17 countries.

Although there is less information available as to *identification, assessment and orientation,* the detailed entries for 22 countries illustrate a variety of approaches. The dominant theme is assessment, there being an apparent assumption that special educational needs will be identified by parents, schools, or organisations concerned with disabled people. A major feature of the assessment process is inter-disciplinary professional co-operation, in consultation with parents and, in 4 cases, expressly with the pupil. There is some evidence of diverging views as to categorisation, but it remains the prime method for determining orientation. Fewer bodies and individuals are involved as decision-makers regarding orientation of a pupil following the assessment. In 8 countries there are bodies which make such decisions alone or jointly. The decision is made by the parents in 5 countries, by the school in 3 countries, and by the school inspector or adviser in 3 countries. There is little formal provision for documentation, and reviews are only specified in 5 countries.

An interesting feature of the *age range* covered by the legislation is that 22 countries provide pre-primary or nursery special needs education, 'pre-primary' being defined by reference to the legislation overall as under the age of six years. There is primary provision in 44 countries and secondary provision in 42 countries. The upper age limits vary from 16 to 18-19 years (with 5 countries above those ages, and 4 countries below them). There is provision for higher and other "post-school" education in 9 countries (subject to the proviso that vocational education has been analysed separately).

The legislation discloses two approaches to *integration*. The first is a definition which depends upon integration into ordinary, regular or mainstream schools. Because this approach is based upon teaching and learning criteria, this Study has described it as 'mandatory pedagogic integration', for which legislation provides wholly or partially in 27 countries. It goes beyond a presumption in favour of special education in mainstream rather than special schools, as demonstrated by various strategies which include locational and collaborative aspects. Above all, integration in this sense involves dealing with the individual needs of each child, subject to the capacity of a mainstream school to meet those needs. The second approach to integration is described as 'socio-economic', in the sense of integration into society, the world of work, leisure, or the community, as specified by 20 countries. These two approaches are not mutually exclusive, the legislation in 15 countries referring to both. Thus, mandatory pedagogic integration is the dominant approach, and 5 more countries have legislation to this effect in draft or in process. Socio-economic integration is more than permissive or discretionary and should be seen as setting goals in terms which constitute mandatory guidelines.

The pedagogic nature of integration is to a large extent reflected by the *curriculum entitlement* of a pupil with special needs. In 22 countries this is based on a regular curriculum, adapted for special needs, whereas in 12 countries there is express provision for a special curriculum for children with special needs. Within those two figures there is substantial variation in detail. It is interesting to note that a total of 23 countries have set broad curricular objectives, expressed by 17 countries as meeting individual needs or aptitudes or disabilities, and by 12 countries in terms of vocational training or personal or social development (6 countries incorporating both objectives). The position is different when it comes to measuring outcomes, where only 6 countries between them provide for monitoring progress by way of special individual teaching plans, counseling, provision for records, and formal reviews. The most likely explanation for this low figure is that monitoring progress is regarded as a matter of practice rather than appropriate for legislation.

So far as *post 16 vocational education* is concerned, the dominant objective, expressed by 15 countries, is integration into the world of work and the acquisition of skills, but this is qualified by the important proviso that there is also emphasis on education in the wider sense of the personal development of an individual with special needs, and equal opportunities as a citizen. The main ages referred to are within the range of 15-16 to 18-19 years. In 11 countries special vocational education is delivered by professional or vocational training centres or training schools; in 6 countries delivery is in upper secondary or secondary schools; and 7 countries deliver special vocational education in special or special vocational schools.

The main emphasis in references to *parents* in the legislation is their role in identification, assessment, orientation and integration. This is not surprising, because it is the central aspect of special needs education. The legislation sets out parental rights and duties in that connection in 24 countries. Only 2 countries specify any appeal procedure, for which the explanation suggested by this Study is that the parents (and also public authorities) are expected to resort to the general law in order to enforce their rights, and that there is no perceived requirement for resolving disputes through a mechanism of appeals in the sole context of special needs education. The other statutory role of parents (and pupils) is participation in the governance of schools in 4 countries.

Lastly, this Study has been an analysis and synthesis based strictly on the data provided to UNESCO by 52 Member States. Considerable trouble has been taken by them to provide a wealth of information.

REFERENCES

1. The Irish constitution restricts required provision to primary education, but see Table 20.1 as to compulsory school age.
2. The constitution of Sri Lanka refers to "...the advancement of...disabled persons" (emphasis added), which has been taken to include education.
3. 'Legislation' includes Acts, Laws, Regulations, Decrees and Government or Ministerial Resolutions or Orders, and also (in the case of France) executive Circulars.
4. In Ireland, Namibia, Uganda and Zambia, legislation is proposed and special education provision exists, or is being introduced (Namibia).
5. References to 'anti-discrimination' include disabilities, equal opportunities, race or ethnicity, gender and religion.
6. Germany has no national legislation, responsibility for education being within the jurisdiction of Federal Districts. The education system is described as "co-operative federalism", provision for special education being made by each District. Five new Districts from the former German Federal Republic (GDR) must also have their school law adopted as a result of the GDR joining the Federal Republic of Germany in 1990. The tenor of the legislation is not clearly mandatory, but the school law of the Districts may ultimately prove to be so.
7. The legislation in Greece is expressed as "immigrant children and other pupils with learning difficulties."
8. As to Germany, see note 6 (supra). In New Zealand there is a Statement of Intent by the Ministry of Education (1991), outlining major legislative changes and which envisages special provision for those with disabilities and those with learning or social difficulties, thus changing the emphasis from a general reference (class D) to an explicit combination of disability and learning difficulties (class B).
9. Both public and private institutions or sectors are referred to by 11 countries under various headings.
10. The expression 'Department' includes bodies such as a National Department, Commission or Crown Agency, on the basis that their work is within the scope of the responsibility of the Ministry of Education. El Salvador, Jordan and Pakistan have relevant Directorates as well as National Councils corresponding to those described in note 12. Zambia also has an Inter-Ministerial Steering Committee.

11. This category arises from an overall focus on disability.

    Education and Health: Bulgaria (where a Medical and Pedagogical Board determines admissions);

    Education and Social Welfare: Finland;

    Education, Health, Social Welfare: China, France, Italy, Malaysia;

    Department of Employment, Education and Training: Australia.

12. *Delegates sent from Ministries of Education, Employment, Health, Social Welfare and others*: Nicaragua (but where in practice only Health and Social Welfare are active and support only the rehabilitation of victims of war), Tunisia (delegates also sent from additional Ministries).

13. *This phrase includes Provincial, Regional, District and Municipal authorities generally and States, Provinces or Districts within Federal systems*: Austria, Canada (based on New Brunswick as an example), Germany, Holland.

14. In Iceland, the Philippines and Sweden there is an emphasis in favour of increased decentralisation.

15. These are a separate category from the National Bodies identified in Table 18.1 as having responsibility for special needs education. In Tanzania such bodies are voluntary and charitable, national and international, in providing materials and training special needs teachers.

16. In Venezuela the objective of the relevant Foundation includes research as well as assisting in implementing policy and international participation.

17. This is a function of the Cuba Association of the Physically Disabled at the provincial level.

18. 'Decisions' includes recommendations or opinions as to appropriate schools.

19. The National Institute of Handicapped (NIH) in Pakistan in an example of a body with a wide brief which also includes research.

20. Under the General Law in El Salvador, diagnosis and evaluation of disabled students will take place in special schools or by professionals hired by the child's family.

21. Pupils are entitled to be consulted in Belgium, Denmark and France. In Bulgaria, a child need not stay more than 3 years at a convalescence school unless the child so chooses.

22. In Austria, where parents decide whether they wish to send their child to an elementary school adapted to their child's needs or a special school, in the absence of a suitable elementary school the child is required to attend a special school. As to the rights of parents in Hungary, Ireland is included, because all children are required to attend school from age 6 to 15 unless their parents choose to make some other educational provision for them.

23. See Table 23.1 note 39 as to higher education in Zimbabwe.

24. Education in Spain is compulsory between age 6 and 16, but it may be expanded up to age 18.

25. In Venezuela special education is developed for children from birth until they

are 16 years old, first in centres at pre-school level (0-4) and then in Institutes of Special Education (4-16).

26. Some pupils in Belgium stay inspecial education after age 21 due to the lack of a sheltered job or home.

27. Pre-Primary, nursery or kindergarten is not always expressly stipulated, but where countries have specified ages for special needs education lower than 6 years old but there is no express mention of a school, this has been classified as 'Pre-Primary' for the purposes of this Study (Canada, Holland, Norway, Pakistan, Zimbabwe). In Malta the minimum compulsory age is 6 and there is also Pre-Primary education. 'Pre-Primary' is defined in the text.

28. This includes countries in which compulsory school education ends at age 16 (Bulgaria, Hungary, Nicaragua, Portugal, Spain), although in Nicaragua there is no special needs legislation as to age. It excludes 3 countries (Pakistan, Tanzania, Ugnada) with upper age limits of 12, 13 and 14 respectively.

29. Local ('States and Territories') policies on integration vary significantly in Australia, from one of integration (Victoria) to another (Queensland) which avoids the use of 'integration', 'handicap' and 'mainstreaming'. Integrations is partial in Bulgaria, where there are special classes in Pre-School and Primary regular schools. Canada has given the Province of New Brunswick as an example, which is included in this figure. Japan is included because there is provision for "mildly handicapped" children in special or ordinary classes with special arrangements.

30. This comprises Germany (Districts), Greece, Ireland and Uganda (all of which are also included under the heading 'policy alone' due to existing policies), and Holland (as at June 1994). This does not, however, include Austria, where pilot "integrative classes" have been created and which, if judged to be successful, will result in amending legislation which will take them into mainstream education.

31. In 3 countries there is partial integration on what appears to be an informal basis only. In Malaysia, students who are visually and hearing impaired are present in mainstream classrooms. Malta has no policy for integration, but children with mild learning difficulties and the physically handicapped are integrated into regular schools. In Nicaragua, efforts have been made to integrate at primary level, but with no legislation or formal policy or plan to support this initiative.

32. This classification comprises those countries where the predominant emphasis is on a regular, compulsory or national curriculum, adapted for children with special needs. The State of Queensland is the basis for including Australia. The classification includes also those countries where there is, exceptionally, a separate curriculum for specific needs, as, for example, Bahrain, which aims to provide an integrated curriculum for all with "compensating" facilities, but which compels special centres such as the Blind Institute to have their own curriculum addressing particular needs. El Salvador is included on the basis that the curriculum in special schools is "related to the official programmes of the regular schools". In Germany the autonomy of the Districts leads to "differences as well as parallels in policy" but there are "remedial programmes in addition to and in connection with the basic instruction courses". All schools in Iceland are required to implement the national curriculum, but a Regulation defines special

eduction according to "a significant change in teaching objectives, content, situation or method" relative to children of the same age. Sweden provides for adult education.

33. There is discretion as to the extent of the adaptation. In some countries this is express, as, for example, in Cape Verde, where the obligatory school curriculum "may" be adapted to the needs of the student, and in Greece, where there are no separate special education curricula, but teachers and school advisers jointly have the "right" to make adjustments to the ordinary school curricula.

34. Although in Belgium the special education curriculum is 'more or less similar to the curriculum of regular education", special provision is based on explicit types of special education, each with their own objectives. In Bulgaria, for every special school and according to the type of school there is a specific methodological programme. Holland has legislation as to integration pending. (See Table 21.1) Pakistan has different priorities in the learning and pace of progress, with curriculum guidelines for teachers and use of regular textbooks with some adjustments. The Department for Education in Venezuela must see that each student receives an individualised teaching programme. Zambia express the provision as "modified supplementary curricula".

35. The country entry for Italy as to curriculum entitlement states that there are no differences between disabled students and normal ones, but a student who has a very severe disability can obtain only a certificate of frequency (instead of the normal title) at the end of the compulsory education. In Tunisia a Decree is restricted to vocational training for persons with motor impairments. Uganda's national curriculum does not mention curriculum entitlement for children with special needs. While there are no formal programmes in Zaire, there are projects to create national programmes for the different levels of schools.

36. Argentina proposes a plan of co-operation between special education schools and professional training institutes. In Ireland, where there government agencies provide post-school education and training, most post-primary schools offer vocational preparation and training courses. Children in Malta with mild learning difficulties are admitted to a trade school, and pupils with sever learning difficulties are admitted to adult training centres. Norway offers the choice of vocational training or upper secondary education. Some vocational training colleges in Tanzania, which train disabled youths, are privately owned by non-governmental organisations (NGOs), such a churches, associations of and societies for the disabled.

37. There are three relevant forms of teaching in Belgium, Form 2 giving pupils a chance to learn some vocational skills in order to find a job in a sheltered workshop, with practical outside training; From 3 is comparable to regular vocational training, but with a more individual approach; and Form 4 is the regular vocational curriculum for youngsters with a normal mental ability. Under the Constitution in Brazil, preparation for labour and citizenship is an objective of the education system, all people with special needs having the same rights as others.

38. In Greece there is a small number of special lyceums for deaf and physically handicapped children; deaf and blind students who finish the lyceum may enter University without entrance examinations. In Venezuela, vocational orientation

is initiated during education in special schools and is developed further in units such as those caring for young people and adults with mental retardation and centres for the rehabilitation of the blind. Although there is a network of special vocational schools in Romania, many local special sections/classes for vocational training have been opened recently in ordinary/vocational training schools.

39. There are current preparations in some Districts of Germany to improve vocational training and job prospects for young people with special educational needs. In Zimbabwe, the Ministries of Social Welfare and Health work hand-in-hand with NGOs to provide vocational education for children with special educational needs.

40. Costa Rica defines special education as "the responsibility of the school, the family and the community".

41. This classification excludes two countries which make both a general and a particular reference to the status of parents.

42. In El Salvador, the diagnosis and evaluation (i.e. assessment) of disabled students may be by professionals hired by the family. (See Table 19.2).

43. In Canada (New Brunswick) if a child is not able to receive a special educational programme in a regular class, the Minister "may" provide such a service at the child's home (or an approved institution). In Ireland, parents may choose to have their children educated other than in school (See Table 19.3). There is also a home teaching service in Malta.

44. The parents' formal consent to special education is required in 5 countries unless (in Austria) there in so suitable elementary school (See Table 19.3). One of the fundamental principles of integration in France is "building relationships between...parent-teacher associations...and parent associations in order to consider the manifold aspects of integration". Parents in Uganda who are unable to pay the normal fees in integrated schools will receive the normal assistance under current proposals.

45. Each school board in Denmark comprises 5-7 elected parents' representatives, 2 staff representations, 2 pupil representations, school chairman and head teacher. The school board "shall lay down the criteria pertaining to the school, including: organisation and instruction, number of lessons for the pupils at each form level, elective subjects offered, special education at the school, and the distribution of pupils in classes" (emphasis added). Holland requires every special school to set up a Participation Council, comprising elected staff and parent representations in equal numbers (varying form 6 to 18, depending on the size of school). A Parents' Council advises the parents' representatives in the Participation Council and co-ordinates parental activities. In Uganda, there are proposals whereby an integrated school should have a PTA.

46. Chile and China.

COUNTRY SUMMARIES

ARGENTINA

1. Extent and Nature of Legislation

The 1981 Law for the Integral Protection of All Disabled Persons (Ley de Proteccion Integral Para Todos Los (Discapacitados) establishes a system of social protection of the disabled in order to include them into normal community life. A disabled person is defined as one who "possess a permanent or prolonged physical or mental defect. That implies considerable disadvantages for the person's familiar, social, educational or integration."

Chapter 2 of the above law states that disabled children will be educated in regular schools and offered necessary support at no cost. Children will be accepted into special schools only if their disability cannot be accommodated in a regular school.

The Law No. 17.11 on The Legal Situation of the Disabled (Situacion Juridica de las Personas Discapacitadas) defines different categories of disability and social protection.

2. Responsibility and Organisation.

Article 13 of the 1981 Law states that The Ministry of Education is to be concerned with the education of disabled students and their integration into the school system. They are to define the criteria by which children are to be accepted in regular school, and detect severe disabilities to be treated in special institutions. They also are to create centres for evaluation, orientation, and training teachers.

There is a sub-direction for Special Education as a part of the Ministry of Education.

3. Identification, Assessment and Orientation

Law No. 22.431 gives authority to the Ministry of Public Health to evaluate disabled persons using a team of specialised personnel.

4. Age Range Covered by Legislation

Primary and Secondary school are covered.

5. Integration

The integration of disabled children into regular schools is a guiding principle in the Law of 1981.

6. Financing of Education for Special Needs

Information unavailable.

7. Curriculum Entitlement

Information unavailable.

8. Post 16 Years—Vocational Education

The Department of Special Education Circular No. 1001, 1987 proposes a plan of co-operation between special education schools and professional training institutes. The professional training institutes will illicit community participation and train qualified personnel. The objective of these training schools is to integrate the disabled into a self-sufficient working life.

9. Teacher Training

The Ministry of Education is involved in teacher training.

AUSTRALIA

1. Extent and Nature of Legislation

An Anti-Discrimination Act was passed in 1991. The Disability Discrimination Act was adopted by Parliament on the second of November 1992. This act renders it illegal to discriminate against a person on the grounds of disability Division two of the Act No. 135 deals specifically with education. It stipulates that an educational authority cannot refuse admission to a disabled student, cannot deny access, may not expel the student or subject the student to any other detriment. The educational authority, however, may not allow a student to enter an institution that caters to a certain kind of disability if the student does not have that particular disability. Also, a student may not be allowed to enter an institution if the school does not have the facilities or services to provide for the student's disability thus putting the student in a situation of hardship.

In 1986 the Department of Education developed Policy Statement 15, "Integration-mainstreaming students with special needs." Between 1986 and 1990, services for the disabled began to expand, however, the policy statement lacked a management plan to facilitate implementation. Following the state-wide review of education in 1990 "Education: Have Your Say," it was recommended that a management plan to implement Policy Statement 15 be adopted.

In Queensland, The Education (General Provisions) Act of 1989 requires the Minister of Education to provide appropriate educational programmes for students of school age. The key issue in the 1990's has been the availability of educational provisions for students with disabilities regardless of their classroom setting. The Policy Statement and Management Plan: Educational Provision for Students with Disabilities is the result of state-wide consultation with the educational community. Some of the policy principles in Queensland include making provision for equitable educational provision, recognising difference and catering for difference, acknowledging that local schools are responsible for initiating evaluation procedures, a commitment to inclusive curricula through a range of options, support of collaborative processes and staff development, and recognition of parental contribution.

2. Responsibility and Organisation

The Department of Employment, Education and Training provides supplementary funding for special education provision. The responsibility for the implementation of special education rests with the State and Territory governments. Specialist schools/facilities, like all schools, are responsible to the General Manager (Schools) in each region. The regional General Managers, in turn, are responsible to the Director of School Education in each State and Territory.

3. Identification, Assessment and Orientation

Information unavailable.

4. Age Range Covered by Legislation

Primary and secondary education are covered.

5. Integration

States' and Territories' policies on integration differ significantly. A 1984 review of eduction in Victoria, for example, states the following principles for integration:

1) Every child has the right to be educated in a regular school;

2) Provision to be organised according to student needs rather than disability;

3) Resources and services should be school based;

4) Decision-making should be collaborative;

5) All children can learn and be taught; and

6) Integration is a curriculum issue.

To mention another example, in Queensland, The Policy Statement and Management Plan: Educational Provision for Students with Disabilities avoided the use of the terms "integration", "handicap", and "mainstreaming." The focus is on a recognition that all students can learn and that the organisational process requires flexibility of programmes, organisation and structural arrangements.

6. Financing of Education for Special Needs

Financing of special needs education varies between States and Territories. In Victoria, a new funding model of resource allocation for students with disability will be introduced. The model will use an index based on the educational needs of students. The resources required to meet the individual needs of the student will be provided at the school the student attends. Each student will be allocated resources in dollar terms which the school will have the capacity to convert to appropriate support.

7. Curriculum Entitlement

In Queensland, the general school curriculum provides the basis for instruction modified according to individual needs.

8. Post 16 Years—Vocational Education

Information unavailable.

9. Teacher Training

In Victoria, The I.S.I. (Inclusive Schooling-Integration) Programme was developed as a professional training workshop and curriculum approach. It was designed to assist schools in the provision of a comprehensive and inclusive curriculum supporting the goal of integration The programme is to resource and support existing regional, district and school based procedures which support the implementation of curriculum. It offers to school support staff further professional development in curriculum.

AUSTRIA

1. Extent and Nature of Legislation

In 1962, The "School Organisation Act" (Schulorganisationsgesetz) was passed. This act paved the way for reorganising the Austrian school system. The Federal School Inspection Act established that school inspection be carried out by Federal authorities with the provincial school boards as subordinate. The 13th amendment of the "School Organisation Act" (1991) stimulated the creation of pilot projects concerning the joint instruction of disabled and non-disabled children. These "integrative classes" constituted no more than 20 per cent of the special education classes in a province. The pilot projects were started in the Hauptschulen (compulsory secondary schools), the lower bracket of the AHS (top-level secondary schools), Polytechnische Lehrgange (pre-vocational courses). The pilot projects continued in 1992-3. The ratio between handicapped and non-handicapped children in these classes is approximately 1:4. The number of pilot classes rose from 50 in 1988-1989 to 206 in 1991-1992. If these integration projects are judged to be successful, they will be taken over into mainstream educational system by an amendment to the School Organisation Act.[1]

2. Responsibility and Organisation

While the School Organisation Act was passed at the national level, implementing the legislation was left to the Austrian Federal States. For example, co-operation between primary school classes and special school classes was fuelled by the efforts of local teachers. This kind of cooperation between "regular" and special education classes may be seen as the basis for the new integration policy.

On July 8, 1993, the Austrian Parliament adopted amendments pertaining to special education and social integration of children. (Features of this legislation are discussed below).

In order to co-ordinate special educational measures at the regional level, certain special schools are to serve as 'Centres of Special Education'. They are to ensure the transfer of special education competence, the quality of instruction, counselling of teachers and parents, as well as supporting human and material resources.

3. Identification, Assessment and Orientation

In order to follow special education courses, children must be physically or mentally handicapped. Before being enrolled in special education, a child must make full use of all pedagogical possibilities in general education (remedial courses, counselling, etc.) Parents, educators, therapists and doctors may give an opinion on the child's ability. Experts may also be invited to give parents detailed information on their child as a kind of "remedial committee". Parents then decide if they wish to send their child to an elementary school adapted to the child's needs or a special school. The School Board is to assist parents in finding the most appropriate school nearest to the child's home. If an elementary school cannot be found which meets the child's needs, the child is nevertheless required to attend a special school. Children with disabilities may also complete their first year of compulsory education at the pre-school stage of an elementary school.

4. Age Range Covered by Legislation

Primary and Secondary are covered. See details in the legislation section.)

5. Integration

See above as related to legislation Integration is to be primarily seen in relation to the pilot projects designed to develop new curricula and teaching methods.

6. Financing of Education for Special Needs

School maintenance is based upon the School Development Programme. The programme is concerned with the maintenance of school facilities as well as the promotion of handicapped students. The actual financing of schools is determined by the budget of the Federal Ministry of Education and the Arts and the budget of the Federal Ministry for Economic Affairs. Allocations are made on a flexible basis depending upon need.

7. Curriculum Entitlement

Curriculum is to be tailored to a child's specific handicap(s). Special schools, (Sonderschule) are to have a flexible and differentiated curriculum. The syllabus is based upon the syllabus for compulsory school adapted to children's needs. An essential aim of the special school in the lower secondary bracket is preparation for vocational education, therefore, subjects as history, geography, science as well as technical and trade instruction assume special importance.

In elementary schools that have integrative curricula, classes should be formed with particular consideration for the children with special needs. The District School Board decides whether children should be instructed according to a different syllabus. The School Conference decides what subjects may be taught according to the syllabus of another class level. Any deviation in the child's prescribed class level must be recorded in the school reports. Pupil advancement is also determined by the school conference. Counselling sessions and individual appointments are to be scheduled concerning integrated teaching.

8. Post 16 Years—Vocational Education

Information unavailable.

9. Teacher Training

Training for "integration teachers" is offered by the teacher training academies (Padagogische Academien) and Teacher-further-training-institutes (Padagogische Institute). Generally it is special education teachers, trained for a specific type of disability that are involved in integration.

The pilot project "Supporting Teachers" included approximately 3,000 pupils at mainstream schools receiving integrative special education.

BAHRAIN

1. Extent and Nature of Legislation

Legislation pertaining to Special Education is included in the Ministry of Education March 29, 1986 decision on plans and programmes. Special education is offered throughout all stages of education, including Adult Education. Services provided for special and regular classes should be equitable. The aim of special education classes is to offer the same learning environment for all pupils and to promote learning. There are approximately 10-12 pupils in special education classes, school hours are approximately 15-18 per week.

2. Responsibility and Organisation

In the Ministry of Education, the Commission for Special Education has the responsibility to differentiate between the different categories of disability, to create rehabilitation programmes and to co-ordinate their work with other commissions.

The International Centre of Bahrain was created in 1979 for the purpose of integrating disabled persons into society. The centre promotes the elimination of discrimination of disabled persons.

3. Identification, Assessment and Orientation

A commission made up of the school director, social assistant, special education teacher and class teacher under the supervision of the division for special education and the Persian Gulf University will decide if a student is to be admitted into special education classes.

4. Age Range Covered by Legislation

Information unavailable.

5. Integration

On a policy level the aim of special education is not only to offer the same learning environment but also to encourage, as far as possible the Progressive Integration of disabled persons.

The Educational Technology Centre at the Ministry of Education contributes to this integration by producing and developing various Teaching Aids which support disabled in regular classroom activities.

6. Financing of Education for Special Needs

The State provides all the financial requirements for educational services. These services are free for all at all educational levels, thus eliminating the need for special funding.

7. Curriculum Entitlement

The aim is to provide the same learning curriculum for all pupils and students and to promote as far as possible the integration of the disabled by providing compensating facilities.

However centres such as the Blind Institute and the Hope House Centre are compelled to have their own curriculum addressing their own special needs. The Ministry tries to make this curriculum as equitable as possible.

8. Post 16 Years—Vocational Education

The Ministry of Labour and Social Affairs runs the National Vocational Centre, now known as the Bahrain Training Institute in Essa Town. This Institute offers vocational training from the basis core level up to the national diploma level.

In addition to the training offered by the Blind Institute and the Hope House Centre, mentioned above, various societies such as the Red Crescent, Womens Societies and National Clubs have their own Voluntary Training Programmes for the disabled.

9. Teacher Training

Information unavailable.

BARBADOS

1. Extent and Nature of Legislation

The Special Education Act of 1981 specifics that when a child reaches compulsory school age and is perceived to be disabled, the matter should be reported to the Minister who will see to examining the child. Children in need for special education are defined as those who are blind, deaf, educationally subnormal, or physically handicapped . According to the child's disability, the child will be put in a special school. If the child develops a handicap during the course of general education, he may be removed to a special school. A child compulsory school age amy be exempted from compulsory attendance if the child is receiving special education of if the child is unable to attend school because of sickness or other sufficient cause.

2. Responsibility and Organisation

The Minister may make regulations in order to specify, in respect to public institutions, the curriculum of study and examinations. He also defines the categories of pupils requiring special education and prescribes cases in which fees may be charged at public institutions for such care. The Minister also defines school inspection.

3. Identification, Assessment and Orientation

Information unavailable.

4. Age Range Covered by Legislation

Pre-primary, primary, secondary and vocational are covered

5. Integration

Information unavailable.

6. Financing of Education for Special Needs

Information unavailable.

7. Curriculum Entitlement

Information unavailable.

8. Post 16 Years—Vocational Education

Information unavailable.

9. Teacher Training

Information unavailable.

BELGIUM

1. Extent and Nature of Legislation

The July 6, 1970 Act.

The law of 6 July 1970 passed by Parliament deals specifically with special education. The special education system is meant for children and young people who need special education because of their pedagogical needs and possibilities. It helps them develop their physical, mental and social skills in order to prepare them for a family life and/or a job in the regular or a sheltered environment. The Act has two basic principles:

1) As a general rule a child should attend a regular classroom and attendance at a special school would constitute an exception. Therefore, The Act gives only a pedagogical definition of 'handicap' and not a medical, psychological or psychometric one. In this way the 1970 Act made an important departure with the former philosophy in the way it stressed an educational rather than a therapeutic approach for ameliorating disability. Children are defined as 'handicapped' in terms of the (un)ability of regular education to deal with pupils with extra educational and didactical needs. It more or less depends on the adaption degree of the regular school whether a child is called 'handicapped' or not in terms of the 1970 Act. Special education is a right but entry into a special classroom must be justified by a comprehensive examination conducted by a guidance service independent of the school.

2) Special education would be divided into eight types or pedagogical settings in order to meet the needs of the individual student. These types are described in the June 28, 1978 decree.

The principle on which this legislation is based, says that integration into a normal life is considered to be a general aim of the system. Therefore, the principle of integration of pupils with a handicap into normal education is explicitly included in article 5b of the Act.

The June 28, 1978 decree.

In this decree the different types of special education are described. Each of them is characterised by its own target objective and its own didactic content, teaching methods and organisation, and is adapted to the specific educational needs of the pupils for whom it is intended.

Type 1 is intended to meet the educational needs of children and young people with a mild mental handicap. It is not organised as nursery-school.

Type 2 is intended for pupils with moderate or serious mental handicap.

Type 3 is intended for pupils with serious emotional and behavioural problems.

Type 4 is intended for pupils with a physical handicap.

Type 5 is intended for pupils who have to stay in a hospital or other medical institutions for a long period of time.

Type 6 is designed for pupils with a visual handicap (the blind and partially sighted).

Type 7 is designed for pupils with an auditory handicap (the deaf and hard of hearing).

Type 8 is suitable for children with serious learning disabilities which cannot be explained by a mental disorder. It is not organised at nursery or secondary school levels.

Regardless of the types of special education, there are four forms of teaching within special secondary education. These differ mainly as far as their objectives go.

Form 1 aims to contribute to providing an active and worthwhile life for those who, because of the seriousness of their handicap, are unable to take part in active work life even in a sheltered workshop. This form of training can be organised for types of education 2,3,4,6 and 7 and lasts for at least four years. Pupils are taught to live as independently as possible in a sheltered environment.

Form 2 can also be organised for types of education 2,3,4,6 and 7. In addition to general and social learning, it also provides work training in order to enable pupils to integrate into a social and work environment (sheltered workshop). The training lasts for at least four years and is divided into two phases. Practical training courses outside the school are also organised.

Form 3 provides pupils with general and social training plus professional training. It can be organised for types of education 1,3,4,6 and 7. The pupils are prepared for integration into a normal social and work environment. The training is comparable with standard professional education and lasts five years.

Form 4 provides secondary education similar to the general, technical, vocational or artistic curriculum of regular full-time secondary education and is also structured in the same way.

2. Responsibility and Organisation

"The Ministry of Education and the Ministry of Welfare are the two bodies that deal with disabled persons.

For the Flemish Community the 'Flemish Fund for the Social Integration of Handicapped Persons' was established by the June 27, 1990 Act. The objectives of the Fund are to provide for the services that handicapped people need, except education. For instance the Fund subsidises initiatives to integrate handicapped people in the regular work environment, provides for professional education and finances different residential and semi-residential institutions and mobile assistance services for handicapped people. Though the subsidisation for both domains is separated, schools for special education and institutions subsidised by the Ministry of Welfare often cooperate. The Ministry of Education is responsible for the financing and subsidising of schools, but in the case of public education it also finances the residential and semi-residential institutions that care for the pupils after school. The discussion is going on whether or not these institutions come under the responsibility of the Ministry of Welfare. In the Flemish Community, special education is a service integrated within the general administration and inspectorate at nursery school, primary and secondary levels.

In the French Community a specific special education administration and a specific pedagogic advisory staff is established.

3. Identification, Assessment and Orientation

In principle, special education is only provided to pupils whose needs are insufficiently cared for by the education resources available within regular education. For a child to be enrolled in a special school, two documents from a counseiling service (a psycho-medical-social centre) or, in the case of some disabilities, an authorised medical specialist need to be obtained.

A) a certificate stating that a child is not able to benefit from a regular classroom and should attend a special school with the indication of the appropriate level and type of special education and, if applicable, the form of teaching within special secondary eduction.

B) a document which justifies this certificate and contains a synthesis of the psychological, medical, social and pedagogical examination. The counselling service plays mainly an advisory role; the parents ultimately make the decision. Special education is a right, never an obligation.

4. Age Range Covered by Legislation

Special schools are available at the nursery school (age 2-6 years) primary (6-13 years) and secondary level (13-21 years). In special cases, depending on the type of education, these age limits can be extended. The reason why some pupils stay in special education after their 21st anniversary is the lack of possibilities to get a (sheltered) job or home.

5. Integration

The 1970 Act allows a pupil enrolled in a special school to attend regular classes; such an attendance may be full-time in the Flemish community, but only part-time in the French community.

Integrated education started on an experimental basis in 1980.

In 1983, it was officially organised for children with a motor, visual and hearing impairment (types 4,6 and 7 of special education). It is meant for those pupils who will be integrated from special education into normal education with a good change of success provided they are offered some help by special education in terms of educational (e.g. braille) and/or para-medical (e.g. physiotherapy, speech therapy) support.

In accordance with the Act on integrated education of March 11. 1986 a broader application has recently been given to integrated education.

The Minister of Education of the Flemish Community issued a circular letter on August 30, 1994, the basic innovations of which are;

— extension to all the types of special education,

— different forms of integrated education: not only the full-time integration is possible but also forms of temporary (not the whole school year) and partial (not the whole programme of regular education),

— extension to the level of higher education (academic education not included),

— the acceptance of the 'equivalence' principle: this means that although some pupils cannot follow all the lessons of the regular programme as a result of their disability they can graduate from a programme by replacing lessons approved by the inspector.

— differentiation within the types of special education on the basis of the nature and seriousness of the child's disability which varies with the nature and amount of additional aid (both financial and educational and/or paramedical).

Admission to integrated education requires a certificate of acceptance, just as special education does. This certificate is based on an integration plan which is necessary for integration. It is the result of consultation between all parties involved:- the pupil or his/ her parents;- the regular school;- the school for special education;- the counselling centres which counsel both schools. This plan is regularly evaluated and adapted, and if necessary, updated. Pupils referred to types 1,3 and 8 of special education can only benefit from the additional aid provided by integrated education when they already attended special education for one year.

In the French community, it has been claimed that a child has to be enrolled in a special school first, in order to benefit from the Act.

In the Flemish community, 933 pupils attended integrated education in the 1993-94 school year (391 types 4, 173 type 6, 26 type 6 (braille), 343 types 7).

In the French community, about 300 "official" instances of pupils are integrated into regular schools.

6. Financing of Education for Special Needs

Schools of regular or special education are financed/subsidised by the government by means of wage subsidies and operation subsidies. The number of pupils are the basis to calculate the operation subsidies and the amount of periods to organise the lessons. On this basis the school can employ personnel. For pupils who attend integrated education, a supplementary number of periods and an extra sum of operation subsidies is attributed to the school for special education in order to organise the additional aid in the regular school. Recently the Minister of Education worked out an experimental system of additional periods in order to help pupils with extra educational needs in the regular school. These additional efforts are made on the nursery and primary school levels.

7. Curriculum Entitlement

Depending on the type of special education, the curriculum is more or less similar to the curriculum of regular education. However, there is a lot of freedom for individual schools to have a curriculum of their own, taking their specific school population into account.

Type 1 of special education is meant to impart elementary knowledge and skills necessary for their vocational training and with the aim of integrating them into the normal social and professional environment. For pupils who attend the *Type 2* of special education, the accent lies on social training, the improvement of the ability to take care of themselves, psychomotor skills and, on the secondary school level, an adapted vocation education. The aim is to prepare those children and young people for a sheltered social and working environment.

Type 3 of special education, adapted to the needs of children and young people with severe emotional and behavioural problems, also focuses on orthopedagogic and psychotherapeutic measures. It also depends upon the mental abilities of the pupils, on how close their curriculum fits in with the programme of regular education.

In *Types 4, 6 and 7* for education with a physical or sensorial disability, the curriculum focusses on the direct effects of the disability (e.g. braille and walking with a stick for the blind). In these types of special education, the mental abilities of pupils play a role in determining whether or not they can attend to a curriculum similar to the one of regular education.

In general, pupils of *Type 5* of special education attend the most important subjects out of the programme of their 'home school'.

The type of special education in which the curriculum is most similar to that of regular education is *Type 8,* meant for children with severe learning problems. Only the didactic methods, the composition of the group and the way to handle these children vary.

Special basic education (nursery school and primary school) comprises 28 periods a week.

On the level of special secondary education, not the types but the forms of teaching determine the content of the curriculum.

Form 1 aims at giving the pupils a social training in order to prepare them to a life in a sheltered environment (at home, in an outpatients' clinic or another sheltered community). The educational situations are connected with real life events intended to increase the ability to do things independently and to improve social, communicational and sensorial-motor skills. 30 periods a week are provided in that purpose.

Form 2 special secondary education gives pupils a chance to learn some vocational skills in order to find a job in a sheltered workshop. Beyond a general and social training (16 periods a week), they also get vocational education (16 periods a week). Practical training courses outside the school are also organised).

In *Form 3,* training is comparable to regular vocational training. The difference between special and regular education lies in the more individual approach concerning the subjects, teaching objectives and duration. It prepares to an integration into a normal social and work environment.

Form 4 provides secondary education with the same curriculum as general, technical, artistic or vocational training. It is only meant for youngsters with a normal mental ability.

8. Post 16 Years—Vocational Education

Mentioned above.

9. Teacher Training

The 1970 Act required that provision be made for further training for special education teachers. However, a comprehensive system of teacher training in this area has not been established. One reason is that it has not been decided whether a teacher working in special education should be a specialist or should be able to teach in regular as well as in special schools. The required qualifications have also not been defined.

In the French community, in December 1990, a Decree established both in-service education and continuing education. In the Flemish community, a decree in 1989 made regulations regarding the permanent training of teachers at various levels in the school system. Recently, as part of the discussion about broadening the range of care within regular schools for children with special needs, the Flemish Minister expressed the intention to change teacher training in the near future.

BRAZIL

1. Extent and Nature of Legislation

Law 5692/71 on Special Education, Basis and Guidelines, specifies in its article 9 that students with mental and physical disabilities and gifted students will receive special treatment in accordance with the regulations elaborated by the Council of Education. The national policy on Special Education contains a set of objectives aiming at guaranteeing the education of students with special needs.

The Federal Constitution of 1988 provides for the rehabilitation and vocational training of the disabled in order to integrate them into society. The Constitution stipulates that the State will promote the integration of the disabled through rehabilitation programmes in education and labour. The law affirms the right of the disabled to education, health, labour, leisure etc.

Chapter III, Article 206 states that "education will be administered according to the following principles:

1) equality of access to school,
2) the freedom to learn, teach, freedom of thought and knowledge,
3) pluralism of ideas and pedagogical approaches, coexistence of public and private institutions."

The 1993 "Ten Year Plan for the Education of All" supports the policy goal of equal access to education. Article 3 states that "the basic educational needs of persons with deficiencies requires special education. The need to define strategies which enable an equal access to education taking into consideration all kinds of deficiencies is an integral part of the education system."

2. Responsibility and Organisation

The Secretary of Special Education in the Ministry of Education and Sport, established by Law 8., 490 dated 19.11.92, has the responsibility for the development of special education in the whole country.

The Public Ministry (Ministerio Publico) and the Federal Public Administration (Administracao Publica Federal) is involved in social integration. The independent body, C.O.R.D.E. (Coordenadoria National para Integracao da Pessoa Portadora de Deficiencia) acts as a coordinating body.

3. Identification, Assessment and Orientation

Directives concerning the above is given by the Ministry of Education and Sport.

4. Age Range Covered by Legislation

The law provides for special education at the pre-school, primary and secondary level and vocational training.

5. Integration

Article 208, III, of the Federal Constitution specifies that the State must guarantee special education to people with disabilities preferably within the regular education system.

The 1992 document "National Integration Policy for Disabled Persons" developed by the C.O.R.D.E. states that integration into society is a fundamental goal for the disabled. Chapter 3 on the disabled states that the State is to "protect and integrate persons with disability." This is to be incorporated into the 1988 Constitution.

6. Financing of Education for Special Needs

Special Education is financed mainly by public, but also to some extent by private, sources.

Article 211 of the Constitution mention that the Union will organise and finance the Federal System of Education, and will support the Federal District and Municipalities technically and financially for the development of their educational systems.

7. Curriculum Entitlement

The programmes, projects and actions related to people with special educational needs are designed by a technical unit and then approved by the Federal State or the Municipal Government.

8. Post 16 Years—Vocational Education

Articles 7, 24, 37, 203 of the Federal Constitution ensure that people with special needs have the same rights as others, and that they can fully exercise their rights as citizens and actively participate in labour life.

Law 5692/71 stated in Article that the general objective of the education system must be the preparation for labour life and a conscience of citizenship.

9. Teacher Training

Teacher training for Special Education is governed by the Federal Constitution, Law 5, 692/71, and by specific guidelines of the Federal Council of Education.

Middle Level: After an initial three years period of training as regular teachers one may follow an additional one year specialisation on Special Education.

High Level: Some institutions also offer teachers and specialists specific courses on Special Education on a higher level.

Teacher training on Special Education may also be provided through the National Programme on distance education.

BULGARIA

1. Extent and Nature of Legislation

The March 1992 Education Act adopted by the National Assembly stipulates that special schools are established for pupils who need special care including pupils with chronic diseases, injuries or mental and physical disabilities. The Act also provides for "convalescence" schools, specialised secondary boarding schools and vocational boarding schools for children with mental and physical disorders such as respiratory and cardiovascular diseases, stomach and kidney disease.

2. Responsibility and Organisation

Admission of pupils in special school is determined by the Medical and Pedagogical Board. The members of the board are chosen by the Ministry of Health and the Ministry of Education and Science.

Selection and admission of pupils into the convalescence schools is carried out with the assistance of the Ministry of Health, the Ministry of Education and Science and the Ministry of Work and Social Affairs. A child is not required to stay more than three years at a convalescence school unless the child chooses to do so and the case is approved by the Pedagogical Board.

3. Identification, Assessment and Orientation

The regional medico- pedagogical commissions are composed of experts who identify and evaluate children with special needs. These commissions are subordinated to a national commission. The different commissions are specialised according to type of disability.

4. Age Range Covered by Legislation

Children are allowed to continue their education in professional schools if their health is sufficiently good. In schools for the mentally retarded students are enrolled up to the eighth grade level. At the end of their schooling, these students receive a proficiency certificate and are entitled to receive a professional qualification in a vocational school. They do not have the right to progress further. Children with eyesight or hearing difficulties may complete secondary general or vocational education.

5. Integration

Integration is partial. In pre-school and primary regular schools there are special classes.

6. Financing of Education for Special Needs

The Ministry of Science and Education fiances about 90 per cent of the education of children with special needs. There are also some non-governmental organisations which contribute to the financing, but their contribution is limited.

7. Curriculum Entitlement

The curricula are elaborated by groups of specialists and then validated by the Ministry of Science and Education. For every special school and according to the type of school (primary, secondary or vocational) there exist specific methodological programmes.

8. Post 16 Years—Vocational Education

Further education in professional schools is provided to students between 16 and 18-19 years old.

9. Teacher Training

At the University 'St. Kliment Ohridski' and the University of Blagoevgrad there exist departments for the training of special education teachers. The studies last for 5 years and are related to different categories of disability.

CANADA

1. Extent and Nature of Legislation

In 1981, the Canadian Constitution containing the Charter of Human Rights was proclaimed. The Charter guarantees certain basic human rights and freedoms. The Charter prompted growing awareness for accepting the disabled in society.

2. Responsibility and Organisation

In New Brunswick, Bill 85, an Act to amend the schools was proclaimed. The Minister of Education and school boards are responsible for the education of all children. The Auxiliary Classes Act and the section of The Schools' Act which allowed school board to refuse certain children admission to the public school system have been repeated. All children qualify equally for all educational programmes and services.

3. Identification, Assessment and Orientation

Bill 85 emphasises individual programming. It defines a special education programme as one which provides for services based on a student's individual needs rather than a categorisation of handicap. It requires schools to integrate. School boards are instructed to place exceptional pupils in the same classrooms as non-exceptional pupils as long as it is not detrimental to the needs of the child. A case must be made to remove an exceptional child from a regular class.

Exceptional children will receive special education programmes. While participating as much as possible in regular classes. If a child is not able to receive a special educational programme in a regular class, the Minister may provide such service at the child's home or an approved institution.

Parents are consulted in the process of a child's education in order to develop partnership between school officials, teachers and parents. Parents are encouraged to support and share information on the child.

4. Age Range Covered by Legislation

The Minister shall provide free school privileges for persons from three to twenty-one years including pupils receiving special education.

5. Integration

Integration is an integral part of Bill 85.

6. Financing of Education for Special Needs

The Provincial Department of Education is responsible for the development of policy and guidelines, and provides the funding to support programmes developed and facilitated by the local school district. There is a branch of the Department of Education Student Services that is required to support professional educators in the School Districts. The Department also integrates programmes with other government departments both federal and provincial.

7. Curriculum Entitlement

Information unavailable.

8. Post 16 Years—Vocational Education

Information unavailable.

9. Teacher Training

Information unavailable.

CAPE VERDE

1. Extent and Nature of Legislation

The law of 29 December (Chapter 1, Article 4) states that the State will promote equal access for all citizens and equal opportunity for educational success.

Article 32 deals specifically with Special Education. The law stipulates that young people with mental or learning deficiencies benefit from appropriate educational provision and initiatives that will permit their rehabilitation and social and educational integration.

The goal of special education is to provide an equitable education to young people from at risk social environments, develop to the maximum the mental capacity of those mentally deficient, support at risk families, support student's emotional equilibrium, reduce limitations caused by a student's deficiency and prepare the student for integration to active life.

2. Responsibility and Organisation

The Ministry of Education, in co-ordinating with other state agencies will create centres for young people with deficiencies. These centres will support students' social and professional integration and offer assistance concerning the educational system and alternative education.

3. Identification, Assessment and Orientation

Information unavailable.

4. Age Range Covered by Legislation

Information unavailable.

5. Integration

The integration of young persons with deficiencies into regular classes will be promoted in situations which support the student's learning, taking into consideration assistance from teachers.

6. Financing of Education for Special Needs

Information unavailable.

7. Curriculum Entitlement

Special education is to be adapted to the needs of each group. Special education may take place in separate institutions. The curriculum of special education in accordance with the obligatory school curriculum may be adapted to the needs of the student.

8. Post 16 Years—Vocational Education

Information unavailable.

9. Teacher Training

Special education teachers and elementary school teachers are defined as those persons who obtain qualification in the curricula for special schools.

CHILE

1. Extent and Nature of Legislation

The Decree of the Ministry of Education of April 3, 1990 considers that it is the State's obligation to guarantee the right to an education for all citizens. It is the responsibility of the Ministry of Education to improve quality and modernise the educational system. According to these principles, there is an initiative to better the education of young persons with intellectual, sensory or motor deficiencies. The general objective is that disabled persons should have equal opportunities to live like other citizens.

Article 1 of the 1990 Law states that dating from the 1990 school year, disabled students will be integrated into regular schools at the pre-primary, primary and secondary level. Disability is characterised according to the following deficiencies: intellectual, visual, auditory, and motor.

2. Responsibility and Organisation

The Ministry of Education, Health, Labour Social Welfare and Justice are involved in the prevention, rehabilitation, and integration of disabled persons.

The regional secretary of the Ministry of Education is required to implement integration projects, taking into consideration the different categories of disability, acceptance of disabled children in school, the existence of trained personnel and school resources. For this purpose, a committee of persons supporting the integration project will be convened with the objective of establishing the conditions that will guide the project, taking into consideration the specialists necessary and the gradual orientation of disabled students into their scholastic orientations and working life.

3. Identification, Assessment and Orientation

In Law No. 19.284 of 1994, Article 7 states that the Commissions for the prevention of disability (COMPIN) of the Ministry of Health or other public or private institutions will carry out the diagnosis and evaluation of people with disabilities.

The characterisation of a student's deficiency according to the above categories will be established by a transdisciplinary team from the Ministry of Education's Diagnostic Centre. The team produces a qualitative report that specifies the various areas concerning student's development. The team is to promote the disabled student's social integration, assist in maximising the student's potential, ensure that the student is no more than two years older than the other students in his/her class, assist in creating a positive attitude in integrating the disabled child into the school community, and attempt to eliminate barriers in the child's education.

4. Age Range Covered by Legislation

Legislation applies to pre-school, primary and secondary education.

5. Integration

Law No. 19.284 establishes the conditions for the social integration of people with disabilities. Article 27 mentions the right of people with special needs to have access to education in regular schools. Teaching will be provided in special schools only when the type and/or degree of disability impedes the integration to regular courses.

An integration project may be realised according to the following three possibilities:1) Special education courses in parallel to regular classes in city and urban schools for children with mental, sensory or motor deficiencies with the assistance of special educators, 2) Integration workshops in regular schools for children with mental, sensory or motor deficiencies with the assistance of special educators, 3) Common courses at the pre-primary, primary and secondary level in urban and rural schools for children with mild or moderate disabilities.

6. Financing of Education for Special Needs

Information unavailable.

7. Curriculum Entitlement

The Educational authorities goal is to teach the common school curriculum to disabled students adapting it to the child's physical, intellectual or sensory needs. The education authority is to develop methods and define resource to implement the integration programme, and develop an appropriate approach to pedagogy and evaluation.

If significant adaptations are made to the common curriculum, details must be provided in the student's record and a copy made for the class' record. The student's record must include an extract of the procedures used for the student's evaluation. The results of the student's evaluation and the student's promotion to the following grade are to be registered in the student's report card and in the class' record. The student will be promoted to the following grade if there is no evidence to prove the contrary.

To retain a student in the same grade an interview must take place in cooperation with the head teacher and the special education teacher. If there is a disagreement between this professional team and the child's parents or guardians, the school principal will decide the matter.

The "Licencia de Education Media", secondary school degree, will be granted to the disabled student upon completion of the minimum scholastic requirements stated in the Constitutional Educational Law," Ley Organica Constitutional de Ensenanza". If a secondary school degree is not obtained, the student will receive a certificate accrediting the level of schooling achieved.

A student participating in an integrated course will be subject to review by the Diagnositc Centre to determine if they no longer need any kind of specialised assistance.

In Law No. 19.284, Article 4, it is mentioned that the State will conduct programmes for disabled persons in accordance with their specific needs. It further states, in Article 32, that the Ministry of Education will adapt the programmes to facilitate the integration into formal education or training of persons who, as a consequence of their disability, have not started or completed their compulsory education.

8. Post 16 Years—Vocational Education

In Law No. 19.284, of 1984; Articles 33 to 38, it is outlined that vocational education will be provided by the State in order to allow for integration into the labour market.

9. Teacher Training

Special education teachers are called into regular classes where there are disabled children for technical assistance. They are to co-ordinate their activities with the head teachers. In the absence of a special education teacher, the local school authority is to contact the Diagnostic Centre which will assume the responsibility for the progress and development of the disabled child.

CHINA

1. Extent and Nature of Legislation

Law of the Peoples Republic of China on the Protection of Disabled Persons (1990) states that:

— the state shall guarantee the right of a disabled person to an education;

— the state shall set up grants in order to assist poor and disabled students; and

— education of disabled persons shall be carried out according to physical and psychological needs.

Law of the people's Republic of China on Compulsory Education (1986) states that the government shall establish special schools or classes for children who are blind, deaf, mute or retarded.

2. Responsibility and Organisation

The Ministry of Education, the Ministry of Health, and the Ministry of Social Welfare are involved in the education of students with special needs. The Education Commission of the Provinces and the education bureaux of the countries are involved in implementing special education.

3. Identification, Assessment and Orientation

A team of experts from the Ministry of Education decides if a child should be placed in a special school, special courses in a regular school or in an ordinary class.

4. Age Range Covered by Legislation

Primary and Secondary education are covered.

5. Integration

Regular primary and secondary schools must admit disabled students who are able to participate in regular classes. Parents may appeal to the school authorities if their child is not admitted.

6. Financing of Education for Special Needs

Information unavailable.

7. Curriculum Entitlement

Information unavailable.

8. Post 16 Years—Vocational Education

Information unavailable.

9. Teacher Training

Information unavailable.

COLOMBIA

1. Extent and Nature of Legislation

Chapter One of the Colombian Constitution states that "all persons are born equal under the law, and will receive equal protection and equal treatment by the authorities so as to benefit from equal rights and opportunities without any kind of discrimination..." The State, in particular, "will especially protect those persons who because of their economic, physical or mental condition, find themselves in a situation of difficulty."

Article 67 states that "education is a personal right and a public service..." Article 68 states that "the education of persons with physical or mental limitations, or exceptional capacities, is the special responsibility of the State."

On 22 January, 1976, Decree number 088 was passed by the Colombian Congress regarding the reorganisation of the Colombian educational system and the Ministry of Education.

Article 5 defines Special Education as designed for persons who have physical, mental, emotional, and social deficiencies or persons who have special learning difficulties. Special Eduction will be integrated into formal or non-formal education. The Government will establish adequate provisions, stimulate private initiative and the training of special education teachers, as well as to promote research in Special Education.

The Colombian Congress passed Law no. 24 in 1988. Article 38 states that pilot projects should be conducted in relation to special education.

In Law No. 115 of February 1994, Law on Education in Colombia, Articles 46-49 are specifically linked with he rights of people with special needs and gifted persons.

2. Responsibility and Organisation

The Ministry of Education is primarily responsible for the education of persons with special needs. The National Institute for the Blind, INCI and The National Institute for the Deaf, INSOR are parts of the Ministry of Education.

3. Identification, Assessment and Orientation

Information unavailable.

4. Age Range Covered by Legislation

Information unavailable.

5. Integration

The social and academic integration of people with disability is the responsibility of the State, the family and the society as mentioned in Law 115 of the Constitution.

6. Financing of Education for Special Needs

Information unavailable.

7. Curriculum Entitlement

The Division of Curriculum Programming and Design is to establish the curriculum for special education and to certify special education teachers.

8. Post 16 Years—Vocational Education

Information unavailable.

9. Teacher Training

Information unavailable.

COSTA RICA

1. Extent and Nature of Legislation

The "Ley Fundamental de Education" Fundamental Educational Law, covers all national education including special education. Policy concerning Special Education was approved in 1987 by the Superior Educational Council, "Consejo Superior de Education" in the publication: National Prevention of Deficiency and Disability Policies and Integration and Rehabilitation, "Politicas Nationales de Prevencion de la Deficiencia y de Rehabilitation Integral".

Chapter two of this document deals specifically with Special Education. Special Education is oriented "to maximise the development of the person with special needs, which implies self-esteem, independence, and integration into society and work."

Special Education is defined to be the responsibility of the school, the family and the community.

2. Responsibility and Organisation

The Ministry of Education is responsible by law for the instruction of all persons. The Department of Special Education deals in particular with the education for persons with special needs. This Department is organised in three different sections:

1) *School-based education* (Educación Escolarizada) which is divided into seven units (Asesorias): Learning Disabilities, Mental Retardation, Emotional and Behavioural Disturbances, Language and Hearing Impairments, Multiple Handicap, Visual Impairments and Giftedness. Its main goals are both towards special schools, and integrated services and classes in regular schools for pupils with special needs.

2) *Community-based education* (Educación Comunitaria). Special programmes for disabled persons are organised and run by the community with technical support from the Ministry of Education.

3) *Vocational development*. Vocational-based programmes are implemented at high-schools or in community educational institutions for persons (14 to 18 years old) with mild and moderate disabilities.

3. Identification, Assessment and Orientation

Identification of persons with special needs is to be seen within a national plan for the prevention of disabilities. This action usually takes place at hospitals and health centers. Infants with severe disabilities (deafness, blindness, cerebral palsy and retarded psychomotor development) are referred to special schools for attention and care.

Evaluation is to be used as the point of departure for determining individualised education for persons with special needs. The evaluation will be conducted by qualified personnel (teachers, and other professionals when necessary) familiar with the child's environment.

It will include an assessment of the child's social, emotional as well as academic level, and be complemented by information on the child's socio-cultural and economic background.

The placement of a child in a special school or self-contained classroom will be conducted by a team of specialists in conjunction with hospital centres, called the Special Education Regional Bureau (Asesoria Regional de Educación Especial).

4. Age Range Covered by Legislation

Pre-school, primary, secondary and vocational education are covered.

5. Integration

The concept of no-discrimination has initiated the creation of services designed to integrate disabled children into regular schools. At present, a commission has been appointed by the vice-Minister of Education to write up the policies and procedures for the implementation of the integration principle in the regular school.

6. Financing of Education for Special Needs

Special education administered in special schools, in regular schools or in other institutions serving persons with disabilities is financed by the Ministry of Education.

7. Curriculum Entitlement

The curriculum for special education should promote the maximum development of persons with special needs and be tailored to each student's needs and sociocultural background.

The Department of Special Education is responsible for designing, developing and implementing the curriculum approved by the Superior Council for Education (Consejo Superior de Educación). The aim of the curriculum is to reach full integration of pupils with special needs.

8. Post 16 Years—Vocational Education

Vocational training based on community rehabilitation is given when the student reaches the IV Cycle of Special Education. Because this modality of education started this year (1994) there are few students enrolled.

9. Teacher Training

Since 1974, the training of special education teachers is the responsibility of the universities. At present the training of special education teachers has a general approach with an emphasis on integration at the bachelor level. There used to be a specialisation in the areas of mental retardation, communicative disorders, learning disabilities, emotional and behavioural disturbances and visual impairments.

Today there are post-grade studies in mental retardation, multiple handicaps and rehabilitation, at the levels of Licenciatura and Master's Degree.

CUBA

1. Extent and Nature of Legislation

The Ministerial Resolution No. 13/85 states that the Cuban Constitution establishes in its 50th Article, Chapter 4 on Rights, Obligations and Fundamental Guarantees that all citizens have the right to an education.

The Special Education sub-system is designed for children, adolescents and young persons who possess mental or physical deficiencies. The goal of special education is to integrate these persons into social life.

Ministerial Resolution 112/76 states that as a part of the movement to perfect the system of national education, it is necessary to draw attention to children with disabilities in primary schools. In particular, it is necessary to create special schools for children who are not able to follow the regular school curriculum. This resolution authorised the creation of schools for the mentally retarded in 1976/1977.

Ministerial Resolution 112/76 also authorises the creation of special education classes in regular schools under the supervision of the school director. These special education classes will be created in *areas where there are no special schools.*

The Ministerial Resolution No. 562/80 authorises the creation of special schools for blind children at the primary and pre-primary level in the province of Villa Clara starting in 1980-81. Prior to 1980 there was only one school for the blind on the national level. An associated resolution creates seventeen more schools for the visually impaired.

Another Ministerial Resolution creates special schools for the hearing impaired, children with language difficulties and children with behavioural problems.

2. Responsibility and Organisation

The Law-Decree No. 67 of the 19th of April 1983, of the Central State Administration Organisation, establishes that The Ministry of Public Health is the Organisation in charge to direct, execute and control the application of state policy concerning the disabled.

Article 70 of the same law establishes that the education of disabled children is primarily the responsibility of the Ministry of Education in conjunction with other authorities except for higher education. The Cuban Association of the Physically Disabled is to co-ordinate at the provincial level the inscription of children with physical and motor difficulties into local schools.

3. Identification, Assessment and Orientation

The Centre for Orientation and Diagnosis is responsible for the identification of a child's disability. They determine if a child is able to attend an educational institution and in all cases, propose a study plan. There are two kinds of study plan: "A General Polytechnic on Labour Education" or one of the specialisations of special education. Children with severe disabilities who are not able to attend special school will be evaluated by the MINISAP, a medical-psychopedagogic institution. This centre communicates its results to the Orientation Centre.

Pilot projects will be undertaken for children with severe physical disabilities so that they may be taught by special education teachers at home.

4. Age Range Covered by Legislation

Pre-school, primary and secondary education are covered.

5. Integration

The school director, teachers and staff in a school where there exist special education courses should promote the integration of disabled children into the normal school life including participation in all cultural and recreational activities.

6. Financing of Education for Special Needs

Information unavailable.

7. Curriculum Entitlement

Information unavailable.

8. Post 16 Years—Vocational Education

Information unavailable.

9. Teacher Training

The selection of special education teachers will take place in the months of May and June. Special education teachers will be selected among the nations' best teachers and will follow a special training course conducted by the School for the Formation of Special Education Teachers.

The Provincial Department for General and Special Education in the month of June will run a seminar for all teachers in schools where there are special education courses. The seminar will contain preparation in school organisation for the mentally handicapped, interpreting the diagnosis from the Centre for Orientation and Diagnosis, learning methodology according to each grade, and school administration.

DENMARK

1. Extent and Nature of Legislation

A fundamental principle in Danish educational policy is that everyone regardless of sex, social and geographical origins, physical and mental handicap should have the same access to education and training. This principle influenced the establishment of the (Folkeskole) comprehensive basic school in 1975.

Chapter 2 of the Act on the Folkeskole, Consolidation Act No. 509 of 1 August, 1994 states that "Special education and other special education assistance shall be given to children whose development requires special consideration or support." The basic idea of the new law is *education differentiation*. That means an education adjusted according to the options and needs of the individual student.

Reform of Danish educational policy has been combined with normalisation of the conditions of the handicapped in all walks of life.

Legislation since 1990 has focused on three basic principles: 1) normalisation, an effort to put the handicapped on an equal footing with other members of society 2) decentralisation, whereby administrative responsibility has been transferred from the State to the countries and local authorities in order to promote grass-roots democracy and 3) integration (discussed separately).

2. Responsibility and Organisation

At each school there is a school board made up of 5-7 elected parents' representatives, 2 staff representatives and two pupil representatives, school chairman and head teacher. The school board shall lay down the criteria pertaining to the school, including: organisation and instruction, number of lessons for the pupils at each form level, elective subjects offered, special education at the school, and the distribution of pupils in classes.

The municipal council shall be responsible for the establishment of preschool classes and for the educational provision in the basic school and the 10th form, including special education and other special educational assistance for children and young people under 18 years of age, who live or have their residence in the municipality, and whose parents wish them to be enrolled in the Folkeskole. The municipal council shall furthermore be responsible for the provision of special educational assistance to children who have not yet started school. Outside of the municipalities of Copenhagen and Fredriksberg, it shall however be the responsibility of the county council to see to the special educational provision for children and youth under 18 years of age, who live or have their residence in the county, and whose development calls for special, extensive consideration or support. The county council shall also be responsible for the provision of special educational assistance to children who have not yet started school. (Consolidation Act, Chapter 3, Article 20.)

The municipal council shall submit a recommendation to the county council about special education and other special educational assistance to children who are enrolled in the schools of the municipality, if the development of the children calls for special extensive consideration or support. It is also the municipal council which shall recommend that special educational assistance be given to children who have not yet started school. The county council (in the municipalities of Copenhagen and Fredriksberg the municipal council) shall decide on the provision of special education and other special educational assistance to children enrolled in the pre-school class and in the 1st to 10th form levels, if the development of the children calls for special extensive consideration or support. It is also the county council, (in Copenhagen and Fredriksberg the municipal council) which shall decide on the provision of special educational assistance to children who have not yet started school. (Consolidation Act, Chapter 3, Article 21.)

The Ministry of Education and Research is the national body responsible for the education of disabled children.

3. Identification Assessment and Orientation

Chapter 2, Article 12 (2) of the Consolidation Act states that "referral to special education which is not of a temporary nature shall be made upon pedagogical and psychological counselling and upon consultation of the pupil and his/her parents."

There is a strong belief in the Danish system that each child should be treated case by case, not as a part of a group that has a similar handicap. Children are placed in school on the basis of their individual abilities; the traditional division of handicap into groups is considered "invalid and superfluous".

4. Age Range Covered by Legislation

Disabled students have the same right to attend compulsory schooling as other students, there is no legislation that specifically mentions them.

As mentioned above it is the county council (in the municipalities of Copenhagen and Fredriksberg the municipal council) that decide on the provision of special education and other special educational assistance to children enrolled in the pre-school class and in the 1st to 10th form levels, if the development of the children calls for special extensive consideration or support.

5. Integration

Integration is believed to be related to the principles of normalisation and decentralisation. However, it is thought that integration cannot be promoted directly through legislation. It may be impeded or prevented directly or indirectly by the manner in which legislation and public information are built. Normalisation and decentralisation are embodied in laws which pave the way for integration.

Special laws in relation to the handicapped have been repealed as part of the normalisation process. A number of Ministries for example which previously catered to the handicapped have been transferred to Ministries administering general legislation.

A Parliamentary resolution from 1969 is the only political decision which mentions integration: "the primary and lower secondary school should be expanded so as to provide for the teaching of handicapped pupils, to the greatest possible extent, in an ordinary school environment."

Following the principle of progressive integration, there are various degrees of integration in Denmark. This ranges from total integration where a child attends a regular class to segregation of children in a special institution. The degree of integration depends on the child's individual needs and the availability of teachers and resources.

6. Financing of Education for Special Needs

As countries have taken over the responsibility for special education within the Folkeskole, the financial, administrative and educational responsibilities are delegated to the local authorities.

Chapter 8, Article 49(2) of the Consolidation Act states that "expenditures relating to special education...shall rest with the countries, with the exception of an amount per pupil determined by the Minister of Education, which shall rest with the municipalities."

7. Curriculum Entitlement

Disabled students follow the same curriculum offered to all students in the Folkeskole. The school is required to provide special instruction and special education assistance. Educational assistance includes special instruction, stimulation and training, counselling and guidance and educational aids.

8. Post 16 Years—Vocational Education

Information unavailable.

9. Teacher Training

Information unavailable.

ECUADOR

1. Extent and Nature of Legislation

The Law on Education and Culture, Article 2, establishes that "all Ecuadorians have the right to an education and the obligation to participate actively in national education."

The Ministry of Education and Culture, in its Decree No. 1292, states that "The principle of integration is to orient special education considering that all disabled persons have the same right to an education as other citizens, and that the integration should promote as fast as possible an environment of normalisation."

Decree No. 257, Article 1 of the Ministry of Education and Culture approves the National Plan for Special Education. Article 2 determines that the Plan for Special Education be included in general educational planning and in the project "The Amelioration of School Quality" and in all other Ministry of Education projects.

2. Responsibility and Organisation

Article 2 of The Ministry of Education and Culture Decree 258 states that "The National Department of Special Education will plan, programme, execute co-ordinate, evaluate and put into effect the National Integration Plan". The Plan is to have started in 1991 and to continue for three years with an evaluation period.

3. Identification, Assessment and Orientation

The Centre of Psycho-pedagogical Diagnosis and Orientation is responsible for the evaluation of all handicapped persons.

4. Age Range Covered by Legislation

Information unavailable.

5. Integration

As part of the policy to promote integration, Ministerial Decree No. 258 affirms the principle of normalisation. Normalisation "establishes that exceptional persons, in order to be assimilated into society should not use or receive special services unless it is strictly necessary."

Further, "The principle of normalisation is effective in terms of the strategy of school integrction, permitting access to students with special educational needs in regular classes."

Total integration is intended to be complete insertion of the disabled student in the regular class, partial integration takes place when the student spends part of the day in the regular class complemented by special education classes.

6. Financing of Education for Special Needs

Information unavailable.

7. Curriculum Entitlement

Information unavailable.

8. Post 16 Years—Vocational Education

Information unavailable.

9. Teacher Training

Decree No. 258 of the Ministry of Education and Culture says that "The integration of disabled children into regular schools demands the implementation of new methodologies for classroom teachers with the support of special education teachers in order to improve the quality of teaching."

EL SALVADOR

1. Extent and Nature of Legislation

Decree No. 111 of November 1993 established the creation of a National Council for the Integral Support of persons with disabilities.

Article 56 of the El Salvadorian Constitution stipulates that: "All citizens of the Republic have the right and should receive basic education that enables them to comport themselves as useful citizens. The States will promote the formation of special schools."

The Law of the Salvadorian Institute for the Rehabilitation of Disabled Persons (ISRI) established in 1990 that the Institute would seek to rehabilitate the disabled with the goal of integrating them into society. The Institute is comprised of sections for the blind, mentally and physically handicapped, persons with learning and behavioural disabilities.

2. Responsibility and Organisation

The General Law on Education, Article 51 states that the Ministry of Education will co-ordinate public and private institutions in order to establish the policy, strategy structure and services that assist in the development of special education. Local authorities are further concerned with the implementation. The Ministries of Justice and Labour are involved in defining legislation for the handicapped.

In accordance with the General Law of Education, the National Council is responsible for building up support services for people with disabilities, for monitoring the actions, and for proposing policies concerning in this area.

3. Identification, Assessment and Orientation

Article 52 of the General Law states that the diagnosis and evaluation of disabled students will take place in special schools or by professionals hired by the child's family.

Article 52 also states that the education of disabled children will take place in special schools, however if a child is able to attend a regular school, he or she may do so with the assistance of a special education teacher.

In Special Education Schools, there are classes for the physically handicapped, the blind, hearing impaired, severely and moderately mentally retarded.

4. Age Range Covered by Legislation

Special education pertains to all persons of school age, covering basic education.

5. Integration

Integration is mainly mentioned in relation to the general goal of integrating the disabled into society. However, there is no specific policy on integration.

6. Financing of Education for Special Needs

There is no specific budget for Special Education. However, there is some financial support from some international organisations.

7. Curriculum Entitlement

Article 54 of the General law states that special education programmes should be adapted to children's aptitudes and needs at the appropriate grade level.

Special Education School are related to the official programmes of the regular schools.

Curriculum is defined as the organisation and systemisation of children's learning experiences in accordance with national and local realities, having as its central goal the integration of the disabled into the family, community and work.

8. Post 16 Years—Vocational Education

Emphasis is put on the importance of identifying the abilities, skills, expectations and wishes of the students disabilities in order to prepare an adequate vocational education.

9. Teacher Training

Article 53 states that the Ministry of Education is responsible for training special education teachers.

FINLAND

1. Extent and Nature of Legislation

New legislation on comprehensive and upper secondary schools came into force in 1985. The responsibility for special education for the moderately and severely mentally handicapped was transferred from the social authorities to the school authorities. This legislation stipulates that all children should attend ordinary schools as far as possible. The main part of children with special needs are integrated into ordinary schools and are provided special support when necessary.

2. Responsibility and Organisation

Comprehensive schools provide special education for children with special needs who cannot follow ordinary teaching. Part-time remedial teaching is available for students with minor learning impediments.

Most pupils with severe handicaps are taught in regular schools. These schools implement advanced objectives set for the comprehensive schools. All schools are supervised by the National Board for Education, but rehabilitation and health care are supervised by the Ministry of Social Affairs and Health.

The responsibility for initial education of pupils with special needs is shared by educational and social authorities. The education of the most severely disabled children is provided by teaching units of special care districts.

3. Identification, Assessment and Orientation

The municipality decides on the arrangement of special education and the grouping of the pupils takes place according to the pupil's needs.

The school board arranges the special education taking into consideration the options of parents and experts.

4. Age Range Covered by Legislation

Legislation covers the age range between 6 and 18 (general and vocational education.

5. Integration

Integration of students with special needs into regular schools is emphasised in the legislation on pupils with special needs.

6. Financing of Education for Special Needs

The state finances special schools which provide comprehensive school education to children of compulsory school age with all kinds of special needs.

7. Curriculum Entitlement

Children with special needs follow the comprehensive school curriculum. Teaching methods and curricula are geared to the pupil's abilities.

8. Post 16 Years—Vocational Education

Orientation to working life is offered in upper secondary school. Schools may devote two weeks to work orientation over a period of three years, Traineeships are provided in co-operation with employers.

9. Teacher Training

Teachers are trained in universities in Finland. Students can opt for special education on the advanced level. These studies qualify them as special class teachers or as special needs teachers.

FRANCE

1. Extent and Nature of Legislation

Article 1 of Law No. 75-534 of 30th June 1975 states that handicap should be prevented, that the education, care, professional training and orientation, right to work, the guarantee to minimum resources and the access to sports and leisure activities for disabled persons constitutes a national obligation. This has been further strengthened in the Circulars of 29 January 1982 and of 29 January 1983.

Article 5 of the same law states that disabled children will be admitted into regular classes or educational establishments under the jurisdiction of the Ministry of Education or Agriculture. These institutions are free of charge; all students are to be admitted despite their handicap.

The Ministry of Education Circular No. 76-156 of April 1976 states that only when a child is not able to attend regular classes will the child be enrolled in a special school. In regular schools, special education support, psycho-pedagogic support as well as transition classes are to be made available.

Since 1982 most of the important documents covering this area, issued by the Ministry of Social Affairs and Health and the Ministry of National Education, adopt the principle of integration. Another principle has been the decentralisation of administration. This concerns the Decree of 30th August 1985, and the Circular of 19th November and 27th December 1985.

The Law on the Orientation of Education of 10th July 1989 reaffirms the right to difference and the importance of integration within the education system.

2. Responsibility and Organisation

The Ministry of National Education is in charge of the education of all children including handicapped children. Specialised establishments are the responsibility of The Ministry of Social Affairs.

The integration of children in a CLIS integration course or in a regular school is often based on a 'Integration Project' involving the two Ministries mentioned above.

3. Identification, Assessment and Orientation

The Law of 30th June 1975 established in each local department a commission on special education (CDES). The decisions of the commission take into consideration the analysis performed by a 'technical team'. These decisions concern the estimated 'rate' of disability (established with respect to national standards), orientation, financial assistance and school orientation.

Since the Decree of 9th January 1989 pupils with special educational needs are divided into two categories; those officially registered as disabled (through a CDES), and those with disadvantages of social, familiar or cultural origine.

Circular 76-156 defines the Committees of "Circumscription" or Enrolment or the "CCPE". There are two committees, primary and pre-primary, and secondary. The Primary committee is made up of pedagogical psychiatric and medical experts, and school social workers.

Circular 91-302 of 18 November 1991 establishes a pedagogical committee which is responsible for integration at school. The committee is lead by the school head and persons from the special education section of the Ministry. The committee is to determine the conditions for integration in school.

Circular 91/304 of 18 November 1991 states that for a child to enter a CLIS integration course, the child must have a handicap recognised by one of the Special Education Commissions, gain permission from the CCPE and in some cases permission from the local department of education, CDES, that will partially finance the student's education.

Circular 93-248 of the 22 of July 1993 states that the interventions of all specialists who examined a child in order to determine the child's disability will be recorded in a confidential document. This document is intended to be an individualised record of the student's progress at school and the frequency of medical appointments.

4. Age Range Covered by Legislation

All levels are covered; pre-primary, primary, secondary, university and professional training.

5. Integration

Circular No. 82/2 of 1976 establishes a policy for the integration of disabled students into regular schools. Integration should offer individualised solutions for each particular student taking into consideration their disability pedagogical and medical support should be available. It is mentioned that integration will be most successful if it is supported by the child, parents, teachers and the administration. Integration is guided by three fundamental principles: 1) *concerted actions*: building relationships between government, professional organisations, local communities, parent-teacher associations, disabled children and parents associations in order to consider the manifold aspects of integration; 2) *decentralised co-ordinated action*: reorganisation of initiatives, clarification of objectives, evaluation of national initiatives in conjunction with other parts of the administration including the Ministry of Health; 3) *flexible laws and regulations*: past experience has shown that it is necessary for non-rigid administrative structures so that specialised personnel may intervene and fully participate in school life.

Circular 83/082 of 29th January 1983 describes the conditions under which integration may take place in schools: 1) integration of an individual student into a regular class with the aid of a special education teacher, 2) integration of a group of a disabled students with the aid of special education teachers, 3) partial integration, individuals or small groups participate in regular classes from time to time.

Circular No. 91-304 of 18th November 1991 establishes the "classes of school integration" (CLIS). The integration classes are to substitute special education classes, and are designed to promote the transition of disabled students into regular classes.

6. Financing of Education for Special Needs

Special education is financed by the State (the Ministry of National Education) and local authorities. The social security system, through the "caisse assurance maladi" finances the main part of the private sector.

7. Curriculum Entitlement

Disabled students in regular schools or in transition classes are required to follow the regular school curriculum adapting learning methods to suit their individual needs.

8. Post 16 Years—Vocational Education

Circular No. 89/036 of 6th February 1989 discusses general and professional education at the secondary level. The Section of Specialised Education (SES) and The Regional Establishment for Adapted Education (EREA) are open to disabled students. Starting at the level of the "college", classes will be interdisciplinary drawing from the contents of general and technical education. After three to four years of study, students are able to obtain a certificate in professional education (CAP).

9. Teacher Training

Circular No. 90/082 of 9th April 1990 constructs a network of special education aids for students with difficulties. If a child needs extra assistance in class, the classroom teacher may request a special education aid. The goal of the *pedagogical* teaching aid is to assist children with learning difficulties, help them with the methods and techniques of classroom work, and monitor a student's progress. The role of the *rehabilitative* teaching aid is to assist children in building their self-esteem by helping them to adjust emotionally, physically and intellectually to the classroom.

For a teacher to participate in a CLIS class, additional professional training will be made available for special education teachers.

All teachers (primary and secondary level) have to follow courses of altogether 42 hours to sensitize them to rehabilitation and social integration.

Special education teachers must have a minimum of three years experience in regular classrooms. After working as a special education teacher it is possible to follow a one year training on the management of rehabilitation and special education centres, (CAPSAIS) established by the Decree of 15th June 1987.

GERMANY

1. Extent and Nature of Legislation

The Federal Republic of Germany was founded in 1949 and consisted of eleven Länder, or Federal States, until 1990. To a large extent the Länder manage their own affairs in education, and they also influence law-making at Federal level via the Bundesrat, a Parliament of the Länder representatives that exists in addition to the Bundestag, the elected Parliament.

In 1990 the former German Democratic Republic (GDR) joined the Federal Republic of Germany in the form of five new Länder". The introduction of democratic institutions in these "new Länder" also involves a fundamental restructuring of the educational system.

In the Federal Republic of Germany there are now sixteen Länder, to each of which the "Grundgesetz" (Basic Law, i.e. Constitution) gave cultural autonomy. Accordingly the Länder in the Federal Republic of Germany exercise both legislative and administrative authority over school affairs.

There is no national legislation in Germany. Legislation is enacted in and applicable to each Land or District. Each Land (district) has a school law of its own. Due to this fact the German education system is characterised by a cooperative federalism. The education system of what used to be Eastern Germany (now the "new Länder"9 will also have to be reconciled with the structures of the "old Länder".

2. Responsibility and Organisation

In the field of education the Federal Government represented by the Ministry of Education and Science plays among other things an important role in the general planning of education and in the promotion of innovation.

The "KMK" ("Die Ständige Vertretung der Kultusminister der Länder in der Bundesrepublik Deutschland"–The Standing Conference of the Ministers of Education and Cultural Affairs of the Länder) serves to co-ordinate the work of the sixteen ministries.

One of the four standing committees of the "KMK" is the Schools Committee. If examines all matters of national interest in primary and secondary education, teacher training, and, in close co-operation with the sub-committee for vocational training, all matters pertaining to vocational and technical schools. It submits its proposals to the plenary session of the "KMK", in which resolutions must be planned unanimously. The ministers commit themselves to put these resolutions into practice or to support them in the cabinets and parliaments of their Länder.

Supervision of the school system is the responsibility of the Ministries of Education and Cultural Affairs of the Länder in their capacity as the highest educational authority.

School administration, which has different forms of organisation, is in many cases structured as a three-tiered system with the Ministries forming the upper level, the district school departments or independently existing secondary schools' offices ("Oberschulämter") the middle level, and the school' offices ("Schulämter") local authority, the lower level.

3. Identification, Assessment and Orientation

Early assistance for disabled children is a necessary and important target for inclusive education. In 1973 the education committee of the German Board for Education ("Deutscher Bildungsrat") adopted recommendations about "The Pedagogical Support of Handicapped and Handicap-Threatened Children and Adolescents".

The setting up of institutions to diagnose disability at the earliest possible stage, and the provision of appropriate educational and therapeutical assistance in good time for those children who are threatened by disability was recommended and put into practice.

A flexible system of support measures, located at integrated settings of kindergartens and general schools, was provided for the children concerned, at an early age. Special pedagogical, educational and therapeutical support is still provided by counselling services which are, in some cases, located in special schools.

The purposes of these counselling services, often functioning as remedial committees (Förderausschuss"), is to identify disabilities as early as possible, and to overcome or prevent them. For this reason experts work in close co-operation with educators, physiological therapists, school psychologists and medical services at these services or resource centres. Special educational needs are determined by the school administration based on the assessment and orientation (recommendation) given by the remedial committee.

According to the recommendation of the remedial committee the administrator or supervisor (school inspector) decides whether the child will attend a regular school, stay there to get special support, or obtain education at a special school.

In the process of identification, assessment and orientation the following points have to be considered:

— type and range of support,

— intervention of parents and recommendation of external services,

— opportunity of support in a regular school,

— availability of necessary special education.

— equipment of technical, and other special media, constructional conditions.

Various external services influence the procedure, e.g.

— Child Guidance and Counselling Services

— School Health Service

— School Helpers.

4. Age Range Covered by Legislation

Legislation applies to pre-school (kindergarten and regular school facilities), primary and secondary education. Germany has 9-10 year compulsory schooling for all students.

5. Integration

'The joint policy of the different Länder is aimed at schools promoting inclusive education. More and more Länder modify their school laws at present. The main consideration being to find the right kind of special education suited to each child's individual needs.

In the last decade, attempts to teach disabled and non-disabled children in a common environment have increased. Children and adolescents with special educational needs may attend mainstream schools if the necessary educational equipment is available.

The following factors are seen as of priority in order to achieve inclusive education: a high standard of competence for teaching and training staff, comprehensive knowledge of all rehabilitation measures and co-ordinated collaboration between vocational training, regular schools, social welfare and medical services.

To help about an effective inclusive provision for all students with special educational needs a well-elaborated network may serve to implement all forms of special needs education. In order to achieve this aim, Resource Centres ("Förder-zentren") were founded. They function in close co-operation with the external services mentioned above and operate the following tasks;

— providing expertise and remedial programmes,

— preparing and arranging meetings of remedial committees,

— taking care of the necessary assistance for teachers with competence in special education,

— giving advice to parents of disabled children,

— brining together, in a multi-disciplinary way, all the provision the disabled child depends on in his/her classroom, primary or secondary school.

In principle the demand for integrated support in regular schools is now legally ensured in most of the Länder.

6. Financing of Education for Special Needs

Responsibility for financing lies within the Länder. At present an increase in funding for inciusive education can be observed. Additionally, disabled children and adolescents are provided with extra financial support.

The financial framework of schools does not differ in the Länder, i.e. it is comparable to all students. Social Welfare Services often help to improve the technical equipment of inclusive and special schools.

However, in the organisation of special schools, the private sector has been relatively important. In 1987, approximately 27 per cent of all special schools functioned by private donations.

7. Curriculum Entitlement

Integration reflects all kinds of disabilities and different types and forms of schools. According to the cultural and educational autonomy of the Länder one can find differences as well as parallels in policy, responsibility and organisation of fundamental curriculum attainments and standards.

For children with special learning difficulties, remedial programmes in addition to and in connection with basic instruction courses are offered in primary and secondary schools.

In general, children with special educational needs are given support for their mental, physical and social development by the curricula of the differentiated systems of schooling under the guidance of special education.

8. Post 16 Years—Vocational Education

At present preparations are underway in some Länder to improve vocational training and job prospects for young people with special educational needs.

9. Teacher Training

The training of teachers requires the study of at least 8 semesters in a teacher training college ("Pädagogische Hochschule") or at a university. The training of teachers for regular schools includes a survey concerning the instruction in special educational needs. The special education training of the teaching staff at general schools, however, in a vital issue.

Professional and in-service training of staff has to take into account the educational, teaching, therapeutical and care facilities, and moreover, consider close co-operation with extra-curricular areas of support.

After graduating from university or college special education teachers can receive further training at university in the form of 3-4 semester courses.

GREECE

1. Extent and Nature of Legislation

Law No. 1143/30-3-1981 was the first one concerning the organisation of Special Education in Greece. This law was enriched and incorporated into the Law No. 1566/1985 dealing with general education (K-12 grades). Law 1894/90, Article 2 refers to supporting the teaching of immigrant children and other pupils with learning difficulties, and Article 8 refers to the establishment of the Council in the Ministry of Education responsible for the special personnel of special education units and to other organisational subjects of Special Education. Beyond these there is a number of decrees concerning Special Education.

2. Responsibility and Organisation

The Ministry of Education is responsible for the education of disabled children. Within the Ministry of Education, there is a directorate for Special Education, which cooperates with all educational services in the country and especially with the 16 special education school advisors, each one being responsible for one district.

Today (1994) there are about 200 small special schools and 650 special classes in regular schools. Most of them are at the level of primary education.

3. Identification, Assessment and Orientation

Disabilities are identified firstly by teachers and parents. For severe handicaps, assessment is undertaken by a medico-pedagogic service. There are about 45 such centres in Greece and 35 ambulatory assessment units in the different prefectures. Guidance and orientation is offered by the school advisors and the school psychologists of special education.

4. Age Range Covered by Legislation

According to Law 1566/85 the age range covered by Special Education extends from 3-18 years, that is during pre-primary, primary and secondary education.

5. Integration

The integration of the disabled into regular schools is one of the main targets of the educational policy. At the present there are two channels in the regular schools for the implementation of this policy; the programme of special classes, and the programme of supporting teaching.[2]

6. Financing of Eduction for Special Needs

Financing of Special Education is provided by the State. It is incorporated into the financing of primary and secondary education.

7. Curriculum Entitlement

There are no separate special education curricula. The teachers who are working in special education programmes, in cooperation with the school advisors of Special Education, have the right to make adjustments of the ordinary school curricula according to the needs and abilities of their pupils.

8. Post of 16 Years—Vocational Education

Disabled children who can continue their studies at lyceums (upper secondary) or tertiary education, are given the possibility to do this. There is a small number of special lyceums for deaf and physically handicapped children. Deaf and blind students who finished the lyceum may continue their studies in the university without entrance examinations. Vocational Education for the disabled has not been developed enough. There are only 7 special vocational education schools and some workshops in different institutions. Sporadically one can meet disabled students in regular vocational schools.

9. Teacher Training

Beyond the four year basic studies at university departments, the teachers working permanently in special eduction units of primary level have taken a two-year in-service education course in special education or approved special education diplomas. Some courses of special education are offered during the basic studies of teacher education as well as during in-service education programmes.

HOLLAND

1. Extent and Nature of Legislation

The Special Education Interim Act (ISOVSO) came into force on 1st August 1985 and is intended to remain in force for 10 years. It requires that special primary and secondary education be provided for children who need a "primarily orthopedagogic or orthodidactic approach."

The Special Education Interim Act defines the objectives of special education and its division into different types of schools, and provides regulations for the organisation of teaching in special schools (the educational and development curriculum, the school work plan and the number of school hours and school days). It governs the status of the staff, pupils (admissions) and parents. There are also provisions with regard to the establishment and closure of schools, their accommodation an funding. The main implementing orders pertaining to special education (primary and secondary) under the Special Education Interim Act are the;

— *Special Education Pedagogical Decree* (Onderwijskundig Besluit ISOVSO). Regulations with regard to teaching in special schools.

— *Special Education Staff Establishment Decree* (Formatiebesluit ISOVSO).

— *Special Education Funding Decree* (Bekostigsbesluit ISOVSO/ OISOVSO).

— *Special Education Building Decree* (Bouwbesluit ISOVSO).

Regulations relating to the dimensions, construction siting and lay-out of special schools.

2. Responsibility and Organisation

Special schools may be either publicly or privately run. Public schools are run by the municipalities. There are no special schools run by the provinces or the state. Of the 1004 special schools (1990/ 91), 27 per cent are publicly run and 73 per cent privately.

Every special school is legally required to set up a participation council (Education Participation Act 1992) (WMO 1992), whose membership comprises equal numbers of elected representatives of staff and parents, varying in total from 6 to a maximum of 18, depending on the size of the school. Parental participation can also take place through the parents' council, which advises the parents' representatives in the participation council and coordinates parental activities.

3. Identification, Assessment and Orientation

A child is admitted into a special school only if it is clear that an orthopedagogic or orthodidactic approach is needed.

A disability may be identified by parents, teachers or counselling services. Parents decide in consultation with school staff if a child should attend a special school suited to the child's needs. There are schools for children with learning difficulties, physically handicapped, deaf, hearing impaired, speech disorders, blind and visually impaired, multiple handicapped, the chronically ill, and the mentally retarded.

The school board decides if a child is to be admitted into a special school. It is advised by a committee of experts who test the child. The committee consists of the head of the school, a doctor, a psychologist, a social worker and an educational expert. The composition of the committee may vary. The committee makes a recommendation to decide if the child is suitable for the school. The parents have access to the committee's report. If a child enters a special school, he or she is re-assessed in two years to determine whether the child is at the right school or if he or she should be moved to another special school or an ordinary school.

4. Age Range Covered by Legislation

Primary and secondary education are covered. There is no general age range within special education; it varies depending on the school type, from 3,4,5,6 years in primary special education up to the age of 20 in secondary special education.

5. Integration

Special education is provided in separate schools.

The Act: "Together to School Again" concerning the integration of children with learning and behavioural disabilities has been accepted by the Second Chamber of Parliament and is now sent for approval to the First Chamber (June 1994).

6. Financing of Education for Special Needs

Special schools (both primary and secondary) are funded by central government.

The "Special Education Funding Decree" discusses the cost of special education. It states that "administrative regulations relating to the commencement and termination of funding for special schools (primary and secondary), and their financial security; regulations concerning pupil records and school rolls and providing the basis for reimbursement claims".

7. Curriculum Entitlement

The Special Education Pedagogical Decree discusses the curriculum content of special education.

8. Post 16 Years—Vocational Education

There are three tracks possible; a) reintegrate in (regular) vocational education, b) take an exam in the school type secondary education for pupils with emotional and behavioural disturbances, c) be a guest-pupil in regular education (following a part of the programmes).

9. Teacher Training

The Special Education Staff Establishment Decree discusses staffing in special education. It states provisions for fixing the staff establishment budget.

HUNGARY

1. Extent and Nature of Legislation

Section 6 of the 1993 Act LXXIX on Public Education states that "education is compulsory for every child...Compulsory education (begins at age 6) and lasts until the end of the school year when the student reaches the age of 16. In the case of students with sensory, speech or other handicaps, compulsory education may be extended as long as the end of the school year when they become 18 years of age."

Section 30 of the Act stipulates that children with physical, a mild degree of mental, sensory, speech or other handicap have the right to receive special pedagogical provision, kindergarten education and school education in accordance with their condition from the time the handicap is diagnosed

Boarding schools are set up for children with moderate handicaps and special vocational schools are set up after compulsory education.

2. Responsibility and Organisation

The Ministry of Culture and Education is primarily responsible.

3. Identification, Assessment and Orientation

Section 6 off the Public Education Act states that it is the head of the school that makes the decision about a child's physical, mental, sensory, speech or other handicap on the basis of an expert's report and the opinion of the rehabilitation committee.

Section 30 states that on the basis of the expert's report and the rehabilitation committee's advice the parents may choose the special education institution where the child is to be enrolled.

Section 30 also states that in the interest of a child or student, the notary of the local authority can oblige parents to take the child to an expert's examination which is a pre-requisite for enrolment at an appropriate institution. If there are no places available at the preferred institution the child will be put on a waiting list at another school.

4. Age Range Covered by Legislation

Compulsory education may be prolonged until a student is 18 years old.

5. Integration

Information unavailable.

6. Financing of Education for Special Needs

All education is to be state run, free of charge to parents.

7. Curriculum Entitlement

Information unavailable.

8. Post 16 Years—Vocational Education

Information unavailable.

9. Teacher Training

Information unavailable.

ICELAND

1. Extent and Nature of Legislation

The Primary School Act of 1974 stipulates that the school shall adjust its function in accordance to the nature and need of its pupils and strive to support all children in achieving all-around development, health and education. Children who deviate significantly from normal development and cannot follow regular classes will be taught in special schools.

The Act on the Affairs of the Handicapped (no. 59/1992) aims to provide all handicapped people with equality and living conditions comparable with those of other citizens, and to provide them with conditions that enable them to live a normal life. This includes entitlement to children with disabilities to attend play-school operated by local authorities.

The Play-school Act (no. 78/1994), covering the age range 0-6, entitles all children with disabilities to necessary special support within preschools and stipulates that all pre-schools shall be physically accessible to handicapped children.

The Compulsory School Act (no. 49/1991), dealing with the age range 6-16, stipulates that the school shall adjust its function according to the nature and needs of its pupils and strive to support all children in achieving an all-round development, health and education. Children who need special educational support shall get it in their own home school, unless his/her parents, teachers or specialists consider a special unit or school more suitable. Regulation of Special Education (no. 106/1992) pertaining tot he Compulsory School stipulates that ordinary schools shall be organised as a whole to take account of the educational needs of all children.

The Upper Secondary Act (no. 57/1988), covering the 16-20 age range, grants the right of entry to secondary education of everyone who has finished compulsory school or has reached the age of 18. Students with disabilities are entitled to appropriate education, training and support in their studies.

2. Responsibility and Organisation

The Ministry of Education and Culture has the main responsibility for special education.

At the Pre-school level administrative responsibility is in the hands of Local Authority Play-school Committees and Play-school Head Teachers.

Under the present law, power of administration at compulsory school level is transferred to District Education Officers by allocating a certain proportion of total number of teaching hours for special education in regular schools. A Bill of Law, shortly to be presented to the Legal Assembly, proposes a transfer of all primary schools and District Education Offices to local Municipalities on August 1st 1995. School principals are responsible for the planning in their School Curriculum, and class teachers for constructing teaching plans for individuals and groups of pupils.

At Upper-Secondary Schools Head Teachers are responsible for services.

Special education services are organised as support either inside or outside classes, as special units inside regular schools or as special schools.

At pre-school level children with disabilities are fully included.

At compulsory school level there are special units or schools for the dear, blind, mentally retarded, emotionally disturbed and multiple disabled encompassing 0.6 per cent of the population. In every major regular school a Student Welfare Committee, comprising the Principal, the Special Educator, the Guidance Counselor, the School Nurse and the SPS representative, coordinates the special education services.

At the upper-secondary level a new Bill of law proposes a pre-secondary option for those who have not passed minimum grade in compulsory school and special units for students with disabilities.

3. Identification, Assessment and Orientation

The State Diagnostic and Counselling Centre is responsible for the assessment of people with disabilities, counselling and giving advice to parents and professionals as well as registration and storage of data. This is done in collaboration with social, educational and health authorities. It concentrates on the pre-school population deriving most of its referrals from paediatricians and pre-school teachers.

Mobile Psycho-pedagogical Services, providing assessment and counselling for pre-schools exist in some of the larger Local Authorities. Area committees for the Affairs of the Handicapped (Law no. 59/1992) provide consultation in some areas.

At the compulsory school level Schools' Psychological Services, located in all District Education Offices, are instrumental in evaluating the needs of individuals in regard to special education. A third of their referrals comes directly from parents. Their role is the assessment and consultation concerning children with special educational needs in regular and special schools. Special Educators in the schools also do a considerable amount of assessment.

According to the Regulation on Special Education parents have the right to access all information pertaining to their child's schooling.

At the upper-secondary level Guidance Counselors within the schools are prominent in providing evaluation, support and referral for students with special needs.

4. Age Range Covered by Legislation

Pre-school, primary, secondary and vocational education are covered.

5. Integration

The Circular on Special Education 1 August, 1990, stresses integration. It states" Integration of handicapped and non-handicapped children shall be an aim of systematic school development."

The Circular assumes that special schools will continue to function, however, no labels or handicap categories are mentioned, and it is envisaged that provision will be organised according to individually assessed need.

The Play-school Act, the Compulsory School Act and the Upper-Secondary School Act all stress that students with disabilities should obtain their education alongside non-disabled students wherever possible. Categorisation of handicaps has been discounted, decisions on provision now being based on individually assessed needs.

The Regulation on Special Education for the compulsory school level stipulates that "Integration of disabled and non-disabled students in their home-school shall be approached through systematic school development". The Regulation assumes, as does the law, however that special schools continue to function for those students whose home schools fail to provide appropriate education for them. The special schools also serve as advisory centres for pupils with disabilities in regular schools.

6. Financing of Education for Special Needs

At the pre-school level all funding comes from the municipality. Funds for the compulsory schools go through the hands of the District Education Officers. Special schools and units serving the whole country are financed separately from the regular schools.

7. Curriculum Entitlement

No formal National Curriculum exists for pre-schools, but play-school Head Teachers are responsible for writing a School Curriculum with reference to an Education Plan for Play-schools (Uppeldisáætlun fyrir leikskóla. 1993) published by the Ministry of Education and Culture. All children at that level are entitled to access to the regular programme.

All compulsory schools are required to implement the National Curriculum for all children. Special Educational Needs are defined in the Regulation for Special Education as "... a significant change in teaching objectives, content, situation or methods compared to what other pupils of the same age are offered". Special Education involves"... the construction of educational plans for individuals or groups...containing short and long-term objectives ... teaching according to the plan (and) recording and review of the plan". Special needs and special education are thus defined in curriculum terms.

Upper-secondary schools have no National Curriculum, decisions on entitlement of access to the school syllabus being in the hands of the Principal.

8. Post 16 Years—Vocational Education

Students with special needs, after finishing compulsory school at the age of 16, are offered vocational education as part of the Upper-Secondary School system based on that law.

9. Teacher Training

Icelandic College for Pre-school Teachers offers experienced pre-school teachers one year of further education in special needs in accordance with Law on the College (no. 10/1973). Many pre-school teachers carry on their education abroad.

Education of special education teachers at compulsory school level is offered as a post-graduate programme for teachers with minimum of two years experience. The programme is offered at the University College of Education and leads to a diploma after one year full-time study and a Master of Education degree after two years. This is based on the Law of The University College of Education (no. 29/1988). The Ministry of Education and Culture grants certification on the basis of the qualification commensurate with Law on the Protection of Title and Praxis of Primary School Teachers, Secondary School Teachers and Principals (no. 48/1986). A Diploma qualifies for certification as a Special Educator in regular schools and an M.Ed. degree qualifies for certification as a Special Educator in special schools and special units.

INDONESIA

1. Extent and Nature of Legislation

The Law of the Republic of Indonesia, No.2 1989 on the National Educational System, Article 8 states that "Citizens with physical and/or mental disability shall get special education." Article 11 states that, "special education is specially designed for those who are physically or mentally disabled."

Government Regulation for the Republic of Indonesia No. 72, 1991 on the chapter on Special Education states that "special education is aimed to help citizens with physical and or mental disabilities in order that they can develop their attitude, knowledge and skills... in communication with society, culture and environment, also they can develop their abilities in the job market or continue their education."

2. Responsibility and Organisation

The Ministry of Education and Culture, the Ministry of Health, and the Ministry of Home Affairs are concerned with the education of the disabled. The Ministry of Education and Culture is responsible for the education of disabled children. The Directorate for Primary Education, Sub-Directorate of Special Education is specifically concerned with educational provision for the disabled.

3. Identification, Assessment and Orientation

Information unavailable.

4. Age Range Covered by Legislation

Special education is offered in primary and secondary school.

5. Integration

Information unavailable.

6. Financing of Education for Special Needs

Information unavailable.

7. Curriculum Entitlement

Chapter 9, Article 38 of the Law on the National Education System states that, "The conduct of educational activities within an education unit shall be based on the national curriculum and the curriculum which is adjusted to the situation, and to the need of the environment and the special identity of the educational unit concerned."

8. Post 16 Years—Vocational Education

Presidential Decree Number 29 dated 10 July 1990 on Secondary Education, states that "technical and vocational education priority is to prepare students to enter the world of work and develop professional attitude" (chapter 2 article 3) and "students have the right for special service if disabled" (chapter 8 article 17).

The Ministry of Education and Culture Decree Number 0490/U/1992 dated 30 December 1992 on Technical and Vocational Schools states that "technical and vocational schools are education units which conduct education as continuation of basis education and prepare the students to enter the work force and develop professional attitude" (chapter 1 article 1) and "to be admitted as student of a technical or vocational school, the candidate has to fulfil the following criteria; 1) Have a diploma of a lower secondary school, 2) Physically and mentally healthy, 3) Physically suitable for the study programme, that he/she chooses, 4) Not more than 21 years old, 5) Pass an entrance test held by the school, 6) Not getting married during education.

This implies that acceptance of disabled students varies according to study programme and relevant field of work.

9. Teacher Training

Information unavailable.

IRELAND

1. Extent and Nature of Legislation

The Irish Constitution (1937) requires that "The State shall provide for free primary education."

The only legislative provision governing attendance at school dates from 1926, The School Attendance Act. This Act requires all children from the ages of 6 to 15 years to attend school unless parents choose to make some other educational provision for the education of their children. The 1930 Vocational Education Act incorporates legislation on the education of some pupils of post-primary age.

A Green Paper "Education for a Changing World" was published in June 1992. This document is intended to generate discussion and proposals which will define educational policy into the next century.

The result of the Green Paper discussions will be a While Paper on education. Its publication will form the basis for an Education Act Legislation is to be enacted in 1994-1995.

A Special Education Review Committee completed a report in 1993. This report will most likely guide policy for the disabled. Some of its recommendations have been implemented or will be implemented in the future as resources permit.

2. Responsibility and Organisation

Primary education is provided for by the Department of Education within the framework of "Rules for National Schools", while about 1.5 per cent of pupils attend private primary schools.

Each national primary school has Principal teacher, a Board of Management and a Patron. The Board is responsible for managing school affairs, to which the Patron nominates the chairpersons and three members. The Department of Education deals directly with the boards of individual schools. A special education section is responsible in relation to special schools in such issues as enrolment and staffing levels.

The Special education system is comprised of three broad levels: 1) supported enrolment in mainstream classes with assistance from a specialists teacher; 2) special classes in mainstream schools; 3) Special school some of which are managed by religious congregations.

The Department of Health, through the Health Boards provides services for children before they reach compulsory school age. Care centres are available to offer medical, therapeutical and psychological assistance.

The "Special Education Review Committee Report" (1993) mentions that second-level education is provided in Secondary Schools, privately owned but almost entirely State funded, and in Comprehensive, Community and Vocational Schools and Colleges.

3. Identification, Assessment and Orientation

Children with severe and profound mental handicaps do not generally attend school. About 200 of these children, out of an estimated 2,000 are being provided for in an educational service as part of a pilot project by the Department of Education. This service is being expanded at present.

4. Age Range Covered by Legislation

There is no current legislation that deals with special education.

5. Integration

Educational provision for pupils with special needs is made in both ordinary and special schools. Today, about 0.9 per cent of all primary and post primary pupils are receiving their education in special schools.

Approximately 2,300 pupils with various types of physical, sensory, and mental handicaps and with language disorder are enrolled in special classes in primary schools. Another relevant development has been the appointment of additional teachers to primary and post-primary schools in areas of socio-economic disadvantage.

The 114 Special Schools (National Schools) have a combined enrolment of about 7,600 students.

6. Financing of Education for Special Needs

The special education system is grant aided; the Ministry of Education is responsible for teacher salaries and approximately 85 per cent of capital costs and grants towards operating costs.

7. Curriculum Entitlement

All pupils are entitled to access a curriculum which aims to enable them to achieve in accordance with their potential.

8. Post 16 Years—Vocational Education

Post-school education and training are provided by three government agencies responsible for industry and employment (FAS), for hotel, catering and tourism (CERT) and for agriculture (TEAGASC). Many post-primary schools offer Post-Leaving Certificate Courses (PLC's) including Vocational Preparation and Training II (VPT II) courses.

Vocational training centres for trainees with serious learning difficulties and handicaps are provided by the National Rehabilitation Board and by voluntary agencies.

9. Teacher Training

The Colleges of Education provide the initial training of all teachers. After some years of teaching experiences, teachers who teach in special schools and classes may spend a year of full time study to receive a Diploma in Special Education. There is also a wide range of relevant inservice courses available at present.

ITALY

1. Extent and Nature of Legislation

Law No. 118 of the 30th of March 1971 recognises "civil invalidity". This law formed the basis for the insertion of disabled children into regular classes assisted by specialised personnel.

Law No. 517/1977 states that disabled children may be enrolled in a regular school with the assistance of a specialised teacher and psychopedagogical services. These classes shall not be composed of more than 20 pupils. The child's school programme will be planned by teachers.

Law of 5 February, 1992 n. 104 concerning the assistance, social integration and the rights of disabled persons.

This law affirms that disabled persons should be integrated into regular schools. The law covers primary to university education.

Decree of the Minister of Public Education of 19 December 1992 containing the rules for examinations within state and private schools of primary and secondary level for the year 1992/1993.

2. Responsibility and Organisation

The Ministry of Public Education, Public Health and Social Affairs on the national level is involved in the education of disabled students. Since 1970, regional authorities were granted greater authority. The local authorities are to organise educational activities and vocational education for the disabled.

3. Identification, Assessment and Orientation

The national health service provides a diagnosis of a child's health at the entrance to pre-primary or primary school. The school and local health unit define the child's programme of study. The child's results are reviewed twice a year.

4. Age Range Covered by Legislation

Primary, secondary and higher education are covered, including the university.

5. Integration

Law No. 517/77 abolished some examinations which allowed pupils to move up from a class other than of the same school cycle; it also provided different forms of integration of disabled children by means of special education support teachers.

The same law states that classes in which there are disabled pupils, shall number at most 20 students. There will be a support teacher in each class, and he/she can teach a child with special needs individually for six hours a week. Classes in which there is a disabled child shall also have the support of specialised personnel from the psychopedagogical services, under the responsibility of the State and local Authorities, according to each one's competence and within the limits of their resources, on the basis of the programme established by the District Council of the school. The teachers college planning the programme of activities of the disabled child shall also have the support of specialised personnel from the psychopedagogical services, under the responsibility of the State and local authorities, according to each one's competence and within the limits of their resources, on the basis of the programme established by the District Council at the school.

The Frame Law of 1992 on assistance, social integration and the rights of Disabled Persons was enacted to integrate and improve previous legislation. For such matters which are not directly addressed by the Frame Law, its articles refer to legal instruments to be issued by the State, and administrative regulations enacted by regional, provincial or municipal authorities, which have promtly to be put out.

The Ministry of Public Education has created an Observatory Committee to evaluate current integration practices and to make proposals for future integration projects. Persons on this Committee include: the Chief of the Office for Studies and Programming, representatives from the Ministries of Social Affairs, Youth, Work, Interior, Health and Treasury, and representatives from handicapped organisations.

6. Financing of Education for Special Needs

The Law NO. 104 of 1992 includes many articles in order to determine the financial responsibility of the single national bodies. In brief, some activities are at the charge of different ministries, moving from and coordinated by the Ministry for Public Education. Also local authorities (which sometimes depend on the single national bodies and sometimes have their own specific competences have the duty to intervene even if "within their own resources". On 24 February 1994 the President of the Republic has promulgated a decree aimed at the determination and coordination of the duties of health units regarding the disabled pupils.

7. Curriculum Entitlement

There are no differences between disabled students and normal ones. When the disability is very severe, the student can obtain only a certification of frequency instead of the normal title to which he/she has right. This happens at the end of the compulsory education and no obstacles are provided till that moment.

8. Post 16 Years—Vocational Education

This kind of education is provided at the end of compulsory education even when the pupil has got the simple certification. Normally vocational education is given both in public and in private structures under the control and with the financial support of local authorities.

As already specified, the law no. 104 allows disabled people to get ordinary degree-if they are in condition to-of university.

9. Teacher Training

Teacher training is entrusted to public schools and to schools held by private associations, and the courses are funded by the Ministry of Public Education. Such courses last about two years, with 1.300 hours of lectures and resulted in the qualification of high-school support ordinary teachers.

JAPAN

1. Extent and Nature of Legislation

A 1979 Government order established nine years of compulsory education for disabled pupils.

The Order for the Enforcement of the School Educational Law defines the degree of handicap that allows children to be eligible for special schools. Education for severely handicapped children is provided in special schools, education for mildly handicapped children is provided in special classes or ordinary classes with special arrangements. There are seven categories of special schools: blind, deaf, mentally retarded, physically disabled, emotionally disturbed, speech and health impaired.

2. Responsibility and Organisation

The Department of Education and Culture is primarily responsible for the education of disabled students.

3. Identification, Assessment and Orientation

Information unavailable.

4. Age Range Covered by Legislation

Primary and secondary education are covered: nine years of compulsory schooling.

5. Integration

Information unavailable.

6. Financing of Education for Special Needs

The Ministry of Education provides almost half of the total public expenditures on education. Special schools are funded by the national government, prefectures and municipalities. Subsidies are offered to parents who are forced to put their children in special education boarding schools far from their homes.

7. Curriculum Entitlement

Information unavailable.

8. Post 16 Years—Vocational Education

Information unavailable.

9. Teacher Training

Information unavailable.

JORDAN

1. Extent and Nature of Legislation

The 1993 Law for the Welfare of Disabled Persons defines a disabled person as one who possesses "a permanent, partial or total impairment in any of his senses or physical, psychological or mental abilities to the extent that the ability to learn, to be rehabilitated or to work is limited in a way which renders him/her short of fulfilling his/her normal daily requirements in circumstances similar to those of able-bodied persons."

The 1993 Law recognises "the right of disabled persons to education and higher education commensurate with his/her abilities."

2. Responsibility and Organisation

The 1993 Law established the National Council for the Affairs of Disabled Persons. This Council is comprised of Members from the General Ministry. Ministries of Labour, Education, Health, Higher Education, Youth, Information, a representative from the Armed Forces, Queen Alia Voluntary Fund, General Union of Voluntary Agencies, Director of Special Education and representatives from disabled persons groups. The main goal of the Council is to "draft the general policy for the welfare, rehabilitation and education of disabled persons...Lay down a national plan for the protection against the occurrence of disability...soliciting grants...laying down internal executive organisational structures."

According to this law, the Ministry of Social Development is responsible for the welfare of disabled citizens. The Ministry of Education and the Directorate of Special Education is responsible for the education of the disabled.

3. Identification, Assessment and Orientation

Article 4 of the same law states that, "The Ministry shall provide the social assessment required for the determination of the nature and degree of disability. The Ministry shall provide to those with multiple and severe disabilities the special services for disabled persons in the fields of welfare, care, relief, and training as well as family and information services."

The Ministry of Education "shall provide the educational assessment required for the determination of the nature and degree of disability...They shall provide primary and all forms of secondary education for disabled persons as commensurate with their capabilities, among which the educational provisions that include programmes of special education."

4. Age Range Covered by Legislation

Primary, secondary and vocational education are included in the 1993 law.

5. Integration

Article 3 of the 1993 Law states that, "The philosophy of the Hashemite Kingdom of Jordan…stresses the following principle: The right of disabled persons to be integrated into the general life of the society. "

The 1993 Law defines special education as, "educational and teaching services offered to disabled persons for the purpose of fulfilling their needs, developing their capabilities and helping them integrate into society."

6. Financing of Education for Special Needs

The 1993 Law exempts all educational and medical materials used by the disabled from customs duties and other taxes. Also, centres and other establishments belonging to the government concerned with the welfare of disabled persons are exempted from real estate taxes.

7. Curriculum Entitlement

Information unavailable.

8. Post 16 Years—Vocational Education

The Ministry of Labour and the Vocational Training Corporation shall provide "the programmes and plans and the evaluation services necessary to achieve the appropriate vocational training for disabled persons, and the development of their capabilities, creation of appropriate employment opportunities and support for protected workshop projects."

9. Teacher Training

Information unavailable.

MALAYSIA

1. Extent and Nature of Legislation

The provision for Special Schools and Special Educational Treatment for Disabilities in the 1961 Education Act establishes the basis for special schools. Special schools are defined as schools which provide special educational treatment for pupils with disabilities.

2. Responsibility and Organisation

Chapter 4 of the 1961 Act provides that the Minister shall establish and maintain educational institutions including special schools.

The 1981 Mahathir report and the Recommendations of the Cabinet Committee pertaining to the Education of Children with Special Needs emphasises a greater governmental role and commitment with the participation of voluntary organisations as supplementary and complementary in nature.

Recommendation 169 stipulates: "realising that the government should be responsible for the education of handicapped children, it should recommend that the government should completely assume this responsibility of providing education from the organisations that are managing it at present. Besides, the participation of voluntary organisations improving the education of handicapped children should continue to be encouraged."

In response to the 1981 report, a committee comprised of the Ministries of Education, Health and Welfare Services and Labour was convened to delineate the functions of each ministry in the education, rehabilitation, vocational training and job placement of the handicapped.

The Ministry of Education is concerned with the education of the hearing impaired, visually handicapped and the "educable" mentally retarded.

NICARAGUA

1. Extent and Nature of Legislation

The Constitution of Nicaragua, Chapter, I, Article 121 stipulates that, "access to education is free and equal for all Nicaraguan citizens. Basic education is free and obligatory."

Article 62 of the Constitution states that, "the State will establish programmes for the benefit of the disabled persons and their physical, psycho-social and professional rehabilitation and their integration into work."

2. Responsibility and Organisation

Since 1980, various government institutions have been concerned with the disabled. In 1990, Decree No. 511 was designed to create The National Commission for Nicaraguan Rehabilitation (La Comisión Nacional de Rehabilitación Nicaraguense CONAREN).

Article 2 of the Decree states that the final goal of this commission is to, "allow full integration of disabled persons into society and work."

Further, the objective of this commission is to:

1) promote and direct the design, implementation and evaluation of the programmes and sectors concerned with rehabilitation, and

2) promote and co-ordinate the mobilisation of government offices, the private sector, the disabled and the general population towards social integration.

The Commission is composed of delegates from the following Ministries and Institutions: Ministry of Health, The Nicaraguan Institute for Social Security and Welfare, Ministry of Labour, and Ministry of Education. Also, representatives from organisations for the disabled, unions and professional organisations will be present.

At the present time (1994), the Ministry of Health and the Nicaraguan Institute for Social Security and Welfare, through a programme named INVICTA-National Institute for Victims of War (Instituto Nacional para Victimas de Guerra) are the only two institutions of the commission that are active. They support only the rehabilitation of victims of war.

3. Identification, Assessment and Orientation

In coordination with the Ministry of Health children are identified when parents seek information and assistance in clinics, health centers and hospitals, and through the community workers in the non-formal education programmes of the Ministry of Education.

The non-formal Programme Coordinator (attending children age 0-6) performs a functional assessment with each child and develops a plan for intervention designed to meet his/her individual needs.

In more urban areas children are referred to a diagnostic center where a more detailed psycho-educational assessment to determine functional level is performed.

A large percentage of teachers are also trained to evaluate functional level. Services are provided according to the specific needs of each individuals. Local promoters follow up by visiting the homes of identified children on a regular basis to assist families to integrate the child in the family and community life. Through Community Based Rehabilitation they attempt to involve the community in the planning, implementation and evaluation of the programmes. Children of school age will attend special education school if available in his/her district. Some children presenting mild disabilities are integrated fully in primary education schools when certain conditions are met and teacher training permits.

4. Age Range Covered by Legislation

There is no legislation for special needs education. Basic education is free and obligatory for children up to 16 years of age.

5. Integration

Legislation in Nicaragua does not contemplate integration. Nevertheless, for the past four years, great efforts have been made to integrate children in different modalities with relative success (full integration in regular primary schools and partial integration through special classrooms in regular primary schools). To this date, no formal policy or plan supports this initiative. Community awareness efforts have opened great possibilities for integration, but lack of legislation and policies to this respect or governmental support do not sustain integration efforts.

6. Financing of Education for Special Needs

Financing of education for special needs is assigned by the Ministry of Education.

7. Curriculum Entitlement

A curriculum transformation is presently taking place for the whole country's educational system. This transformation includes children with special education needs and will allow, through its flexibility, a greater possibility for adaption in order to meet the special learning needs of all children.

8. Post 16 Years—Vocational Education

Vocational education is available for young adults with special educational needs up to age 18 in Special Education Schools.

9. Teacher Training

The training of special education teachers is done through short courses and seminars provided by the Division of Special Education of the Ministry of Education.

NORWAY

1. Extent and Nature of Legislation

Legislation for Special Education dates from 1951. In 1975, The Education Act of 1969 was applied to disabled children. It was thought that children with special educational needs should be educated in their local regular schools. Following this Act on Primary and Lower Secondary Education, each municipality is responsible for providing education for all children living within its borders, regardless of their abilities. All pupils are registered at their local schools, and all children have the right to receive instruction adapted to their individual abilities and aptitudes.

An Act on Upper Secondary Education gives young people with special needs the right to instruction adapted to their individual abilities.

In June 1991, a reorganisation of special education was adopted by the Storting (the Norwegian Parliament) based on two White Papers, no. 54 of 1989-1990, and no. 35 of 1990-1991. These White Papers set out the division of responsibilities between national, regional and local educational authorities with regard to the provision of training for those with special training needs in all age groups.

A new reform, "Reform 94" gives every young person the right to upper secondary and vocational education. This reform is still in the process of being implemented, which implies that there will be some changes in the legislative provision in 1994.

2. Responsibility and Organisation

In general, the local and regional authorities offer training for the disabled, whereas the development of national expertise and experience in areas which cannot easily be covered at the local level, is incumbent upon the State. Through a re-structuring and a reorganisation of several former special education schools, twenty resource centres for special education were established on the 1st of August 1992. There is one board for the national level and one for the regional resource centres. All are run by the Government.

3. Identification, Assessment and Orientation

The overall aim is to identify children with special needs as early as possible. All local health centres co-operate with education psychological service centres. The Act on Pre-school Education ensures priority entrance for disabled children. The Act on Primary and Lower Secondary Education ensures the right to special education for children below the age of seven, as well as for those in compulsory school. Detection of disabilities is followed up by educational or other provisions at all levels. The educational-psychological service centres constitute a support system for kindergartens, primary and secondary

7. Curriculum Entitlement

Section 1 of Article V (Policies and Guidelines for Special Education) states that "The curriculum for special education shall be based on the curriculum prescribed for the regular school by the Department of Education, Culture and Sports". Three schemes may be adopted for special students; (1) the regular curriculum prescribed for regular children, (2) the modified curriculum which is the regular curriculum with certain adaptions to meet the needs of special children, such as inclusion of orientation and mobility for children with visual impairment, and (3) the special curriculum which is designed for children with special needs and aimed primarily at developing adaptive skills of maximise their potential. Prototype instructional materials specifically designed for the above children are prepared by the Special Education Division and made available to the field.

8. Post 16 Years—Vocational Education

Section 15 Chapter 2 of the Magna Carta for Disabled Persons (R.A. 7277) entitled 'Vocational or Technical and Other Training Programmes', specifies that "The State shall provide disabled persons with training in civics, vocational efficiency, sports and physical fitness, and other skills. The Department of Education, Culture and Sports shall establish in at least one government owned vocational and technical training programme for disabled persons. It shall develop and implement sports and physical fitness programmes specifically designed for disabled persons taking into consideration the nature of their handicaps".

Section 16 entitled 'Non-Formal Education' specifies that "The State shall develop non-formal education programmes intended for the total human development of disabled persons. It shall provide adequate resources for non-formal education programmes and projects that cater to the special needs of disabled persons" In addition Section 13 states that at least 5 per cent of the allocation for the Private Education Student Financial Assistance Programme created by virtue of R.A. 6725 shall be set aside for disabled students pursuing vocational or technical and degree courses.

4. Age Range Covered by Legislation

Legislation covers obligatory education, primary and secondary (16 years).

5. Integration

Decree Law No. 319/91, 1991 provides that, "legislation for the integration of disabled students in regular schools published ten years ago must now be enlarged and implemented."

The law calls for: classification and categorisation of the students based on pedagogical diagnosis rather than medical criteria; regular schools to be made sensitive tot he difficulties of disabled students; and making regular schools accessible for the disabled, in the spirit of "schools for all".

6. Financing of Education for Special Needs

Information unavailable.

7. Curriculum Entitlement

Article 18, paragraph 4 of Law No. 46 186 states that, "basic education for disabled students should develop a curriculum and programmes adapted to the characteristics of each grade of deficiency."

The law also requires that the school curriculum be made accessible to disabled students by using specialised equipment, special education assistants and support services.

Decree Law No. 319/91, 1991 emphasises that special education consists of adapting the conditions of learning for students with special needs.

8. Post 16 Years—Vocational Education

Information unavailable.

9. Teacher Training

Article 33 paragraph 1 of Law No. 46 186 states that, "special education teachers will obtain their qualification in special education courses offered in schools of higher education."

QATAR

1. Extent and Nature of Legislation

In 1981, the Qatar cabinet issued resolution No. 41 to form various policy resolutions. Principle 1 states that, "education being a life necessity and a significant factor for the development of a good citizen is the right of every Qatari citizen."

The Educational Policy of Qatar, 1985, provides that: Educational authorities, under the principle of equal opportunities, should provide teaching for the mentally or physically disabled students through the following approaches:

1) special centres for the teaching of the disabled,
2) developing special curricula that suit the different categories of the disabled,
3) preparing the necessary staff for teaching and administration at the various disabled institutions, and
4) rehabilitating the disabled in a way that conforms with the tasks to be assigned to them after stepping out into public life.

2. Responsibility and Organisation

Information unavailable.

3. Identification, Assessment and Orientation

Information unavailable.

4. Age Range Covered by Legislation

Information unavailable.

5. Integration

Information unavailable.

6. Financing of Education for Special Needs

Financing, general, specialised and technological education is undertaken by the state.

7. Curriculum Entitlement

Information unavailable.

8. Post 16 Years—Vocational Education

Information unavailable.

9. Teacher Training

The Ministry of Education in co-operation with Qatar University has set up a course for a special education diploma.

ROMANIA

1. Extent and Nature of Legislation

The Law Decree 138/1990 of the Provisional Council for National Unity deals with the amelioration of social protection, education, schooling and professional training of children and young people with deficiencies. It has been complemented and amended by;

— Government Decision No. 586/1990, providing the reopening of university training in special education and social work,

— Government Decision No. 1161/1990 dealing with the establishment of The State Secretariat for disabled persons which provisionally took the responsibility of financing and co-ordinating special education, until 1993.

The new Constitution of 1991 has a special article, no. 46, stating that "Handicapped persons are entitled to special protection. The State assures the achievement of a national policy of prevention, treatment, rehabilitation, education, instruction and social integration of handicapped, respecting the rights and the duties of the parents or tutors".

The Law No. 53/1992, dealing with the special protection of handicapped people, contain an;

— Article 6 paragraph A stating the right of handicapped persons to "equal and free access in any ordinary school, day courses, evening courses or distance learning courses, according to existing and rehabilitation potential, respecting the educational legislation", and

— Article 6 paragraph B providing for the instruction of non-ambulatory handicapped persons at home until their thirtieth year.

Government Decision No. 283/1993 for the school year 1993-1994 and Government Decision No. 426/1994 for the school year 1994-1995 defines, "special (adapted) education and schooling as organised for persons with different problems that constitute disadvantages for their educational, vocational and school integration. This education is addressed to children with various impairments, physical, mental, sensory, language disorders, socio-emotional and behavior problems."

Article 54 of the above Decision states that education and vocational training for persons with special problems is achieved through;

— special schools, kindergartens, vocational schools, lyceums and post-lyceums, special schools for re-education and training (of behavior problems);

— educational structures, sections, classes or groups, integrated in other educational institutions from the local community and medico-social institutions;

— alternative educational structures, centres for preventive education, centres for special education, educational complexes for young persons; and

— education at home for the non-ambulatory handicapped persons.

2. Responsibility and Organisation

The Ministry of Health and the Ministry of Education, Labour and Social Welfare are concerned with the social welfare of disabled children.

Article 4 of Decree 53/1992 states that special education in special schools, the structure of the school year, the duration of schooling, the content of activities, the methods of teacher training and teacher qualifications will be decided by the Ministry of Education in concert with the Ministry of Labour and Social Welfare, the Ministry of Health and the Ministry of the Interior.

The Government Decision No. 283/1993 and No. 426/1994 stipulates that organisation, coordination and evaluation of special education is the responsibility of the Ministry of Education.

3. Identification, Assessment and Orientation

Article 1, paragraph A of Decree 53/1992 provides for the identification of children with physical and mental handicaps who cannot be cared for within their families or who cannot attend regular schools.

Paragraph B of the above law provides for the medical and psychopedagogical examination of disabled children as well as their scholastic and professional orientation.

Article 16 of the Law Concerning the Social Protection of Handicapped Persons (No. 53/1992) concerns the definition of handicaps based on specific categories defined by the clinical diagnosis of medical personnel.

Government Decision No. 283/1993 and 426/1994, Article 56, states that the, "psycho-pedagogical assessment of children with special problems for the purpose of their educational and vocational guidance is accomplished by the commission of complex assessment, subordinated to the school inspectorates and co-ordinated by a specialised teacher (psychopedagog)."

4. Age Range Covered by Legislation

Pre-school, elementary, secondary, and post-studies are covered.

5. Integration

Article 6 of Law No. 53/1992 provides that non-institutionalised handicapped persons shall benefit from free and equal access to regular schools, and day or evening courses.

Government Decision No. 283/1993 and 426/1994 stipulates that children with language disorders who attend ordinary kindergartens and primary schools are to participate in "inter schools," centres for speech therapy as a structure of integrated special education, staffed by special education teachers.

6. Financing of Education for Special Needs

Assured by the State, recently through the Ministry of Education.

Government Decision No. 586/1990, the Law Decree No. 138/1990, recently amended by Government Decision No. 56/1994 provides the rights of disabled children which includes free (state subsidised) food, transport, housing, medicine, clothes and equipment.

7. Curriculum Entitlement

Special or ordinary curriculum is delivered in special education institutions according to the learning potential of the pupils. Recent ministry regulations are facilitating equal access of children coming from special elementary or vocational schools to ordinary or higher levels of schooling.

8. Post 16 Years—Vocational Education

A network of special vocational schools for pupils with disabilities coming from special elementary schools, age range 15-16 to 18-19. Many local special sections/classes for vocational training were opened recently in ordinary vocational training schools.

9. Teacher Training

Initial teacher training is stipulated in Government decision No. 586/1990.

Government Decision No. 283/1993 and 426/1994, Article 58 provides that the in service training and appointment of the teaching staff, research activities and curriculum elaboration shall be realised according to the methodology developed by the Ministry of Education.

SPAIN

1. Extent and Nature of Legislation

Article 27 of the 1978 Constitution provides that, "all have the right to an education. The liberty to an education is recognised."

Article 49 of the Constitution states that, "public authorities will bring into being a policy of prevention, treatment, rehabilitation and integration of the physically, auditively and mentally disabled, to whom they will offer special assistance to fully benefit from the rights stipulated in this law for all citizens."

Decree No. 62/1981, article 10 defines special education as education tailored to special physical, mental or sensory needs. Special education is to take place in special schools or in special education classes in regular schools.

The 1982 law No. 13 on Social Integration of Disabled People (LISMI), develops article 39 of the Constitution and establishes measures of a preventive, rehabilitative, educational, laboral and social nature aimed at achieving the integration of disabled people in society.

Decree 334/1985 on Special Education states that education of pupils with special needs shall be carried out, when possible, in regular educational centers. The purpose of Special Education Schools is to provide students having special educational needs associated with extreme handicap or multiple disability, with a place at school.

The 1990 Law on the General Educational System (Ley Organica de Ordenacion General del Sistema Educativo, LOGSE) Chapter 15, Article 36 states that "the education system shall have at its disposal the necessary means for students with special needs, whether they be temporary or permanent, to successfully obtain the same general objectives laid down for all students within the same system".

2. Responsibility and Organisation

The 1978 Constitution determines the distribution of responsibilities between the State and the 17 autonomous communities. Education is a shared responsibility; certain aspects fall to the state while others to the communities. The concept of "basic unity" allows the autonomous communities to add various elements to basic education. Resources are provided by the state, whereas education administration is only undertaken by the central authority in 10 of the 17 communities.

Chapter IV of Decree 620/1981 distributes the following authority to the government agencies:

The Ministry for Education and Science is the highest educational authority for private and public education. They are to oversee Special Education.

The Ministry of Labour is to promote the integration of the disabled in the workforce.

The Ministry of Health and Welfare is to be concerned with medical rehabilitation and general assistance, especially concerning social security. The Ministry of Culture is to promote the socio-cultural integration of the disabled.

Decree 443/1985 established an orientation unit of the Ministry of Education for Special Education. The Special Education unit was charged with the tasks of prevention, early detection and orientation of parents and students.

Decree of 21-5-1986 established a National Support Centre for Special Education. The purpose of this centre is to conduct studies on special education, establish evaluation instruments, develop curricula, create and edit texts, design materials, orient parents and children, train special education teachers, and experiment with new technologies.

In 1990, a resolution was passed creating the Department of Educational Orientation in Special Education Schools. This department is an instructional unit which integrates professors involved in special education. These include psychologists, speech therapy teachers, social workers and physiotherapists.

As stated in the Ministerial Order of 12 December 1992, instructions were given to all teams in order to adjust their performance to the latest demands derived from the development of LOGSE. The functions allocated to these teams are part of a wider frame of action addressed not only to students but also to support given to schools, to cooperation with teachers in tasks related to attention to diversity, curricular planning and development.

Decree No. 27998 of 1993 establishes a team for Educational and Psychopedagogic Orientation. The composition of the team is transdisciplinary. The purpose of this team is to complement the work of the Special Education Unit; co-ordinate with the Teaching Centres and the Inspectorate; and work with the provinces in order to provide pedagogical support. They are to support teachers, assist in curriculum development, facilitate access of the disabled in pre-primary, primary and secondary school, promote co-operation between educational authorities, undertake psycho-pedagogical evaluations and suggest the most appropriate means of schooling.

3. Identification, Assessment and Orientation

Chapter III of the 1985 Decree on Special Eduction calls for, "the prevention and early detection of disability in children." This task is fulfilled by Teams of Educational and Psychopedagogic Orientation.

Paragraph b of the Decree requires that the evaluation of disabled students be multi-dimensional. Paragraph c provides that the elaboration of the "Individual Development Plan" be conducted with the participation of parents and professors. These plans should include a plan of studies and a description of necessary personalised support.

The 1990 Law on The General Educational System (Ley Organica de Ordenacion General del Sistema Educativo, LOGSE), in Article 37, states that the educational administration will encourage the participation of parents and tutors in decisions that concern the schooling of special education students.

4. Age Range Covered by Legislation

Integration of disabled students is mandated in pre-school, primary and secondary education. Education of students with special needs shall therefore cover the same age period as that of the rest of the students. Education is compulsory between the ages of 6 and 16, and it may be expanded up to the age of 18.

5. Integration

The 1982 Law on Social Integration of the Disabled stipulates that "the disabled will be integrated into the regular educational system, receiving as necessary programme support and other assistance".

Special education is regarded as either transitory or permanent. Students who are not able to be integrated into regular schools are to attend special institutions.

The 1985 Decree on Special Education emphasises the total integration of the disabled. "Integration into regular schools is the first step ... facilitated by individualised specialised support ... only when a person does not have the capability to be integrated shall the student be sent to a special school."

Education of the disabled shall be governed by four principles: "normalisation of services, school integration, specialised teaching support and individualised teaching." Further, "in accordance with the principle of normalisation, disabled persons shall not use or receive special services, other than in cases that are indispensable."

Regulation 4763, of March 1985, established pilot schools for integration in the 1985/6 school year in order to implement the 1985 Decree. Integration is to take place in primary and secondary schools. Integration was to be expanded in 1986/7 by Decree No. 30/1986. Decrees promoting the integration of the disabled have been passed up to 1993. Currently most students with special needs are integrated in regular educational centers.

The 1990 Law on the General Educational System, in Article 36, emphasises the principles of normalisation and integration. It stresses principles mentioned in the 1985 Decree. Disabled children should participate in regular classes with the support of specialised personnel and equipment; special education in separate institutions will only be authorised if the students' needs are not met in a regular school. The 1990 Law considers as one of its main points the attention to diversity of interests, abilities and aptitudes of students. It also foresees measures to adjust the curriculum and organisation of schools to the needs of all students.

6. Financing of Education for Special Needs

Decree No. 620/1981 concerns public assistance for the disabled. The disabled are to benefit from public financial assistance in the areas of education, rehabilitation, special assistance, transport, integration to work, and socio-cultural life. Subsidies are available to the disabled and their families.

Education in regular and special school is free for the disabled.

7. Curriculum Entitlement

Students with special educational needs who attend regular schools are to follow the official curriculum with the necessary adaptions. Students who attend Special Education Schools, due to the seriousness of their disability, may follow a curriculum whose main reference is the official curriculum, but has been adapted to their capacities and is aimed at maximising their personal development.

8. Post 16 Years—Vocational Education

A Resolution of January 26,2 1993 expands integration of disabled students in centres for vocational education at the secondary level,

9. Teacher Training

Special education training can be carried out in two different ways:

— on the one hand as special training included in studies resulting in the attainment of title of Primary School Teacher specialised in Special Education. This takes place at University and lasts for three years.

— on the other hand by following specialisation courses lasting one or two years after the primary school teacher dimploma. As the former, this is also studied at university.

The Annex to the 1989 Resolution of the Department for Pedagogical Renovation (Renovacion) defines the special education support teacher as a special education teacher who is to assist with the student's individualised teaching programme. The teacher is to constantly observe the student so as to identify special needs, assist in teaching the curriculum, supplying materials and orientation as well as evaluation and liaison with other support servic.

SRI LANKA

1. Extent and Nature of Legislation

The Constitution of the Democratic Socialist Republic of Sri Lanka establishes the fundamental right that, "all persons are equal before the law and are entitled to the equal protection of the law." It further provides that, "nothing in this article shall prevent special provision being made, by law, subordinate legislation or executive action, for the advancement of women, children or disabled persons."

The Education Ordinance No. 31 of 1939 gives the State responsibility for the "...continuance and discontinuance of schools of different grades including schools for the education of blind, deaf, defective and epileptic children. This ordinance also establishes special schools for mentally and physically handicapped children.

The 1991 Policy Guidelines for the Development of Special Education, states that "The objective of special education shall be the development and maximisation of potentials, as well as the inculcation of value systems to make learners with special educational needs become independent, useful and contributing members of society."

2. Responsibility and Organisation

The Ministry of Education and Cultural Affairs determines the policy pertaining to the Special Education system on the basis of advice and recommendations from the National Educational Commission, National Institute of Education (NIE) and Special Education Advisory Committee. Special Education programmes are implemented in the provinces by the Provincial Departments of Education through Assistant Directors of Special Education and Special Education Teachers. Review of progress and monitoring of implementation is conducted by the Special Education branch of the Ministry of Education and Cultural Affairs.

3. Identification, Assessment and Orientation

The 1991 Policy Guidelines for the Development of Special Education states that The "identification, screening, assessment and evaluation of children with special educational needs shall be conducted in the school and in the community, utilising appropriate instruments of assessment." Further, "early detection, diagnosis and intervention is prerequisite for the successful rehabilitation of children with special educational needs." A multi-disciplinary team comprised of parents, teachers, special education teachers and educators, school managers, health and social workers, paediatricians, psychologists, paramedical personnel and therapists is to evaluate children.

The team will collect data on the child including a history of the child's health, physical deformities, motor co-ordination, hearing, personality, behaviour, learning disabilities and educational difficulties.

School admission is flexible; a student may be admitted at any time in the school year. All schools are required to admit students with special needs.

Parents are to be contributing partners in special education sharing information and experiences.

4. Age Range Covered by Legislation

Primary and secondary education are covered.

5. Integration

The 1969 Cabinet Paper establishes a policy for integrating blind children in regular schools.

The 1991 Policy Guidelines for Development of Special Education, Section 5 states that "the goal of special education shall be the integration of learners with special educational needs into the regular school system and eventually the community."

6. Financing of Education for Special Needs

Information unavailable.

7. Curriculum Entitlement

The 1991 Policy Guidelines for Development of Special Education state that "the emphasis shall be on technical and vocational education in the special curriculum for special educational needs."

The curriculum for special education shall be based on the curriculum for regular schools modified to meet the needs of students.

8. Post 16 Years—Vocational Education

Information unavailable.

9. Teacher Training

The 1979 Education Reform Committee's report recommended, "that the general course of training provided for teachers who handle normal children should include at least a basic knowledge of the skills required for handling handicapped children."

The Maharagma Teachers College conducts a two year educational course for children with hearing and visual impairments and mentally retarded children. Trainers are selected by the Teacher Education Branch of the Ministry of Education and Higher Education.

SWEDEN

1. Extent and Nature of Legislation

There is no separate law aimed at securing the rights of disabled persons. In accordance with efforts to integrate the various issues regarding the disabled special paragraphs concerning the disabled have been incorporated into certain laws. In recent years, there has been a trend towards framework legislation with less and less detailed government control of the local authorities' and county council's activities.

The Social Services Act states the right for a child with physical or psychological or social problems to have priority to a place in pre-school.

In December 1993, the Parliament enacted that upon parental request, all children between 1-12 years of age have the right to public child-care. This legislation will be put into effect on the 1st of January 1995.

The Education Act of 1985 states that every child and youngster shall no matter of sex, geographical residence, social and economical circumstances have the same access to an education within the state system of schooling. The Act differentiates between 'normal' schools and two forms of special schools. One school for the mentally handicapped, and one for students with visual and hearing impairments and speech difficulties. The Act also states that if possible, special education shall be organised within the classroom.

2. Responsibility and Organisation

The Ministry of Health and Social Affairs is responsible for pre-school and child care. The Ministry of Education and Science is responsible for schooling and education of children from the age of 7 and forth to adult education. Recently, there has been a tendency to transfer responsibility of organising and carrying out the education to the municipalities.

3. Identification, Assessment and Orientation

The necessity to give extra support to children with special needs is strongly emphasised in the School Act and in the curricula.

4. Age Range Covered by Legislation

The Social Services Act states the responsibility of the municipality to arrange pre-schooling for all children of age 6 years.

The School Act concerns all children, with or without special needs and covers primary, secondary and vocational education, ages 7-20 and adult education, ages 21 and forth.

5. Integration

As the result of a policy stated in the 1980s almost all disabled pupils are integrated into ordinary schools. There are special schools for students who study by sign language, are mentally handicapped or are multi-handicapped.

6. Financing of Education for Special Needs

There is no separate State grant for Education for Special Needs. State subsidies to municipalities take the form of general equalisation grant. The municipalities are at liberty to deploy the grounds for various service purposes as they see fit. However, they are to see to it that enough resources are given to Education for Special Needs.

7. Curriculum Entitlement

Special education is included in the general curriculum.

In December 1993, the Parliament decided on a new curriculum for the whole of the compulsory school system, *i.e.,* to compulsory school, Lapp (Sami) school, special schools and compulsory school for the mentally retarded. In December 1993, the Parliament also decided on a new curriculum for the upper secondary school, municipal adult education, the special secondary school and adult education for the mentally retarded. This is the first time different types of schools have had a single curriculum with the same goals, the same basic values and the same allocation of responsibilities.

8. Post 16 Years—Vocational Education

After finishing the nine year compulsory school most of the youngsters, in fact 98 per cent, attend the upper secondary school. Municipalities are obliged, under the School Act, to provide upper secondary schooling for all pupils leaving compulsory school. In the upper secondary school all education is organised in study programmes of three years' duration. There are 16 nationally determined programmes, 14 of which are primarily vocationally oriented and two preparing primarily for university studies. Municipalities must offer a comprehensive selection of national programmes and admissions capacity for the various programmes must be adapted to student preferences.

9. Teacher Training

3,5 - 4,5 years of full times studies at university are required to become a teacher in a compulsory school. Part of the studies are completed by inservice training. The Government's goal is that all teachers receive at least 10 weeks of education about methods within special education. If or when a teacher receives a child with special educational needs, he/she will be offered a short course through the National Agency for Special Education through its consultants, resource centres or special schools.

TANZANIA

1. Extent and Nature of Legislation

The 1967 Arusha Declaration states that "handicapped individuals shall be trained and educated so that they too can participate in the nation building."

The 1969 Five Year Development Plan establishes as a basis for educational policy "to give every Tanzanian child basic education as soon as the financial circumstances of Government permit", which includes handicapped children.

The 1978 Education Act affirms the right of every citizen to education. It defines a special school as one which provides education for persons suffering from disability.

The Public Primary School Act requires students to attend compulsory schooling for seven years. However, very few handicapped children have been enrolled in primary schools.

There has been increasing concern for the education of the disabled in a 1992 proposal of the Ministry of Education and Culture on "Education Sector Programme for Internal and External Financing."

2. Responsibility and Organisation

In Tanzania Mainland the provision of basic education to all children of compulsory school age, regardless of their disability, remains the concern of the Ministry of Education and Culture.

Voluntary and charity organisations, both national and international, do help the Ministry of Education and Culture in the provision of educational materials and in the training of teachers on special needs education.

3. Identification, Assessment and Orientation

The process of identifying and assessing children with disability is carried out at a multi-disciplinary level whereby the Ministry of Health and the Ministry of Education and Culture work as one team. The Department of Social Welfare is also incorporated in vocational training programmes. Placement and orientation are done by the Ministry of Education and Culture in collaboration with the Department of Social Welfare of the Ministry of Labour and Youth Development.

4. Age Range Covered by Legislation

By legislation, the school age is between 7 and 14 years of age.

5. Integration

It is the policy of the Ministry of Education and Culture that children with disability should be integrated in regular schools and whenever possible be enrolled in schools near their home. This aims at enabling both the normal and the disabled children to share school resources and local experience together. This on the other hand promotes community participation in moulding the disabled. For example, the visually impaired children are now attending schools in their neighborhood and they are attended by specialist teachers in the Itinerant Programme.

6. Financing of Education for Special Needs

Generally educational services to children with special educational needs are supposed to be fully financed by the government through the Ministry of Education and Culture. However, presently the costs are partially shared between the Ministry of Education and Culture and non-governmental organisations (NGO's). The government pays the salaries to specialist teachers, running costs and purchase of textbooks, while the NGO's facilitate the process by providing transport, buildings, technical equipment and materials.

7. Curriculum Entitlement

The Institute of Education of the Ministry of Education and Culture prepares curricula to all schools in the country including curricula for children with special educational needs.

8. Post 16 Years—Vocational Education

Responsible for provision of Vocational Training is the Department of Social Welfare in the Ministry of Labour and Youth Development.

Some Vocational Training Colleges, which train disabled youths, are privately owned by NGO's such as churches, associations of and societies for disabled persons.

At present there are few pupils leaving schools for the disabled (i.e. the deaf and blind) that are enrolled in to the few existing vocational training centres annexed to the special schools for the disabled.

9. Teacher Training

The Ministry of Education and Culture is the only Ministry charged with the task of training teachers of the disabled locally and abroad. There are now two Teacher Training Colleges training specialist teachers for disabled children.

TUNISIA

1. Extent and Nature of Legislation

The State guarantee all children the right to education and equal opportunities. Law No. 81-46 of May 1981 states that, "prevention of handicap, care, education, vocational education, work, socio-economic integration, constitute a national responsibility."

Law No. 91-65 of July 1991 stipulates that the State, "will assure that adequate conditions permit the handicapped and students with difficulties to benefit from their right to an education."

2. Responsibility and Organisation

Law No. 81-86 of May 1981 creates a National Superior Council whose responsibility it is to assist the Minister of Social Affairs in the elaboration of policy for the handicapped. They are to propose programmes that assure the social protection and integration of the handicapped and to promote inter-administration co-operation. The Council is presided by the Minister of Social Affairs with representatives from the Ministry of Finance, Equipment, Education, Higher Education and Research, Public Health, Sport, Unions and Employers Organisations, Socio-economic Council, Handicapped Organisation, and the Cabinet of the Prime Minister.

Decree 88-2051 of 22 December 1988 established a High Council for Disabled Persons. This council is in charge of assisting the Ministry of Social Affairs on policy matters related to the area of disability.

3. Identification, Assessment and Orientation

Law No. 81-46 May 1981 defines a handicapped person as one who possesses a sensory, mental or motor disability. The Ministry of Welfare assigns handicapped identity cards to the disabled so that he/she is able to benefit from provisions for the handicapped.

4. Age Range Covered by Legislation

Pre-primary, primary, secondary and higher education are covered.

5. Integration

Law No. 81-46 May 1981 stipulates that, "the education and re-education (of the handicapped) will take place as much as possible in regular schools and if not possible in special institutions. The opening up of pre-school, primary, secondary and higher education is authorised by the Ministry of Social Affairs."

6. Financing of Education for Special Needs

Disabled persons receive subsidies from government and certain tax exemptions.

7. Curriculum Entitlement

Law 93-10 of 17 February 1993 concerns vocational training. Decree 93-1474 of 5th July 1993 and Law 91-98 of 31 December 1991 established the organisation of vocational training for persons with motor impairments.

(i) join any school and level commensurate with their qualifications, interests and abilities,

(ii) choose any subject he/she wants and is able to do including the sciences,

(iii) be availed equal opportunity and treatment for and during employment.

R. 6 states "an integrated school should have one P.T.A."

R. 7 Teachers of Special Education not only deal with children who have disabilities, but also with other children with special educational needs.

R. 8.1 In integrated institutions persons with disabilities should pay the same fees charged. Where parents are genuinely unable to pay, the normal strategies for helping children whose parents are unable to meet fees requirements and apply.

6. Financing of Education for Special Needs

A policy for decentralisation of services, which include education has been developed and provides empowerment to district authorities to fund and run services. Each decentralised district now provides funding to Special Education

7. Curriculum Entitlement

There is no mention of curriculum entitlement for children with special educational needs in the National Curriculum.

8. Post 16 Years—Vocational Education

Uganda National Institute of Special Education, which is under construction, has developed a curriculum for Social and Vocational Rehabilitation education. The purpose of this curriculum is to equip various categories of professionals who will prepare post 16 years for education which is ecological and practical. These professionals include special education teachers, occupational therapists, social workers, nurses, probation officers, etc.

9. Teacher Training

Uganda National Institute of Special Education (UNISE) is a component under the Ministry of Education and sports for;

— the training of personnel for persons with disabilities,

— the development and production of teaching and training aids,

— the entailment of research in Special Education and publications for the general public about persons with disabilities.

VENEZUELA

1. Extent and Nature of Legislation

The 1961 Venezuelan constitution states that everybody has the right to education, "Discrimination based on race, sex, creed or social condition is not permitted ... All have the right to an education. The State will create schools, institutions and services sufficient to allow access to education and culture."

Article 32. The objective of Special Education is to take care, with adequate methods and special resources, of people with such special physical, intellectual or emotional characteristics, when they cannot fit in with the programmes corresponding to the various levels of the educational system.

Article 33. Special Education shall be oriented so as to facilitate the independence of persons with special needs and the integration into the community.

Article 34. Policies will be established to create adequate services for prevention, diagnosis and rehabilitation of people with special educational needs and to organise curriculum development and evaluation.

The 1981 Educational Law (Ley Organica de Education) stipulates that "all have the right to receive an education in accordance with their aptitudes and aspirations...without discrimination of any kind."

The above law emphasises that the goal of Special Education is to orient the individual to maximise his/her development, stressing possibilities rather than deficiencies in order to facilitate independence and integration into the community.

2. Responsibility and Organisation

Article 35 of the 1961 Venezuelan Constitution defines the following ministries as concerned with special education; the Ministry of Education and the Ministry of Family and Work. In addition municipal organisations are involved.

Decree No. 2.038, of February 1977, establishes the creation of The Foundation for the Development of Special Education. The Board of the Foundation is presided by a representative from the Ministry of Education, and comprised of persons from the Ministry of Health, and Ministry of Youth as well as representatives from the Foundation for the Child and the Institute of Nutrition. The objective of the Foundation is to assist in implementing policy and programmes developed by the Ministry of Education, train teachers, conduct research projects including in the area of prevention, and participate in international co-operation.

The 1986 Educational Law (Lay Organica de Education) establishes the Department of Special Education within the Ministry of Education. The Department of Special Education is to train specialised teachers, orient family, and to promote integration.

In each State there is a Department of Special Education (23 for the whole country) with different professional supervisors responsible for the application of the policies defined by the Council of Special Education.

3. Identification, Assessment and Orientation

The 1981 Law emphasises prevention and early detection of handicap. An inter-disciplinary team will conduct assessment.

The Council of Special Education establishes programmes on prevention, diagnosis and rehabilitation.

4. Age Range Covered by Legislation

Special Education is developed for children from birth until they are 16 years old. First it is provided in centres of pre-primary level (0-4 years old) and then in institutes of Special Education (4-16 years old).

5. Integration

The 1986 Law mandated the creation of The National Institute for the Integration of the Disabled. This Institute comprised of representatives from the Ministry of Labour, Welfare, Education, and Family will promote the integration of the disabled by conducting research, implementing laws and decrees, orienting public and private institutions in educational programmes, and giving grants to the disabled. Various strategies have been designed to achieve effective integration of people with special needs with respect to the family, the school and the community in cooperation with parents and institutions.

6. Financing of Education for Special Needs

Special Education is financed through the National Budget, by the National Congress, by Foundations for the development of special education and by international cooperation.

7. Curriculum Entitlement

The Department of Special Education is to see that each student receives an individualised teaching programme taking into consideration the child's social and emotional background, and vocational aspirations.

Such a socio-pedagogical model of action tries to facilitate the integration of people with special needs into society by the appropriate adequation of curricula to the different levels of education, through both formal and non-formal programmes.

8. Post 16 Years—Vocational Education

The 1986 Law stipulates that the Ministry of Education will

organise professional education programmes and encourage the participation of the private sector.

Vocational orientation in special education is initiated during education in special schools, and is further developed in institutions such as;

— TEL (Labour Education Workshops). This unit is in charge of taking care of young people and adults with mental retardation (16-45 years old).

— CRC (Rehabilitation Centers for the blind).

9. Teacher Training

Teacher Training in special education is provided by the Department for Special Education. The training is done in different universities and high schools (public and private) in the country. The duration is 3 years for an intermediary level or 5 years for the complete training (Education Licence).

ZAIRE

1. Extent and Nature of Legislation

Law No. 86-005 of 1986, articles 35 to 40, on General Education, defines the organisation of a special education system for children with special needs. It establishes an act of non-discrimination in national education having to do with race or ethnicity, social condition, gender and religion. Special education will be organised in special institutions, in special classrooms and in regular schools at pre-primary, primary, secondary and higher levels.

Decree No. 89-018 of 1989 opens up the provision of special education to the private sector. Private entities are bound to respect the conditions established by the Law of 1986.

The 1991 Decree No. 0492 established special schools and specialised instruction for the deaf, blind, and students with motor and mental difficulties.

2. Responsibility and Organisation

All schools (public or private, regular or special) are under the responsibility of the State through the Ministry of Education for pre-primary, primary or secondary schools (regular or special, also including vocational education) and through the Ministry of Higher Education and Scientific Research.

The direction of special education (mentioned in Decree 8-VII-92 depends on the Ministry of Education. Its responsibilities only concern pre-primary, primary and secondary schools, since special education is not yet operational at higher and university level in Zaire.

In each region it operates within the Regional Division of primary, secondary and vocational education. And at a lower level, within the Regional Sub-division or within the district or municipality in which a special education unit has been created. These services must in particular conduct an assessment of children with special needs and classify them according to the different types of needs.

At the local level special education is represented by special-center schools, covering two sectors;

— a formal sector with schools managed directly by the Public Authority,

— and an informal sector with special schools organised by the State in favour of NGO's.

3. Identification, Assessment and Orientation

No formal identification system of children with special needs has yet been created.

4. Age Range Covered by Legislation

Pre-primary (3-5 years), primary (6-12 years), and secondary (13-18 years) is covered.

5. Integration

Information unavailable.

6. Financing of Education for Special Needs

Special education receives only 0.2 per cent of the National Budget.

7. Curriculum Entitlement

There are no formal programmes for different special educational needs, but there are projects to create national programmes for the different levels of schools.

8. Post 16 Years—Vocational Education

Some vocational training is to be found.

9. Teacher Training

There are two special education teacher training centers in the country for 11 regions.

ZAMBIA

1. Extent and Nature of Legislation

Zambia has had an articulated National Policy on Special Needs Education since 1977. This was reflected in the Educational Reform Document (1977). This document has elaborated recommendations on Special Needs Education. This stated policy has not been adequately implemented owing to no specifications of special needs education in the Education Act of 1966, which is currently being reviewed.

Chapter 551 of the Laws of Zambia establishes a council called the Zambia Council for the Handicapped. Representatives from the Ministry of Education, Health, Labour, the Red Cross, and organisations of handicapped persons serve on the Council. The Council ensures the general protection of the handicapped.

2. Responsibility and Organisation

In 1971, education of the disabled became part of the responsibility of the Ministry of Education. At that time, a Special Education Directorate was created in the Ministry. There is also an Inter-Ministerial Steering Committee on Special Education which deals with the organisation and improvement of education for the handicapped.

There are two main modalities of provision of special needs education;

(a) Residential Special Schools are still the main feature,

(b) Integrated provision, via resource room model, especially at Secondary School level.

3. Identification, Assessment and Orientation

The Education Reform Document of 1977 states that, "Identification of handicaps cannot be carried out successfully unless it receives the co-operation of the parents, the community and the specialists in the medical, social and educational fields. All concerned should appreciate the importance of disseminating information about the varieties of handicap and the importance of surveying and identifying handicapped children early so that appropriate medical, social and educational provision can be made at the right time".

4. Age Range Covered by Legislation

Information unavailable.

5. Integration

The 1977 Educational Reform Document states: "Handicapped children should attend ordinary schools and colleges in view of the importance of socialisation but this should depend on the nature and degree of their disability."

6. Financing of Education for Special Needs

Funds for financing special needs education comes from the Central Government and donor agencies. The funds from the Central Government goes to the recurrent expenditure, whilst capital projects have been assisted by different donor agencies.

7. Curriculum Entitlement

The CDC, Special Education Unit, in conjunction with specialist teachers produce and distribute modified supplementary curricula. However, most special needs pupils have left school without adequate knowledge and living skills to enable them to lead an independent vocational and social life.

8. Post 16 Years—Vocational Education

Information unavailable.

9. Teacher Training

The Ministry of Education established the Lusaka College for the Teachers of the Handicapped. Teachers in ordinary schools interested in special education are trained in this college. It mainly provides inservice training to serve teachers who require additional training and want to advance in the education for children and youth with special needs.

From 1992 all colleges and the University will offer modules on Special Needs Education.

ZIMBABWE

1. Extent and Nature of Legislation

The 1987 Education Act provides for the fundamental rights for all children. It states "every child in Zimbabwe shall have the right to a school education." No child shall be refused admission to any schools on the grounds of discrimination.

This Act is being amended to read "nine years of school education for every child of school age shall be compulsory." Compulsory attendance is to be enforced by enforcement officers.

The 1992 Disabled Persons Act says that "No disabled person shall, on the grounds of his disability be denied the provision of any service or amenity ordinarily provided to a member of the public."

2. Responsibility and Organisation

The Ministry of Education and Culture is concerned with the education of all citizens. The Schools Psychological Service and Special Education sponsors various special education programmes.

Policy decisions on special education are made by the Permanent Secretary with his Deputy Secretaries. The Deputy Secretary (Schools' Division) has under him the Chief Education Officer Psychological Services and Special Education). Below these officers there are two Deputy Chief Education Officers, one for Special Education, and the other for schools' psychological services. In the regions there are educational psychologists, speech therapists special education officers and remedial tutors. These persons are to implement policy decided on the national level.

The Ministry of Social Welfare provides hostels for children with severe to moderate emotional and behavioural disturbances. Schools within these hostels are run by employees of the Ministry of Education.

In 1993 the National Disability Board was established. This Board is made up of representatives from the Ministry of Health and Child Welfare, Ministry of Education and Culture, Ministry of Local Government, Rural and Urban Development, Ministry of Public Service, Labour and Social Welfare, the Zimbabwe Congress of Trade Unions (ZCTU), Employers Confederation of Zimbabwe (EMCOZ), different organisations of people with disabilities and organisations providing services for people with disabilities.

3. Identification, Assessment and Orientation

The policy statement on Special Education (Act 1987) adopts the following strategy: early detection, intervention and prevention of handicaps. Officers of the Ministry in the regions identify special needs children. Educational psychologists do the assessments. The Ministry of Education and Culture works hand in hand with the Ministry of Health, Rehabilitation Unit.

4. Age Range Covered by Legislation

The Ministry of Education and Culture caters for 0-18 years. The Ministry of Higher Education for 18 years and above.

Primary and secondary education is covered.

5. Integration

The policy statement on Special Education promotes integration of children with handicaps into ordinary schools, wherever possible.

6. Financing of Education for Special Needs

Primary school is free and compulsory for all children. Secondary education is universal for those who can afford it.

The policy statement on Special Education encourages the procurement of funds for special education including non-government sources.

7. Curriculum Entitlement

Special needs children follow curricula that is followed in regular schools. Appropriate teaching techniques that meet the specific needs of the special needs child are used and cognisance is given to the children's different pace of learning.

8. Post 16 Years—Vocational Education

At the moment the Ministry of Social Welfare and the Ministry of Health work hand-in-hand with non-governmental organisations to provide vocational education to children with special needs.

9. Teacher Training

The Ministry's policy is that teachers who teach special needs children must have a specialist training in special education. There is one college, United College of Education, that trains Special Education teachers. One must be a conventional trained teacher with three years teaching experience, to be admitted for Special Education training.

REFERENCES

1. *CERI/OECD, Report Prepared for the OECD/Ministry of Education*, Netherlands, December 1-3, 1993, p. 71.
2. *CERI/OECD, Project on Children and Youth at Risk*, Report on Greece, Stelios Nicodemos, 1991.